SAUTERNES

A study of the great sweet wines of Bordeaux

Jeffrey Benson and Alastair Mackenzie

SAUTERNES

A study of the great sweet wines of Bordeaux

Revised edition

SOTHEBY'S PUBLICATIONS

© 1990 Jeffrey Benson & Alastair Mackenzie

First published 1979
Revised edition 1990
Published for Sotheby's Publications
by Philip Wilson Publishers Ltd
26 Litchfield Street
London WC2H 9NJ

Available to the USA book trade from
Rizzoli International Publications, Inc.
300 Park Avenue South
New York
NY 10010

Exclusive distribution to the USA Wine Trade, from
THE WINE APPRECIATION GUILD
155 Connecticut Street San Francisco
California 94107 USA
(415) 566-3532

ISBN 0 85667 370 6

Library of Congress Catalog Number 89-060468

Designed by Andrew Shoolbred
Filmset in Great Britain by Keyset Composition, Colchester,
and printed and bound by Singapore National
Printers Ltd, Singapore

British Library Cataloguing in Publication Data

Benson, Jeffrey
  Sauternes. – 2nd ed.
  1. Sauternes wines
  I. Title II. Mackenzie, Alastair, 1933–
  641.2′222′094471

ISBN 0–85667-360-9

Contents

FOREWORD

The wine of Sauternes is one of the most remarkable in the world. It is however one of the least well known. It is a wine the traditions of which are not old; yet it comes from an ancient wine-growing area.

Sauternes is a wine that has seemed to justify the most prodigal expense, yet today it suffers from lack of appreciation, to the extent that some growers are even thinking of uprooting their vines and not replanting them.

These are paradoxes that have to be resolved. What is needed is the good offices of a third party to enlighten potential lovers of this wine.

I pay tribute to Messrs Jeffrey Benson and Alastair Mackenzie for having seen fit to delve into the mysteries that surround this region and the wine it produces. Their book is the first that seeks to remove the myths surrounding Sauternes wine, thereby restoring its rightful and proper share of mystique. And God knows it is rich in them. This book highlights the miraculous fortuity of the making of 'the greatest wine in the world', given that its genesis is devilishly sophisticated.

Add to this the miracle of the soil and a micro-climate beneficent towards a fickle fungus — the basic factors over which Man has no control. It fell to him to extract from all this, like the musician from his instrument, the most marvellous and harmonious tones; his task to reveal that this is indeed God's chosen country.

It then remains for him to make known to the world, if not his efforts then at least the results of this labour. The authors have contributed all their skill towards achieving this end.

Comte A. de Lur-Saluces, 20th September 1978, Château Yquem

FOREWORD

Le vin de Sauternes est un des plus notables qui soit au monde.
Un des plus mal connus, c'est pourtant un vin de tradition
récent, provenant d'une vieille région de production.

C'est le vin qui a justifié les plus folles prodigalités, et il
souffre de ne pas être mieux apprécié aujourd'hui, puisque
certains producteurs songent, même, à arracher leurs vignes ou
à ne plus les replanter.

Il y a là des paradoxes qu'il fallait éclairer. Il fallait un tiers
attentif pour informer les amateurs potentiels de ce vin.

Je rends hommage à MM Jeffrey Benson et Alastair
Mackenzie d'avoir voulu percer les mystères qui entourent
cette région et sa production. Leur livre est le premier qui
cherche à démystifier le vin de Sauternes, lui rendant ainsi sa
juste et véritable part de mystére. Et Dieu sait qu'il en est riche.
Il met en lumière le hasard merveilleux qui conduit à
l'élaboration du 'plus grand vin du monde' si on veut bien
admettre que sa genèse est diaboliquement sophistiquée.

Ceci ajouté au miracle du terroir et à celui du microclimat
favorisant un capricieux champignon, sont les données sur
lesquelles l'homme n'a pas de prise. A lui pourtant revient de
tirer de cet ensemble, tel le musicien de son instrument, les
merveilleux et plus harmonieux accents. A lui de révéler la
vocation profonde de cette région bénie des dieux.

Il lui restera ensuite à faire connaître, sinon ses efforts, du
moins du résultat. Les auteurs y aident de tout leur talent.

Comte A. de Lur-Saluces, 20 septembre 1978, Château Yquem

PREFACE

It is exactly ten years since we completed the text of the first edition of *Sauternes*. This second edition gives us the opportunity to revise and amplify the original in the light of the many changes that have taken place and much new information that has since come to light.

We have visited and revisited numerous properties and corresponded with all, and, of course, studied everything that has been written about the area and its wines. As before we are necessarily much indebted to very many willing helpers both in France and in this country. In particular we would like to thank MM Pucheu-Planté and Seguin of the Department of Oenology, University of Bordeaux I, for generously allowing us to use the results of their exhaustive researches; M Mercier of the Department of Electronic Microscopy, University of Bordeaux I, for his miraculous photographs of *botrytis cinerea* in action; Sita Garros for supplying invaluable information, and Colin Boden and Paul Lanneluc for supplying much of the photography.

The aim of the book is unchanged. We hope that it will be a useful reference book for professional and amateur devotees of Sauternes. Even more important, we hope to catch the interest of those — still far too many — who think that it is rather unsophisticated to enjoy sweet wines; to convince them that Sauternes and its immediate neighbours can produce wines that are as enjoyable and interesting as any dry wines.

If we can persuade even a few sceptics to try a glass of good-quality Sauternes, Barsac, Cérons, Loupiac, Cadillac or Ste-Croix-du-Mont with an open mind we can confidently leave it to the wine to complete the conversion.

Jeffrey Benson and Alastair Mackenzie, 1990

History

Vines were brought to the Bordeaux area by the Romans, probably about the time of Julius Caesar, and have flourished there ever since. Comte Henri de Vaucelles, proprietor of Château Filhot, and a great authority and theorist about the history of the area, thinks that one of the reasons for Sauternes' rise to vinous eminence, apart from its magical microclimate, of which more later, is the fact that its little line of hills were a sort of frontier between the Gallic Bordelaise, who were Romanised, and the less civilised Ibero-Aquitaneans. The prelates of the early Middle Ages, becoming increasingly powerful, were able to exploit the situation in order to enlarge the Church's estates, on which sweet white wine was first made in this area.

The immense Bordeaux trade with England from the thirteenth century (Bordeaux was technically an English province for 300 years from 1152) was preponderantly in red wine. There is mention in the records of the Guildhall in London of merchants coming from Barsac to sell or promote their wine in the thirteenth century. On 9th July 1363 the municipal leaders of Langon, the nearest town to Sauternes and its canton, took an oath of fealty to the Black Prince in Bordeaux.

The loss of the Holy Land, the dissolution of the Templars and the ruin of the competing vineyard areas of the Loire Valley and Poitou then encouraged the development of the vineyards of the Garonne in making not only light red wine but also sweet white wine, based on Mediterranean models, for sacramental purposes. The latter was not commercialised but made solely for the Church, as was customary in rural Catholic communities, under the aegis of powerful ecclesiastical counsellors, of whom the most famous was Bertrand de Got, later Pope Clement V, who was Bishop of Bordeaux in 1300.

In the sixteenth and seventeenth centuries a prolonged period of cold, a sort of mini-Ice Age, disrupted agriculture in a community already impoverished by crises and troubles, and the formerly powerful princes of the Church with their luxurious life-style gradually disappeared, to be replaced by a new middle-class society. A large part of the Garonne vineyard area fell into disuse but the Langon middle classes kept up the production of Church wines by stabilising with spirits wines made from late-harvested grapes for the Dutch market.

The independence of the Netherlands — the Dutch Republic was declared in 1579 — led to a great increase in the commerce of French wines. Dutch merchants set up in Bordeaux to export wine to the Baltic and the Hanseatic towns. Much of this was sweet white wine from the Sauternes and Langon areas. The trend was maintained and we know that around 1740 approximately ten times as much white wine as red was being exported to Scandinavia, Hamburg and the Baltic ports.

There was an English merchant resident in Bordeaux at that time, too, one Henry Thompson. Malvezin in his *Histoire du Commerce de Bordeaux* (1692) lists among his 1647 purchases Barsac, Bommes and Sauternes, matching Graves and Médoc in the top price bracket.

The improvement of the climate after the last great frost in 1709, when all the rivers of that part of France were frozen over, encouraged the redevelopment of quality wine-making. In 1685 the Edict of Nantes, which had given tolerance to Protestants, was revoked and by the early eighteenth century the middle-class society of Bordeaux and Langon had adopted the ideas of the Counter-Reformation. In viticultural terms this meant a return to the ecclesiastic tradition of making fine wines for keeping without the addition of spirit. The de Pontac family, whose members included important merchants and priests, played an important part in this return to traditional methods. Being so humid the Sauternes area specialised in sweet wines harvested in successive pickings. The grapes were rotten, *pourris* — but the word was never mentioned to the customer, only to the vineyard workers (as specified in the *Rules of Cultivation of Château Filhot* [1740]), since it seemed an inappropriate description of grapes from which sacramental wine for use in the Mass was to be made.

About this time the more Protestant area of Monbazillac in Bergerac was producing fortified sweet white wines which were preferred by some to the now natural wines of Sauternes. Recently some bottles of white Bergerac were discovered in a Dutch ship wrecked in about 1750 and the wine has been said to resemble an old Sauternes. But during the course of this century the better properties of Sauternes and its surrounding areas reduced the yield to produce a heavier must and greater extract and introduced other technical improvements such as the use of sulphur. After the Revolution Monbazillac's importance waned when the Bordeaux laws prohibiting the addition of spirit were extended to Bergerac.

The regained prosperity of the eighteenth century brought about the building of large châteaux, some of which have kept the names of their then proprietors (as Château d'Arche). A new merchant class and the families of the Bordeaux Parlement (a legal court whose appointments were often hereditary) became increasingly wealthy. Until this time there were no large estates in the present sense for the vineyards were worked by peasants or small tenant farmers who received a share of the crop from the landlord; in the 40 years before the Revolution many of the poor tenants, having got into debt, had to sell out and the size of the estates greatly increased.

Naturally the Revolution had a disastrous initial effect on the area of the great sweet white wines and many noble families were bankrupted as early as 1794. Trade was disrupted, prices were frozen arbitrarily and in some areas vines were uprooted and replaced with food crops. Many ecclesiastical domains, too, fell into decline; the towns of La Resle and Langon went along with the anti-clerical feeling of the Revolution to the point of neglecting the production of sweet and liquorous wines, which had *ancien régime* associations. The old reputation of the Langon vineyards disappeared whereas that of Haut-Preignac, Barsac and Sauternes eventually prospered. Once the situation eased and trade picked up a bit, the new owners restored the earlier vineyard names and some families recovered part of their former possessions, grouping vineyards together by intermarriage, the Lur-Saluces family acquiring the largest amount of property as a result.

Even before the Revolution Château d'Yquem had the distinction of being purchased and highly praised by Thomas Jefferson, future President of the United States. Yet it was in a sense the Revolution that helped Sauternes to a wider recognition by encouraging its appreciation in temporarily de-Christianised Paris and subsequently in the whole of Napoleonic Europe. M Bernard Ginestet in his book *Barsac/Sauternes* suggests that the very hardships, suffering and poverty that the Revolution brought helped to popularise the rich, sweet wines which were so sustaining in times of food shortages. This may appear fanciful but he backs it up by pointing to the increased consumption of Sauternes and the other sweet wines in both World Wars. Also the imperial and royal courts of Europe were looking in the nineteenth century for alternatives to the sweet wines of the Rhine and Tokay, whose productions had suffered as a result of the revolutions of 1848. Sauternes provided one, and was established by the great success of the 1847 d'Yquem at the Russian court.

The sweet wine areas, like all others, were hit by the triple nineteenth-century disasters of oidium, phylloxera and mildew. They were particularly badly affected by oidium, which struck in 1852, but sulphur-spraying had solved that problem by 1858. The sand content of much of the Sauternes soil discouraged the phylloxera louse somewhat and the 1893 edition of Cocks et Féret states that most of the vines were still French. Finally, however, they all had to be grafted on to American roots.

A little-known episode of Sauternais history is the attempt in the 1870s by the firm of MM E. Normandin et Cie to produce a sparkling Sauternes. Assisted by a staff of experienced workmen from Epernay and using the Champagne method with Sauternes grapes, they produced at their headquarters at Châteauneuf in the Charente valley a wine which won a gold medal at the Concours Régional d'Angoulême in 1877. Their example was followed by the house of Lermat-Robert who produced a sparkling Barsac which was shown at the Paris exhibition the next year. Apparently the experiment was not a lasting success.

The collapse of the royalist world and various national and international crises made the first decade of the twentieth century a difficult one for the Bordeaux wine trade generally, but one improvement was the restriction of the use of the Sauternes *appellation*, which had become widely abused, and the formation of a producers' association for Sauternes and Barsac. Then came the First World War and the Russian Revolution followed by Prohibition in America and the great slump of the late 1920s and early 1930s. Like clarets, fine Sauternes could be bought for absurdly low prices between the Wars. However, the 1930s did bring the institution of the *Appellation d'Origine Contrôlée* (1935), which limited the title Sauternes to the communes of Sauternes, Barsac, Bommes, Preignac and Fargues. Barsac was allowed to retain its own *appellation* or to call itself Sauternes. Cérons, Loupiac, Ste-Croix-du-Mont and Cadillac also have their own *appellations*.

After the Second World War changes of fashion and austerity combined to undermine the popularity of Sauternes. Many people simply wouldn't pay anything like a proper price for these delicious wines which are necessarily expensive to make. There were few good vintages in the 1960s; many proprietors had to start making dry white and red wine which they could sell (though only as Bordeaux Supérieur) in difficult years. But the 1970s were more fortunate and gradually over the last ten years, since interest in wine generally seems to be on the increase, people have begun to realise what wonderful value these wines are, and both sales and prices have risen. A number of leading properties are making better wine than they were ten years ago and — most encouraging of all — Château de Myrat, the *deuxième cru* which uprooted its vines in 1976 on the grounds that making fine sweet wine was no longer economic, has decided to replant. The situation has certainly improved and it is fair to end on a note of cautious optimism.

THE MAKING OF THE WINE

The fine sweet wines of Sauternes and Barsac, areas which form an enclave in the southern part of Graves some 25 miles south-east of Bordeaux, are unique. As with all the fine wine areas of the world, this uniqueness is the result of a combination of soil, grape variety, climate, microclimate and human endeavour and expertise.

Soil

It is generally agreed that the nature of the soil and subsoil, together with its chemical and mineral content and in particular its ability to drain, is one of the most important determining elements in the character and quality of wine.

In the early Tertiary Age the whole of the Gironde was part of a vast area known as the Aquitanean Sea. As the sea receded it left huge sediments of different kinds. The soil of the Médoc and the northern part of Graves consists mainly of deep gravel banks which drain well and retain the heat of the sun. In the north, in St-Estèphe, there is more clay in the soil, and the southern part of Graves is sandier.

The soils of our area are basically later Quaternary Age formations with outcrops of Tertiary Age Stampian and Aquitanean periods. The late Quaternary formations cover these in varying thicknesses except in the region of Barsac and Preignac, where the Stampian formation appears under a layer of starfish limestone of marine origin, similar to the highest level of St-Emilion.

The main vineyard area is situated on the ancient gravel-sand terraces of the river Garonne and a spring-fed stream, the Ciron. In these alluvial layers carved into hills by the erosion of wind and water one can distinguish small gravel fragments of the Pleiocene (Tertiary) period, which form a plateau dominating the Garonne valley at a height of 70 to 80 metres, and also larger gravel fragments of the Quaternary Age. It is on this combination of sandy gravels, which constitute

14

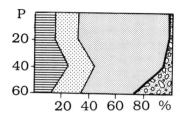

Fig. 1

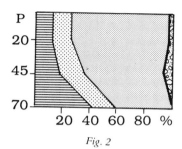

Fig. 2

Samples taken at various depths, separated by size, weighed separately and reduced to a percentage of total soil at that depth.

1. A loam closely related to wind-blown loess. It is a finely grained deposit consisting of wind-blown material subsequently re-sorted by water.

≣	Clay
⋰	Limon[1]
░	Sand
◌	Gravel
⬤	Pebbles

P Depth in cms

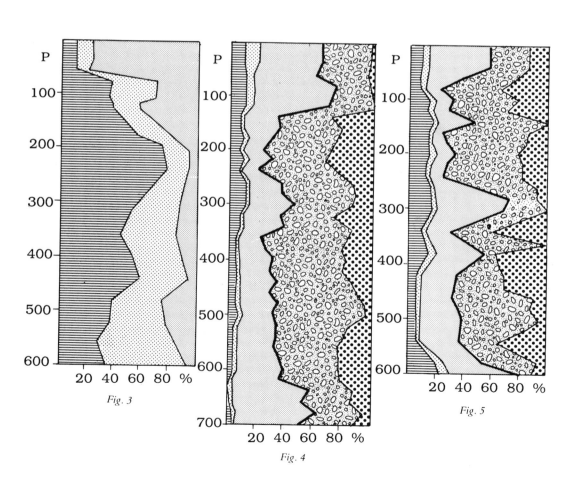

Fig. 3

Fig. 4

Fig. 5

the higher part of the area of Sauternes (Bommes, Fargues, Sauternes and Haut-Preignac), that the majority of the finest vineyards are placed. In contrast to this landscape where little hills and valleys alternate, the region of Barsac and Bas-Preignac is characterised by a comparatively low altitude (12–15 metres). The flattish surface, of the Stampian period, more or less karstified (formed by the solution of limestone), is covered by red sand and supports a good vineyard area with several classed growths.

Put very simply, Barsac and the lower part of Preignac are mainly limestone and clay on a limestone subsoil, while the other three communes are predominantly gravel on a sand, gravel and clay subsoil.

These are essentially generalisations, however, and as so often with wine areas, there are variations (especially of subsoil) — not only from commune to commune and vineyard to vineyard but within the same property — which undoubtedly affect the quality of the grapes grown on them.

To illustrate this we give some examples of experiments conducted by MM Pucheu-Planté and Seguin showing the exact make-up of the soils in four parts of our area. The samples are taken from:

a) Barsac (soft limestone soil)
b) Barsac (hard limestone soil)
c) Sauternes — Yquem (predominantly clay)
d) Sauternes — other (gravel/sand)
e) Bommes (gravel/sand/clay)

a) and b) Barsac is comparatively flat and, as we have seen, contrasts with the hilly contours of the neighbouring communes. The starfish limestone is covered by a thin layer of sediment left by wind and water which is mainly red, and rich in iron oxide — again like some of the St-Emilion soil. It has a browner tinge in areas of more recent alluvial deposits. The depth of the soil explored by the roots varies from 0.3 to 2 metres. The root system is generally spread out near the surface but sometimes penetrates deeper according to the degree of solution in the underlying limestone. The differences in the Barsac soil stem from the fact that there are two kinds of limestone present, one quite soft and the other very hard, compact and very resistant to decarbonation. These play a big part in determining the evolution of the deep strata. (Figs 1 and 2)

c) Sauternes — Yquem. This part of Yquem is 65 metres above sea level; an alluvial crust, only 1 to 2 metres deep at the most, covers a very thick dome of clay with limited permeability. In the nineteenth century a special drainage system was laid to allow water to escape from this clay hill. (Blocked drains can cause vine-plants to wither.) The combination of light surface texture and deep, well-structured clay, with its own drainage system and permitting deep roots, is unique in the area. (Fig. 3)

Average monthly temperatures 1977-86

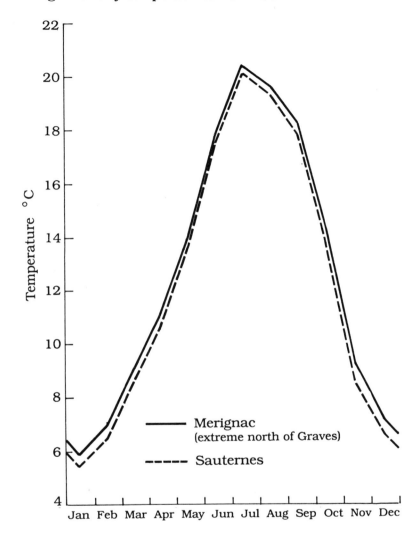

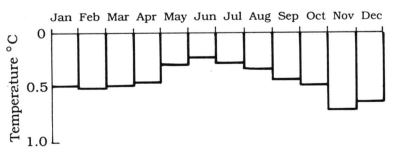

Absolute differences between Merignac and Sauternes

17

Average monthly precipitation 1977-86

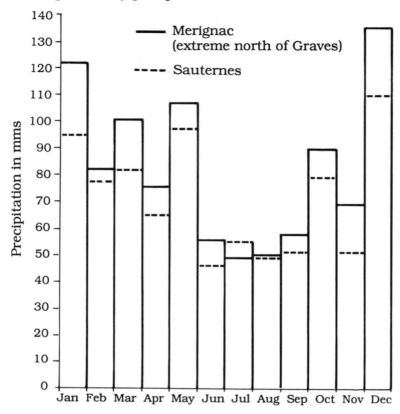

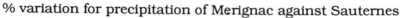

% variation for precipitation of Merignac against Sauternes

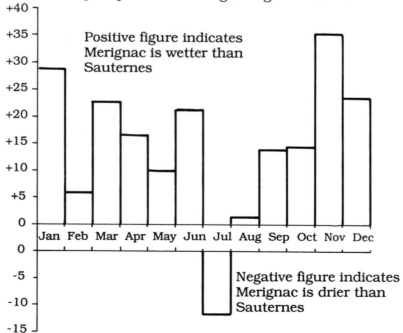

d) Sauternes — This sample is on top of a sand/gravel hill 50 metres high. Thirty-year-old vines achieve roots generally three metres deep, but can reach five. (Fig. 4)

e) Bommes — This sample is on top of a sand/gravel hill 60 metres high. The vines achieve roots only 2.4 metres deep; the very high water level after storms inhibits root depth. The vines are not so vigorous here and are more subject to coulure and millerandage because the water can easily rise and asphyxiate the vine. (Fig. 5)

Conclusion: although the two areas seem at first sight to be homogeneous in soil make-up a study of the deeper strata which the roots reach shows major variations. The hillier gravel/sand areas vary considerably in their clay and stone content. Even in Barsac, which seems more homogeneous, this in-depth study shows two distinct types of limestone subsoil.

With the exception of Château d'Yquem, which is geologically unique in the area, the chemical properties of the Sauternes soils are much the same as those of the rest of Bordeaux. It is physical differences, not chemical ones, that determine variations of character in the wines.

Climate and the noble rot

These two phenomena are so closely interwoven that we must deal with them together.

The Bordeaux climate is an oceanic one known as Aquitanean. It is stabilised by the large amount of water around it: the Atlantic and the huge Gironde estuary, fed by the Garonne and Dordogne rivers. It is also influenced by the Gulf Stream and sheltered from Atlantic winds by the pine forests of Les Landes. All these factors combine to give the area hot summers, long mild autumns, fairly mild, wet winters, and mild springs. There are local variations of course: the differences in average monthly temperature and precipitation between Sauternes and Merignac, near Bordeaux, 1977–86, are indicated in the adjacent diagrams. It is a climate particularly suitable for producing fine wines, but to understand the secret of Sauternes' uniqueness we must examine its special microclimate.

The little river Ciron, rising from springs in Les Landes, runs south-west to north-east past Sauternes and Bommes then between Preignac and Barsac to join the Garonne near the old port of Barsac. Until the end of the nineteenth century it was quite an important waterway, for logs cut in the forest of Les Landes were floated down it to this port. The Ciron makes an important contribution to the microclimate necessary to produce Sauternes (once described by a Bordeaux historian as 'le don du Ciron'). The significantly colder waters of this tree-canopied stream running into the warmer waters of the tidal Garonne cause evaporation, which leads to the formation of mists during the night. In autumn these last until they are burnt off by the late morning sun. They spread over the vineyards on either side of the rivers and the repeated alternation of humid, misty conditions and dry, sunny ones is the perfect breeding-ground for one of nature's strangest contributions to wine-making.

Botrytis cinerea, to give this cryptogamatic fungus its proper name, is responsible for two kinds of rot which affect grapes, *pourriture grise* and *pourriture noble*. The first generally attacks immature grapes whose skins have been split by excessive rain, oidium, mildew, hail, birds, insects or maggots, and is usually accompanied by other fungi, especially penicillium and aspergillus, which impart an unpleasant taste to the grape-juice; it also widens the split and opens the way for destructive bacteria. The second, our 'noble rot', attacks only fully ripened grapes when the grape's resistance to infection has decreased. The researches of MM Pucheu-Planté and Seguin have revealed that the botrytis spores put out filaments, germinative tubes (*hyphae*) which penetrate the grape-skin through micro-

The different stages of the conidian cycle of *botrytis cinerea*.

Microphotographs: M. Mercier, Department of Electronic Microscopy, University of Bordeaux I.

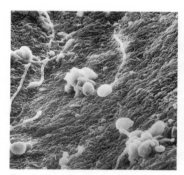

Fig. 1 Detached *conidia* (spores) and emission of *hyphae* (germination tubes)

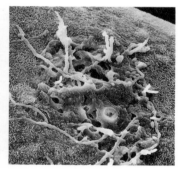

Fig. 2 Early branching of *mycelium* (clusters of *hyphae*)

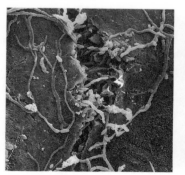

Fig. 3 Later branching of *mycelium*

Fig. 4 Growth of *conidiophores* (spore-carriers).

lesions (far too small to be seen by the naked eye or even to be penetrated by unwelcome bacteria), as well as through the peristomatic breaks which already exist in its membrane. The fungus then grows within the walls of the skin cells while destroying pectic structures such as the middle tissues. After four to eight days *hyphae* emerge from the grape surface and develop into *conidiophores*, spore-carriers which further spread the rot. The length of this conidian cycle is influenced by environmental factors, especially temperature and acidity. The concentration of malic and tartaric acids in the grape also causes variation. It can take anything from 70 to 800 hours.

After the first stages of the 'noble rot' the skin goes brown or violet and the grape is called *pourris plein* — rotten but full. When the process is complete and the grape is a revolting-looking, wizened raisin it is called a *grain rôti*.

Let us look at the alchemy that is taking place inside the now dead grape. The fungus consumes about a third of the grape sugar, five sixths of the tartaric acid, a third of the malic acid and a quarter of the citric acid. It also consumes much of the water content of the juice and by rendering the skin very porous it encourages further evaporation by sun and wind. The grape is between half and a third of its original weight. Important by-products of this digestive process are glycerol, gluconic acid and dextrin, which contribute towards the oleaginous texture of the wine. There is another important by-product, botrycine. An important effect of the breaking down of the molecular structure of the skin by botrytis is that when the grapes are pressed tannins are released into the juice; this is not the case in the making of other white wines.

So the overall effect is considerable metabolising of acidity, an intense concentration of grape sugars, an increase of tannins, a number of by-products which will give the wine its characteristic aromas and texture and, of course, a very considerable reduction in quantity of juice.

There is still some mystery about botrytis. Some oenologists think that colonies of certain strains that have grown up in the area are particularly adapted to the function of *pourriture noble* rather than *pourriture grise*; similarly it is thought that particular yeast strains will gather over the years in certain vineyards and cellars and help to give a particular growth its own individual character.

Sauternes probably has the most suitable climate in the world for achieving its particular miracle. But the perfect succession of night and early morning mists and warm days does not occur every autumn even here. Botrytis can be very haphazard and contrary in the way it spreads its spores over the vineyard area. Richard Olney in his admirable book *Yquem* cites the vintages of 1974 and 1976 as two extremes. In 1974 Yquem, which ideally picks only grapes affected by botrytis, made eleven pickings or *tries* over a period of some two months, despite which no wine was considered good enough to go out under the d'Yquem label. In 1976 there was one preliminary picking and then the entire harvest was collected, in bunches, at the incredibly early date of 13th October, 21 days after the first *trie*, so early and so uniform had been the onset of botrytis; to have left it any longer would have been to risk excessive botrytis and botrycine posing future fermentation problems. The average at Yquem is five or six *tries* and about 45 days. 1983 was another very uniform year (although because the first part of the 'Indian summer' was so dry the botrytis was late in coming) and most recently 1986. Most years fall somewhere in between the two extremes and it is here that the wealthier and the more conscientious proprietors have the advantage over those who cannot afford or will not attempt repeated pickings. Naturally these are costly because the pickers must be highly skilled to select and handle the precious raisins and may have to be on call over a period of several weeks. At any time rain, hail or frost may come and destroy the whole crop within hours. Rain will quickly saturate the now very porous skins and swell the grapes, so that renewed sun — or a drying wind — will be needed to dehydrate them again. If the rain continues the grapes may split and rot. In 1978 there was glorious hot sunshine in late autumn but insufficient humidity and so virtually no botrytis. Even what ultimately prove to be quite good years can prove terrifying tests of nerve and judgement for proprietors. 1985 is a good example: the weather had been very good but, as in 1978, the humidity was too low. Rain brought a little botrytis in late September but then the hot, dry weather returned. Those brave or wealthy enough to take the risk held back and hoped for the best. In late October and November botrytis set in again and the harvest, for those who waited, was finally excellent. But many had picked in early or mid-October and so made wine little affected by botrytis.

As we have said only the wealthiest and most perfectionist of growers can afford to pick exclusively *grains rôtis* over some 6–8 *tries*. It is very costly and labour-intensive. Many pick perhaps two or three times, pick bunches rather than individual grapes, or wait until a fair number of bunches are affected and pick all at once.

There are all sorts of stories about how the wonderful properties of the noble rot were discovered by an accidental delay of the harvest. The most famous are set in Hungary in the seventeenth century, Germany in the eighteenth and Sauternes (Yquem) in 1847. This last must surely be taken with a pinch of salt when one considers the evidence we have. In 1839 M Jouet, librarian of Bordeaux, speaking of the area (including Podensac), says that the grapes were only picked when rotten and after the vines had lost their leaves. The Yquem cellar-book, dated October 1810, proves that late harvests and selective pickings were well established by the early nineteenth century. In that year three *tries* were made between 3rd October and 11th November. M Henri Redeuilh, writing about Cadillac, Loupiac and Ste-Croix-du-Mont at the end of the eighteenth century, says that there were several *tries* ending often in mid-November. M Bidet in his treatise on the nature and cultivation of the vine (1759) says that Sauternes was making sweet and liquorous wines, picking several times and only very ripe grapes. The memoirs of a steward of Guyenne (1716) record that at vintage time one chooses shrivelled grapes and does not cut those that are nearly rotten, so that the harvest lasts till December. It should be noted that he describes this as the norm. Even earlier, in 1666, in a deed of 4th October following a lawsuit between François de Sauvage, 'Sieur Di-quem', and some of his workers who wanted to pick too early we are told that in Bommes and Sauternes picking does not usually start before 15th October.

All these pieces of evidence indicate that in Sauternes late and selective picking has been the practice for centuries and we can hardly doubt that its purpose was to make use of the effect of botrytis on the grapes. Richard Olney conjectures that in the seventeenth century a decision was made to pick the whole harvest when most of the grapes were affected, rather than by successive pickings; so that some vintages would be not unlike modern good ones (1976 for instance) but that there would be considerable variation of sweetness and richness from year to year. He is convinced that the Sauternes *vigneron* can at no time have been unaware of the noble rot and of the wonderful effect it has on the wine.

M Ginestet suggests in *Barsac/Sauternes* that the so-called 'saprian' (rotten) wines of fifth-century BC Greece were made from botrytis-affected grapes, saying that even in the Mediterranean there are some microclimates suitable for *pourriture noble* and that it is often difficult to tell the difference between grapes merely shrivelled by overmaturity and those nobly rotted. He also points to Virgil's advice in the Eclogues: 'To make good wine, harvest as late as possible'. He quotes further from Greek and Roman literature and claims that the practice of making wine from nobly rotten grapes spread over the whole of Europe wherever conditions allowed. But of course he cannot offer any real evidence. What he wants to say is that the stories that place the discovery of botrytis in the nineteenth century are nonsense, which is surely right.

In the previous edition we mentioned experiments being conducted in California in spraying botrytis spores on to grapes artificially. In fact experiments have been proceeding at the University of California (Davis) in the laboratory culture of botrytis spores since the 1950s and still continue. In his book *Liquid Gold* Stephen Brook describes the experiments of Myron Nightingale, starting in the early 1960s. Fertile spores isolated from botrytis cultures are sprayed on to fully ripe sémillon bunches laid out in trays in the temperature-controlled winery. They are wrapped in plastic for 30 hours to gain humidity and then warm and cool air is blown over them alternately to simulate the natural conditions of Sauternes. Apparently this technique has been more successful with Mr. Nightingale's riesling than with sémillon and it would certainly be premature to describe it as a breakthrough. Similar experiments have been conducted in South Australia by Joe Grilli at Primo Estates and Tim Knappstein at Enterprise Wines in Clare. The process is expensive and as labour-intensive as the real thing but Mr. Grilli's wines are said to be indistinguishable from those made from naturally botrytised grapes.

Finally even at traditionalist Yquem there has been some experimenting recently in years when there is a lack of early morning humidity, by laying down water pipes between the vine rows which emit a fine spray to induce the onset of botrytis. Alexandre de Lur-Saluces says that so far the results are inconclusive.

We are again indebted to MM Pucheu-Planté and Seguin for their study on the role of the climate in the vintages 1971–1981. In this period the sémillon grapes reached full ripeness within the normal Bordeaux margin (late September to early October) six times. In 1976 ripening was unusually early (mid-September) and in four consecutive years, 1977–1980, it did not occur until mid-October.

It is interesting to note the considerable variation in must weight from year to year. This is strongly influenced on the one hand by the summer rainfall, which is very variable, and also by the clay character of a number of Sauternes soils; sometimes these poorly formed clay levels can create underground puddles which can temporarily asphyxiate the vine roots. Indeed heavy thunderstorms coming at flowering time or during the period of growth can affect the whole water intake of the plant and cause a physiological imbalance resulting in coulure, millerandage or retarded growth.

The first signs of botrytis may appear on the grape skins quite early but their evolution does not start to speed up until about ten days before the grape is fully ripe, when its biological resistance is much reduced. As maturity approaches grapes are very sensitive to climatic conditions and especially to rain; a few showers may often suffice to induce a splitting of the skins made fragile by the action of botrytis. This happened in various parts of the vineyards in 1973, 1974, 1976 and 1981 to a greater or lesser extent.

As for the other years, 1974 was particularly wet (339 mm in September, October and November), 1977 and 1978 were two late-ripening and dry years, while 1972 was late-ripening, cold and dry; otherwise over-ripening took place in good conditions (slightly rainy and very sunny autumns).

The chemical composition of the musts (table II) showed a satisfactory richness in sugars and acidity except in 1972, 1974 and 1980. The high sugar concentration in 1978 was due to *passerillage* rather than botrytis — the grapes were merely shrivelled and not rotten — in an exceptionally dry year (47 mm of rain from September to November). In 1976 the rainy period before the second picking caused a lowering of the sugar levels of the musts which eight days earlier had been around 340 grams per litre.

From this detailed analysis of eleven consecutive years of Sauternes first and second growths one can readily understand that the uncertainty of the weather does not allow a systematic production of great Sauternes. Yet in most years at least some fine wines were made.

Grapes

The grapes from which Sauternes and the neighbouring sweet wine *appellations* are made are the same as those used in making the neighbouring white Graves, sémillon, sauvignon blanc and muscadelle. Much the most important is sémillon, which, with its thinnish skin, is particularly susceptible to the attacks of botrytis. In many parts of the world it produces rather unexciting wine but here (and in Australia) it finds conditions which suit it perfectly and, if growers prune it severely and aim for a small, high-quality harvest, it makes beautiful wine. The wine it produces is naturally high in alcohol and quite low in aroma and acidity. It ages well and is suited to oak casking and develops what is said to be a waxy or lanolin smell. There are undoubtedly clonal variations. The strain used in California is said to be less susceptible to botrytis and Jancis Robinson in her *Vines, Grapes and Wines* notes that the sémillon bunches at Yquem are smaller and looser than at other properties, though whether this is caused by clonal variation or the unique soil conditions at Yquem must be uncertain.

The sauvignon blanc with its pungent liveliness is used in comparatively small quantities to add acidity and aroma to the sémillon base. The proportion among the *premiers crus* varies from virtually none at Climens to 25% at Rayne-Vigneau. Some properties maintain the old tradition of planting one sauvignon vine at regular intervals along the rows of sémillon, though they are now more generally planted separately. Sauvignon blanc is rather less prone to botrytis than the sémillon.

25

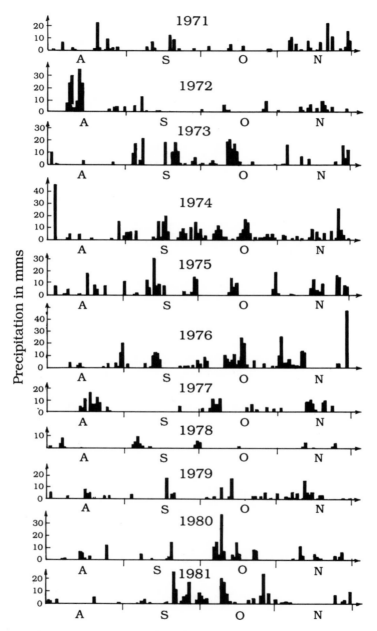

Daily distribution of rainfall in the course of the months of August (A), September (S), October (O) and November (N) during the eleven years of the study

The strong-smelling muscadelle is used in small quantities in many Sauternes to give extra perfume to the wine. The highest proportion in a classed growth is 15% at Romer-du-Hayot.

An average Sauternes vineyard might contain 75% sémillon, 20% sauvignon and 5% muscadelle, although as we have seen there are wide variations.

It is thought that up to the nineteenth century muscadette was the main variety of the area and there was a larger proportion of sauvignon than semillon in the average *cépage*. In the 1850s when the sémillon was found to be more resistant to oidium more of it was planted and no doubt its greater susceptibility to botrytis was increasingly appreciated.

Table I
Chemical composition of musts of sémillon at maturity
(Averages of different parts of Sauternes and Barsac)

Year (Date of samples)	Weight 100 grapes	Sugars g/l[1]	Total Acidity meq/l[2]	Tartaric Acid meq/l[2]	Malic Acid meq/l[2]
1971 (29/9)	186	212	104	106	44
1972 (9/10)	189	201	105	83	71
1973 (26/9)	235	202	84	88	36
1974 (23/9)	198	187	96	82	42
1975 (23/9)	198	210	105	94	42
1976 (8/9)	223	197	98	90	40
1977 (12/10)	189	200	100	94	46
1978 (10/10)	175	226	102	85	41
1979 (4/10)	237	202	106	92	36
1980 (30/9)	222	181	122	89	58
1981 (24/9)	276	223	79	84	37
Average	**212**	**204**	**100**	**90**	**45**

Table II
Chemical composition of musts from nobly rotten grapes during the period of over-ripening
(Averages of different parts of Sauternes and Barsac at the time of the second picking)

Year (Date of Samples)	Weight 100 grapes	Sugars g/l[1]	Total Acidity mew/l[2]	Tartaric Acid meq/l[2]	Malic Acid meq/l[2]
1971 (12/10)	88	343	114	94	53
1972 (30/10)	112★	223★	98★	81★	67★
1973 (16/10)	81	273	80	86	42
1974 (10/10)	164	187	89	74	36
1975 (13/10)	76	433	130	92	65
1976 (7/10)	89	306	126	96	45
1977 (20/10)	77	286	121	118	60
1978 (17/10)	86	338	120	85	56
1979 (10/10)	118	337	145	80	45
1980 (20/10)	136	240	90	122	48
1981 (14/10)	135	282	87	48	21
Average	**105**	**302**	**110**	**89**	**47**

1 grams per litre
2 milli-equivalents per litre (when concentration of an acid in solution is measured, it is done by reacting the acid solution with a solution of an alkali, which neutralises the acid. The term meq/l is a direct measure of the volume of alkali needed in such a reaction. A certain volume of acid of concentration 50 meq/l will require the same volume of alkali to neutralise it, irrespective of the nature of the acids.)

★In this period in 1972 there were hardly any grapes affected by noble rot.

Viticulture

The work in the vineyard is dictated by the annual life-cycle of the vine. It starts in mid-March when the rising sap causes 'tears' to ooze out of the wounds made by the earlier pruning.

At the end of March comes the budding when the 'eyes' (concealed at the base of each previous season's leaf) on the pruned branches begin to swell.

Next is the leafing: the eyes have become shoots and now sprout tiny leaves. At the same time new eyes appear at the joint of the shoot and under each leaf stem ready for next year.

Two weeks later the flower buds appear usually coinciding with the fourth leaf. A tendril forms opposite each leaf and two of these will usually be fertile and develop flower buds, like little grape-bunches. The infertile ones climb and twine.

Flowering and fertilisation take about a month. Flowering often happens in the second week in June but it can be late May or early July. It is a vital time for the crop: pollination is essential for even a partial failure can cause coulure, to which the sauvignon vine is especially susceptible. Millerandage is another condition caused by poor fertilisation which results in stunted and late-ripening grapes.

The setting of the fruit stretches from pollination until about mid-August. The grapes swell up to a good size with little change in their chemical make-up, absorbing, thanks to their chlorophyl content, much of their nourishment from the air. The vine's growth continues with new leaves sprouting.

Ripening and lignification: suddenly everything changes. The grapes ripen and the branches harden and darken. The vine's growth virtually ceases as all its energy goes into maturing the grapes and the wood. The grapes lose their chlorophyl and take their sugar from the leaves as their acidity gets lower and their sugar level rises. Ripening is traditionally supposed to be a hundred days after flowering but of course this is only an approximation. The sauvignon, which flowers slightly later than the sémillon, catches up with it and they ripen at the same time. When the leaves have contributed all their sugar they turn yellow and fall off. In early November the sap falls, the vine becomes dormant and the cycle is completed.

As soon as the harvest is finished any old vines to be destroyed are uprooted and the topsoil ploughed. The soil is sterilised, compost is added and then it is left fallow. Fallow vineyard ready for replanting is manured, ploughed and staked ready for the spring plantation of young vines. Here more manure will be used than for the more mature vines. The main vineyard will be ploughed between the vine rows and soil thrown up at the base of the vine to protect the roots and grafts from the cold. The old year's growth is cut off except for two to four branches. The sémillon and muscadelle are pruned by the *taille à cot* or *gobelet* method: all the previous year's wood is

28

cut off except for two stumps cut very short, each carrying two or three eyes from which the fruit-bearing shoots will develop; then these are trained upwards so that the shape of the mature vine is something like a goblet — hence its name. The less prolific sauvignon is better suited to the *guyot simple* method, also used in St-Emilion. One long arm with six to eight eyes is left and one short arm with two, which will be the fruit-bearing one the following year.

During the winter pruning some of the best branches may be cut from the finest mature quality-producing vines and set aside for grafting. The other cut branches are gathered up and burnt on the spot or set aside for firewood. Finally any faulty stakes are replaced and the wires tightened. In the nineteenth century, before wires were used, each vine was trained to a single stake and the long branches gathered together and tied near the top. This meant that the vines were far less well aerated than today and therefore presumably somewhat less susceptible to botrytis.

In March the vineyard is ploughed and the earth removed from the base of the vinestock. The soil is loosened. Hoeing will continue from time to time during the growing period to destroy the weeds that compete with the vine for nourishment and to aerate the soil.

In March and April any American root-stocks bought from nurseries are planted and those planted the previous year are grafted with vinifera cuttings from the recent pruning. Elsewhere in Bordeaux new plantations are made with year-old grafted nursery plants.

Treatments against pests and diseases start at leafing time with a sulphuring and then a fungicide spraying. The second sulphuring often coincides with the flowering as the circulation of air helps pollination. In good weather two or three sprayings and sulphurings suffice; in wet years more may be necessary.

In the weeks before flowering shoots or suckers emerge from the vinestock and these must be removed as they too compete for nourishment.

In June and July the young shoots are trained between the double wires and moved upwards as they grow.

By July the vine has to be trimmed to keep the passages clear and to direct the sap back to the grapes; it may even be necessary to remove some of the least promising bunches of grapes if too many have formed.

A certain amount of defoliation is necessary to allow air to circulate around the branches. This starts just before the grapes ripen and goes on until early October. This must be done carefully and moderately as until the grapes are perfectly ripened the still green leaves are an important source of sugar supply for them.

Because the appearance of nobly rotten grapes does not

necessarily indicate their sugar level this has to be checked before picking, and throughout the harvest, with a glucometer or a refractometer. M Ginestet mentions that a new method of assessing the condition of the grapes, their sugar and acidity levels and their degree of noble rottenness has been perfected by the Sopra and Novoferment companies. It measures the sensitivity of the enzyme laccase and measures the actual and potential state of the grape using colour criteria. He adds that most growers probably still have not heard of it!

When the picking finally starts — the norm is late September but it has been known, in freak years, to be as early as 28th August (1893) or as late as 20th October (1980) — the pickers' care and expertise are absolutely vital, not only in the selection and delicate handling of the *grains rôtis* but in the rejection of any damaged or diseased grapes which could infect the must with bacteria and perhaps induce volatile acidity.

In our discussion of botrytis we have already noticed the methods and difficulties of harvesting the Sauternes grapes. The latter result primarily from the apparently arbitrary and sporadic arrival of botrytis — although, as we have seen, it is in fact governed by the climatic conditions — and the risk of sudden rain, hail or early frost which can wipe out the entire remainder of the crop.

Cryoextraction
Although we said above that there has been no dramatic breakthrough in the artificial spraying of botrytis spores, in the last five years a process has emerged which could revolutionise the making of Sauternes. It is called cryoextraction and has something in common with the making of German Eiswein although, of course, that occurs naturally.

In essence it is a process which enables the grower to defeat the elements by picking botrytised grapes when they are still wet either from the early morning dew and mists or — more crucially — saturated by rain. The grapes are picked wet and immediately placed in a large refrigerator. The temperature is maintained at about $-5°C$ and the fruit remains inside for about 24 hours. The juice of nobly rotten grapes has a lower freezing point than that of normally ripe grapes (and, naturally, one far lower than water); by submitting grapes to a temperature somewhere between the freezing point of ordinary ripe grapes and that of *grains rôtis* only the juice of the botrytised grapes will be unfrozen and will run off when pressed. The grapes must be at a uniform temperature when pressed. Also during the pressing the formation of crystals inside the tissues exerts a pressure and alters the texture (this is called supra-extraction). Finally the musts are concentrated by the retention of water crystals inside the pulp during pressing.

An extensive series of tests has been carried out at different temperatures by Professors Chauvet and Sudraud of the Laboratoire Interrégional de la Répression de Fraudes and M Jouan of the Institut d'Oenologie, Talence, with the help of the company of Pedia-Kreyer who have the patent for the process. There are some indications that this method might improve musts from normally ripe grapes as well, but it is for botrytis wines that it can play a potentially life-saving role.

The first experiments were conducted, with just two 20-litre *cuvées*, by M Merlaut of Rayne-Vigneau after he was approached by Professors Chauvet and Sudraud, and he was so impressed with the results that he is vinifying more and more of his harvests by this method. The quality of Rayne-Vigneau's wines since 1982 has certainly been markedly improved. Hamilton Narby and his technical experts at Château Guiraud were also involved in early experiments and were equally impressed by the results.

It is not proposed that this technique should be a substitute for the traditional methods in good weather: M Merlaut has conducted experiments with cryoextraction on botrytised grapes picked at 3pm on sunny days and there is no improvement of the must. But it should prove invaluable in saving nobly rotten grapes which are suddenly hit by rain, and it does enable pickers to start early in the morning, if need be, without waiting for the grapes to dry after the early morning mists and dews.

Cryoextraction is now being tried out at a number of the other leading properties including Doisy-Védrines, La Tour-Blanche, Rieussec and even Yquem itself. It is expensive — the initial outlay is very high — but if it can save potentially good botrytis harvests that are hit by rain then surely it will pay for itself in a few years. Those properties that had these facilities in 1987 must have been very grateful for them. It is certainly an exciting possibility that could have a profound effect on the future of Sauternes.

Vinification

When each round of picking is completed the grapes are brought to the *chai*, sometimes very lightly crushed and pressed immediately. When the grapes are picked not individually but in bunches the stalks are usually left on as they help the juice to drain without too much pressure on the skins. The best presses for this delicate operation are the old-fashioned vertical basket type, as used at Yquem, or the modern, and very expensive, pneumatic ones. Most common are the horizontal or cylindrical presses, which are faster but less gentle. There are usually three pressings (two at Climens), sometimes more, of which the third or last, by far the smallest, is the richest in sugar and extract, although unless the grapes have been picked with great care some less desirable flavours can be secreted and passed on into the must. About 80% of the must comes from the first pressing, 10–15% from the second and the rest from the third.

Usually after pressing the juice, lightly sulphured to prevent oxidation, is poured into a vat for about 24 hours to allow any solids to fall to the bottom, then is racked off the deposit into barrels or tanks for fermentation. This can last for less than two weeks or for six or more — generally the richer the must the slower the fermentation, which is usually conducted at around 20°C. As with all wines the balance is all-important: in this case it is the balance between sugar and alcohol in particular that must be correct. In good years the top properties will hope to achieve a must weight of 19–21° Baumé, *i.e.* 19–21% of sugar, or potential alcohol if it could all be fermented out. Usually when the alcoholic content of the must reaches about 14–15% the various yeasts which act upon the sugar to produce alcohol and carbon dioxide are rendered inactive. In addition there are some natural antibiotics created by botrytis, called botrycine, which further inhibit yeast activity, so that in the best and richest musts fermentation comes to an end naturally. Often, however, in poorer years or when growers have felt obliged to pick the grapes early or all together, the must weight will be considerably lower, so that to leave a suitable amount of residual sugar in the wine the fermentation has to be stopped artificially by the judicious use of sulphur dioxide. Sulphur must be used every time the wine is exposed to the air, but great care must be taken not to overdo the sulphur, which in excess can impart a nasty taste to the wine and leave the wine-drinker with a headache. Other ways of stopping the fermentation are to reduce the temperature or, uniquely at Doisy-Daëne, to use a centrifuge.

Sometimes the must weight will be too low to allow the legal minimum of 13% alcohol to be achieved while leaving a few degrees of residual sugar. The way out of this predicament is to chaptalise. This subject is not much talked about in Sauternes but it is widely practised — even by classed-growth properties, although Yquem, Climens and Guiraud, to name but three, never chaptalise. Chaptalising is the practice of adding a sugar solution to the must to increase its potential alcohol by up to two degrees, and is so called after the French scientist Jean-André Chaptal (1756–1832). It has come to be rather an emotive term, but it is neither illegal nor indeed reprehensible provided that it is done in moderation and only when essential. It is the only way in which some of the less well-off growers can avoid going under when climatic conditions are unfavourable. What is less acceptable is to use it as a short-cut to wines with high alcohol and sugar, picking

1. Cooper at work: once there were 300, now only four exist

2. Hydraulic presses in the 'fermenting room'

early and avoiding the risks of waiting for more botrytis. Some wines, even from classed growths, that do not show much botrytis character have a rather unattractive 'eggy' taste which we feel may be the result of some sugar solution, as opposed to grape sugar, remaining in the wine's residual sugar.

After fermentation the wine is racked off into oak barrels or into fibreglass, stainless steel or cement tanks or vats to mature. Those who favour the latter method argue that this keeps the wine younger and fresher and minimises the ever-present risk of oxidation. It also avoids the enormous evaporation losses (up to 20% of each vintage) caused by maturing in new or newish oak. The oak barrels are new each year at Yquem, and were until recently at Nairac; elsewhere the proportion of new barrels varies from a half to a fifth each year. It is a mistake to suppose that 100% new oak casking automatically makes a better wine. The wine must be robust, powerful and massively structured, as indeed d'Yquem is, to marry perfectly and cope with the flavours and tannins of new oak. Some properties mature the wine partly in barrels and partly in vats. It is normal to rack the wine about every three months and to fine it with egg-white or bentonite before bottling, which usually takes place after eighteen months to two years. While d'Yquem is matured for three years, the interesting and unique Gilette is kept for a minimum of twenty years in small concrete vats, which underlines the fact that there are many variations in the methods of pursuing excellence in wine-making in Sauternes. Many proprietors favour filtration while others consider that this can emasculate or damage the wine.

As each picking will be separately fermented and vinified, at many properties there will be many different casks to be 'assembled', when the time comes, into the final wine. At this point any considered not up to standard and which might detract from the reputation of the château will be declassified and sold off as mere Sauternes. This often takes place when the wine is about a year old, although in this as in almost every other stage of the vinification process there is considerable variation from château to château. A number of properties, including Suduiraut, Coutet and Caillou among the classed growths, make a special *crème de tête* in some years. This practice seems, if anything, to be on the increase, though it must militate against the quality of the property's ordinary wine.

The wine

In the first edition we wrote that the sweet wines of Sauternes and the neighbouring communes were, in a sense, the Cinderellas of the fine wine world. Robert Parker, perhaps more graphically, has recently described them as the dinosaurs of Bordeaux because, presumably, of the struggle they have to avoid extinction. Certainly since the Second World War and until fairly recently demand for these luscious beauties has been small and the prices, except for d'Yquem, absurdly low. Some owners started producing dry white wine and planting red wine varieties, although the wine can only be classified as Bordeaux or Bordeaux Supérieur whatever its quality. It seems quite inconsistent and inequitable that dry white wine made in Cérons is entitled to the Graves appellation but not that made in Sauternes. In 1976 the second-growth Château de Myrat actually gave up the struggle on the grounds that making high-quality sweet wine was no longer an economic proposition; the vines were uprooted.

The main reason for all this is that since the War there seems to have been a steadily increasing feeling — or prejudice — that it is not sophisticated to like sweet wines unless, presumably, they are fortified like port or madeira. There were some hopeful signs in the 1970s despite Myrat's demise and we sense that at last, as interest in wine is ever on the increase, that prejudice is gradually being broken down. Other sweet wines like Muscat de Beaumes de Venise from the Rhône and some of the Australian dessert wines have begun to catch the public imagination and Sauternes too have begun to be appreciated more widely for the fine, complex wines that they are.

Part of the problem is that since the last War Sauternes has been thought of, in the UK and the USA at least, as a dessert or 'pudding' wine pure and simple. The French, however, serve younger Sauternes as an aperitif and maturer vintages with *foie gras*, with fish or even meat, with cheese (especially Roquefort) and some not too sweet desserts. This is often regarded rather patronisingly by the British as a quaint and possibly rather promotional practice. Richard Olney, who is not only the author of *Yquem* but also a distinguished writer on food, in his chapter on Yquem and the table reminds us that it is only comparatively recently that Sauternes has been thought of as primarily a dessert wine. In the era of huge multi-course banquets Yquem traditionally accompanied the main fish course (turbot, brill, sole, salmon trout or salmon). This was followed by clarets and burgundies with the meats and game and apparently there were no complaints about ruined palates! At a dinner at Yquem in 1913 the 1918 d'Yquem (*sic*) accompanied the turbot *sauce mousseline*, as specifically recommended by the late proprietor, Comte Bertrand de Lur-Saluces, who added that it is best of all, perhaps, with *foie gras*; alternatively with fruit, or 'towards midnight, when one has just come home, served very cold with a dry biscuit'. André Simon, founder of the International Wine and Food Society, who perhaps did more than any other man to foster intelligent interest in food and wine throughout the world, agreed with the Comte that it should never be paired with ices, chocolate or sugary sweets. He recommended that it should accompany a ripe peach, nectarine or practically any kind of fruit. He added that it is also both helpful and delightful with a biscuit at eleven o'clock in the morning. Another authority whose opinion is worth noting is Raymond Postgate, creator of the Good Food Guide and also a distinguished writer on wine. He agrees with André Simon about the peach, 'slowly peeled', or a bowl of nuts. P. Norton Shand, another well-known wine-writer, claims that to be appreciated at its best it should be iced very slightly and taken with caviar and toast no thicker than a sheet of cardboard. The wealthy are welcome to experiment.

Richard Olney includes two more recent all-Sauternes dinner menus besides the famous one presented at Yquem in 1926 for two hundred French and foreign journalists. One, served in Berkeley, California in 1975, included entrecôte of beef with potatoes cooked in butter and duck fat with mushrooms, paired with d'Yquem 1955 and 1967; and Culpepper, Virginia ham braised in Sauternes and served with prunes stuffed with green olives accompanied by Château Caillou 1947. Both pairings, apparently, were startlingly successful. The other, in Paris in 1985, was partly organized by Mr. Olney himself and matched d'Yquem vintages of 1980, 1945, 1937, 1921 and 1893 with shellfish consommé, braised turbot in Sauternes sauce, ragoût of calves' sweetbreads, truffles, *foie gras* and cocks' combs, charentais melon in champagne, duck in sweet-and-sour sauce and cheese. He confesses that it was nearly impossible to build a menu round such a series of old and outstanding d'Yquem vintages each of which should really have been the climax of a dinner.

Ultimately of course, as with most things in the world of wine, it is a matter of opinion. We have no doubt that a fine Sauternes can be enjoyed with many foods — fish, pâté, meat, game or cheese for example — although the strength and extract of the wine might overpower a delicate dish. The depth and complexity of the Sauternes would not be adversely affected, though whether it would be enhanced is another matter. We cannot agree, however, that it is an ideal accompaniment to desserts of any kind — not even plain fruit. We feel that even a ripe peach, slowly peeled or not, will have some acidity or sweetness which may fractionally interfere with the perfect balance and harmony of a great wine. We also feel that, while it can be delicious as an accompaniment to many different dishes, its richness, complexity and above all its completeness make it most suitable for drinking alone and that it can best be appreciated by itself. It is not so much a dessert wine; it is a dessert in itself and the finest one imaginable.

Some writers suggest that Sauternes should be drunk well chilled and the sweeter the colder. We feel that the finest growths should be served cellar-cold. If the wine is iced many of the most delicate and elusive characteristics of its taste — and for all their richness the best Sauternes do have finesse — and particularly of its smell, are numbed. This can easily be tested by chilling the wine in the refrigerator, smelling and tasting it, and then warming it in the hand for a minute or two and noting the improvement. One often has to do this at large tastings when the white wines tend to be over-chilled. The wines best served as an aperitif or after a meal are probably the ordinary unnamed Sauternes and Barsacs, the wine of a less good and not very botrytis-affected vintage or even, dare one say it, the wines of those properties which are less conscientious even in quite good years and produce what Bernard Ginestet calls 'Sauternes pâles'.

One of the most remarkable features of fine Sauternes is its longevity. It is often enjoyable to drink as soon as it is bottled, provided that it has not been over-sulphured, but its complex character is masked at first by its natural sugar. Gradually, as the wine matures in the bottle, the colour deepens to a full, mellow gold and the subtle flavours unfurl and reveal themselves. The rate at which this happens naturally depends on the particular vintage. There are still bottles dating back to the last century which are in good condition.

Let us examine the appearance, smell, taste and after-taste of a glass of fine Sauternes near its peak. Its colour will be golden, deep or light according to vintage, château and cellaring. It will have a clearly defined bouquet, rich, often honeyed, with plenty of fruit, sometimes soft and peachy, sometimes bigger and more powerful, perhaps with sterner overtones of marmalade or barley-sugar. Sometimes there is a suggestion of the nostalgic smell of cricket-bat (linseed) oil — perhaps this is what others describe as lanolin, for in the smell and taste of these wines inevitably the same scent or flavour will suggest different things to different people. I remember Ted Hale M.W. ('raw sausage-meat') and Michel Bécot ('violets, mignonettes, roses') giving me their personal impressions of the bouquet of limestone St-Emilions. The first thing one notices in the mouth is the characteristic rich, liquorous texture, at once silky and voluptuous in the best examples; then the flavour unfolds. All the hints and suggestions offered on the nose are translated into a more tangible and three-dimensional form on the palate with a harmonious balance of fruit, acidity, alcohol and sugar giving an ethereal sweetness, all-pervading but not cloying. In the finest wines this is not a single taste sensation — as, for example, with a good Beaume de Venise — but an immensely complex and subtle flavour curve. When one has savoured the wine and swallowed it the intricate network of the flavour nuances lingers on and on in the mouth. This reminds one of the authors of his most sybaritic moment — sitting at the top of the pavilion at Lord's on a beautiful June afternoon, watching Cowdrey bat, listening to a Mozart piano concerto through earphones and sipping Château Rieussec 1959.

In 1978 we wrote that the economic situation in Sauternes was extremely serious with expenses, especially labour for the repeated pickings at the best properties, very high and prices still unrealistically low. Then the average price of a tonneau (900 litres) of Sauternes sold in bulk was some 7,000FF, about the same as an equivalent St-Emilion; but as the tonneau of Sauternes would be the produce of about twice the number of vines the difference in profitability was considerable. Happily things have steadily improved in the 1980s. The 1980 vintage was again comparable with St-Emilion (10,306FF against 9,328FF). Since then Sauternes/Barsac has gradually forged ahead until the figures for 1985 are 21,003FF against 14,606FF which puts it third, behind St-Julien and Pomerol, in the bulk wine prices of Bordeaux *appellations* for that year.

For a comparison at the highest level here are some recent prices, ex-cellars Bordeaux, of some of the leading red (1982) and sweet white (1983) wines (in French francs per bottle):

Calon Ségur	156	Suduiraut	132
Figeac	255	Nairac	140
La Conseillante	288	Climens	151
Léoville Lascases	316	Guiraud	167
Margaux	470	Rieussec	167
Lafite-Rothschild	640	d'Yquem	682

This shows d'Yquem ahead of Lafite, the leading red (not

counting Pétrus), and four of the top first-growth Sauternes and Nairac about on a par with the Médoc third-growth Calon Ségur.

Finally let us examine the latest London auction prices (summer 1988), again comparing red 1982s and sweet white 1983s. Here we find d'Yquem (£935 per case) ahead of the red first growths (£385–726) but way behind the absurdly priced Pétrus (£1,980–2,700). Then Climens (£214–264) is fifth among the red second growths and on a par with Magdelaine in St-Emilion; Rieussec and Guiraud are just behind, all three coming between Cos d'Estournel and Gruaud Larose. These prices show Sauternes doing better against their red rivals.

So, despite the fact that the classed growths apart from d'Yquem are still underpriced, the situation is definitely improving and Sauternes is becoming easier to sell at a fair and realistic price, which in turn enables growers to spend money on more modern and efficient equipment.

It would perhaps take an almost unimaginable change in fashion, or public opinion, for Sauternes to be widely accepted in Britain as a table wine, but with evangelists like Nicole Tari and Richard Olney who knows what may happen?

Local gastronomy
In the authors' opinion the very finest Sauternes are best appreciated absolutely on their own. But that is a personal view, not a magisterial pronouncement. There is a considerable body of opinion, admittedly mostly in France but with such distinguished 'foreign' champions as Richard Olney, which does not agree.

There is no more fervent promoter of the combination of Sauternais wine and food than Nicole Tari of Châteaux Nairac and Giscours (Margaux). She advocates accompanying many dishes with Sauternes including melon, *croûte à Roquefort, blanquette de veau, quenelle de brochet,* mussel soup, turbot *sauce mousseline, blanquette de coquilles St Jacques,* terrine of salmon, turkey with chestnut stuffing (d'Yquem with Christmas dinner?), lampreys, almond tart, fruit salad, sorbets, hazelnuts, walnuts and dried prunes and apricots.

Here are a number of restaurants in the Bordeaux area whose chefs serve special Sauternais dishes, with their specialities:

Hotel de France, Auch (André Daguin). *Poulet deux sauces au Sauternes. La pièce de boeuf au Sauternes et au Roquefort.*

Relais de la Poste, Magescq (Bernard Cousseau). *Alose au Sauternes. Filet de veau aux morilles et au Sauternes.*

Le Chapon Fin, Bordeaux (Jean Ramet). *Chauf-froid au Sauternes. Le ris de veau braisé au Sauternes.*

Le Prés et les Sources d'Eugénie, Eugénie-les-Bain (Michel Guerard). *Soufflé léger aux poires.*

La Tupina, Bordeaux (Jean-Pierre Xiradakis). *Miltonée de tripes aux cèpes et au Sauternes.*

Hauterive, Bouliac, near Bordeaux (Jean Arnat). *Le foie gras au Sauternes.*

La Réserve, Pessac l'Alouette (Pierre Bugat). *La dodine de volaille au Sauternes.*

Other good restaurants even closer to hand are *Auberge des Vignes* (Sauternes), *Le Sauternais* (Sauternes), *Le Forge* (Sauternes), *Au Cep* (Preignac) and *Le Grangousier* (Langon).

And finally *Restaurant Claude Darroze* in Langon (Claude Darroze) whose *fricassé de poissons* we described in the first edition.

Here is the recipe for his *charlotte au Sauternes* (to serve 25):

> 16 egg yolks
> 700 gr. sugar
> 30 cl. Sauternes
> The rinds of 2 lemons, grated
> The juice of 2 lemons
> 12 gelatine leaves soaked in a little water
> 1.7 litres cream.

1) Mix the egg yolks and sugar. Add lemon juice and wine and heat gradually. Do not boil; cook like an egg custard. Remove from heat, add moistened gelatine leaves and lemon rind.

2) Beat up cream and incorporate into custard mixture which should now be cold.

3) Place in mould and decorate with biscuits soaked in Sauternes. Place in refrigerator for 12 hours before serving.

Appellations

Sauternes. Decree of 11th September 1936.

ARTICLE 1 (Modified, 14th September 1953, article 2)
Only those white wines which conform with the conditions stated hereunder and are harvested on the following communes have the right to use the *appellation contrôlée* 'Sauternes': Sauternes, Bommes, Fargues, Preignac and Barsac, excepting those areas of recent alluvial deposits and those designated for cultivation other than as white wine vineyards, in particular forest cultivation, according to local practice.

The boundaries of this production area shall be entered on the surveyor's plans of the communes in question by experts appointed by the managing committee of the Institut National des Appellations d'Origine and the plans thus prepared will be registered with the town halls of the communes in question before 1st January 1954.

ARTICLE 2
Only those wines made from vines of the following stock shall have the right to the *appellation contrôlée* 'Sauternes': sémillon, sauvignon, muscadelle.

(Completed 26th December 1960, Article 2) As from the harvest of 1961, any producer of *appellation contrôlée* wine defined by this decree who owns plots of land containing hybrid white wine varieties within his property located in the area described may not claim the right to use this *appellation*.

ARTICLE 3 (Modified 23rd June 1947, article 7)
Those white wines having the right to use the *appellation contrôlée* 'Sauternes' shall only be made from must containing 221 grams of natural sugar and with a minimum alcoholic content of 13° overall (actual and potential) after fermentation with a minimum of 12.5° actual alcohol.

ARTICLE 4 (Replaced 19th May 1982)

The basic yield stated in the first article of decree number 74,872 of 19th October 1974 is fixed at 25 hectolitres per hectare of vines in production. The yield authorised for the particular vintage is the ceiling stated in article 3 of decree number 74,872. It may not be altered for the wines produced in the same area of vines in production except for the *appellations* 'Sauternes' and 'Bordeaux'. In this case the quantity declared in the *appellation* 'Bordeaux' must not be more than the difference between that put forward under the regulations of article 1 of decree number 74,872 of 20th November 1974 (modified) and that put forward under the *appellation* 'Sauternes' having applied an equal coefficient to the quotient of the annual yield established for that particular vintage as applied to the *appellation* 'Bordeaux' and to that of the basic yield of the *appellation* 'Sauternes'. The benefit of *appellation contrôlée* cannot be given to wines produced from vines under three years old.

ARTICLE 5 (15th February 1947)

Within a period of one year proposals aimed at regulating the pruning of vines producing *appellation contrôlée* 'Sauternes' wines shall be submitted by the Syndicat Viticole de Sauternes.

ARTICLE 6 (Modified 24th January 1956; then 9th October 1956, first article; completed by decree number 74,871 of 19th October 1974)

Vinification shall be carried out with grapes that have reached *surmaturation (pourriture noble)* harvested in successive pickings. It will be in accordance with local practice. For wines having the right to use the *appellation contrôlée* 'Sauternes' all oenological practices allowed under current law are permitted, except for concentration and the addition of alcohol which are forbidden. They may not be sold on the market without a certificate issued by a tasting committee appointed by the Institut National des Appellations d'Origine on advice of the Syndicat Viticole of the region of Sauternes and Barsac. This committee will consider whether the wine meets the requirements of current regulations and, in particular, of this decree.

An internal regulation approved by the Institut National des Appellations d'Origine shall determine the procedure to be followed in issuing the certificate.

ARTICLE 7

Those wines which, under the terms of this decree, have the right to use the *appellation contrôlée* 'Sauternes' may not be declared after the harvest, offered to the public, despatched, put on sale or sold unless, in the harvest declaration, in advertisements, on brochures, on labels or on any form of container, the above-mentioned appellation of origin is accompanied by the words *'appellation contrôlée'* in very clear form.

ARTICLE 8

The use of any sign which may lead the purchaser to believe that a wine has the right to use the *appellation contrôlée* 'Sauternes' when it does not conform with all the conditions required in this decree shall be prosecuted under the general laws relating to fraud and to the protection of appellations of origin (1st August 1905, articles 1 and 2; 6th May 1919, article 8; 19th August 1921, article 13) without prejudice to any kind of fiscal sanctions which may be applicable.

The Barsac decree is virtually identical. Those of Loupiac and Ste-Croix-du-Mont differ only in that the basic yield is fixed at the considerably higher figure of 40 hectolitres per hectare; Cérons and Cadillac also have this figure. The Cérons decree is similar again; it states that the communes of Illats and Podensac are also entitled to the *appellation*; the must has to contain 212 grams of natural sugar, as opposed to 221 for all the others. The Cadillac decree lists the other communes entitled to the *appellation*: they are Baurech, Béguey, Capian, Cardan, Donzac, Gabarnac, Haux, Langoiran, Laroque, Lestiac, Le Tourne, Monprimblanc, Omet, Paillet, Rions, St-Germain-de-Grave, St-Maixant, Semens, Tabanac, Verdelais and Villenave-de-Rions. The minimum actual alcohol content is 12% and the residual sugar content must be at least 18 grams per litre.

THE 1855 CLASSIFICATION

The organizers of the great World Exhibition held in Paris in 1855, which was designed to show off Napoleon III's splendid new empire, invited the Bordeaux Chamber of Commerce to produce a representative selection of the wines of Bordeaux. They in turn asked the Bordeaux brokers to get together and propose a ranking list or classification of the finest properties, which they did basing it firmly on the current state of the market. The red wine classification was supposedly of the wines of the Gironde but in fact they were (and are) all Médocs except for the first growth Haut-Brion from the Graves. The extraordinary thing is that this order of merit, designed purely for a specific event which took place more than a hundred years ago, has remained unchanged (apart from the long overdue promotion of Mouton-Rothschild to the first division in 1973).

The other classification made at the same time was of the wines of Sauternes, including Bommes, Preignac, Fargues and Barsac. This too has remained unaltered — apart from the splitting up, assimilation or disappearance of vineyards.

Here is the 1855 classification in its original form:

Premier grand cru

Château d'Yquem	Sauternes

Premiers crus

Château La Tour-Blanche	Bommes
Château Peyraguey	Bommes
Château Vigneau	Bommes
Château Suduiraut	Preignac
Château Coutet	Barsac
Château Climens	Barsac
Château Bayle	Sauternes
Château Rieussec	Sauternes★
Château Rabeaud	Bommes

Deuxièmes crus

Château Mirat	Barsac
Château Doisy	Barsac
Château Pexoto	Bommes
Château d'Arche	Sauternes
Château Filhot	Sauternes
Château Broustet-Nérac	Barsac
Château Caillou	Barsac
Château Suau	Barsac
Château de Malle	Preignac
Château Romer	Preignac★
Château Lamothe	Sauternes

★These properties are actually in Fargues which did not then come under the diocese of Bordeaux.

Not surprisingly there have been some enforced changes since the list was drawn up, though no promotions, demotions or additions. Bayle is now Guiraud. The original Peyraguey has long been two separate properties, Lafaurie-Peyraguey and Clos Haut-Peyraguey. Vigneau has become Rayne-Vigneau and Broustet and Nairac (as it is now spelt) are separate properties. Rabeaud (originally spelt thus) absorbed Pexoto and was later divided into Rabaud-Promis and Sigalas-Rabaud; then they came together as a single property for some time, separating again in 1952. The Doisy estate is now officially listed as three separate properties and Lamothe has recently become two. Myrat (to give it its modern spelling) disappeared temporarily when its vines were uprooted in 1976 but is happily now restored.

This is how the classification stands today:

Premier grand cru

Château Yquem	Sauternes

Premiers crus

Château Climens	Barsac
Clos Haut-Peyraguey	Bommes
Château Coutet	Barsac
Château Guiraud	Bommes
Château Lafaurie-Peyraguey	Bommes
Château La Tour-Blanche	Bommes
Château Rabaud-Promis	Bommes
Château Rayne-Vigneau	Bommes
Château Rieussec	Fargues
Château Sigalas-Rabaud	Bommes
Château Suduiraut	Preignac

Deuxièmes crus

Château d'Arche	Sauternes

Château Broustet	Barsac
Château Caillou	Barsac
Château Doixy-Daëne	Barsac
Château Doisy-Dubroca	Barsac
Château Doisy-Védrines	Barsac
Château Filhot	Sauternes
Château Lamothe	Sauternes
Château Lamothe-Guignard	Sauternes
Château de Malle	Preignac
Château de Myrat	Barsac
Château Nairac	Barsac
Château Romer-du-Hayot	Fargues
Château Suau	Barsac

La Commanderie du Bontemps de Sauternes et Barsac

Like most of the French wine areas, Sauternes has it own wine
fraternity, La Commanderie du Bontemps de Sauternes et
Barsac. It is sponsored by La Commanderie du Bontemps de
Médoc et de Graves, and exists to preserve the high standards
of the wines of the area and to give them publicity. Its members
are proprietors, brokers and dealers in Sauternes wines, and
distinguished visitors from other parts of France and the rest of
the world. The president is called the Grand-Maître (M. Louis
Ricard of Château St-Amand); there are two vice-presidents, a
grand chancellor, a *grand argentier*, an *hérault* and the general
assembly of members. Appropriately, old gold, the colour of
mature Sauternes, is the colour adopted for the traditional
robes which the members wear for their dinners, tastings and
initiation ceremonies. There is also a Commanderie du
Bontemps de Ste-Croix-du-Mont and a Commanderie des
Compagnons de Loupiac.

THE COMMUNES

Sauternes

The small, attractive village of Sauternes, situated 40km south-east of Bordeaux, with a population of only 582, surrounds an imposing church. Opposite the church is a superb restaurant — very unpretentious — called *Auberge des Vignes*, specialising in steak barbecued on old Sauternes vines. A new restaurant nearby, *Le Sauternais*, is owned by Hamilton Narby of Château Guiraud and is much smarter, offering a range of fine *nouvelle cuisine*.

Next to the Maison du Vins, which sells a good range of Sauternes, is *Les Ormeaux*, the local newsagent and petrol station, which has an old unspoilt bar used by the locals.

A little way out of the village, set amongst the vines, is the hotel-restaurant Château de Commarque, which is owned by an English couple, Dr. and Mrs. Reay-Jones, and offers comfortable rooms and good regional cuisine. Their predecessor had replanted the vineyard and Dr. Reay-Jones is now making Sauternes.

The commune of Sauternes covers 1,161 hectares, of which approximately 400 are under vine, on a soil similar to Cérons of gravel, clay and sand and a subsoil mainly of clay (which requires good drainage), gravel and iron.

The wines have a pronounced honey bouquet and taste, and in good years, when the botrytis is concentrated, take on a distinct marmalade bouquet and taste. There is also a little dry white and red wine produced in this area.

In the 1855 classification the commune of Sauternes listed one *premier cru supérieur*, Château Yquem, one *premier cru*, Château Bayle, now Château Guiraud; three *deuxièmes crus*, Château Filhot, Château d'Arche and Château Lamothe, now divided into Château Lamothe and Château Lamothe-Guignard.

An early, unnamed poet described Sauternes as a ray of sunshine concentrated in each glass and the poet Biarnez wrote:

3. The village of Sauternes from the air

Sauternes! At this name alone the Gourmet's heart leaps
And at once his palate with fragrance steeps.
For there, in the humble vine, puissant nature
Secretes, with her spirits, certain essences pure
Which she distils with rays from the glorious sun.
After a thousand detours, the magic is done,
Leading into our cellars these holy springs:
This to man both his strength and his genius brings.

Bommes

This is a very small village (population 416), surrounding the church. It lies 6km south–west of Preignac on the banks of the

4. The village of Bommes from the air

river Ciron. A new restaurant has recently opened, *Auberge Dix Cours*, which has stark décor but good, basic well-cooked food. The commune of Bommes is 580 hectares of which 300 are under vine.

The soil is predominantly gravel with some clay and sand in parts. The subsoil is clay and limestone. In the 1855 classification, the commune of Bommes listed four *premiers crus*, Château Peyraguey, now Château Lafaurie-Peyraguey and Clos Haut-Peyraguey; Château Vigneau, now Château Rayne-Vigneau; Château Rabeaud, now Château Rabaud-Promis and Château Sigalas-Rabaud; Château La Tour-Blanche. There was one *deuxième cru*, Château Pexoto, which is no longer in existence as it is now part of Château Rabaud-Promis.

Fargues

The small village of Fargues (population 1,020) is well named as it is dominated and overlooked by the imposing remains of Château de Fargues owned by the Marquis de Lur-Saluces (of Château Yquem). The castle of Fargues was built around the eleventh century and came into the Lur-Saluces family in 1472. It was burnt down in the seventeenth century and there are no plans to rebuild it. In the village itself (some 4km south-west of Langon) is the Town Hall which originally was the priest's house and a few shops. The commune of Fargues covers 1,541 hectares of which 200 are under vine and it has a clay and limestone soil with a gravel and clay subsoil.

In the classification of 1855 the commune of Fargues listed one *premier cru*, Château Rieussec; one *deuxième cru*, Château Romer, now Château Romer-du-Hayot. The wines are of

5. The village of Fargues from the air

48

similar style to the commune of Sauternes but in years when the botrytis is highly concentrated Fargues seems to have lower acidity.

Preignac

In the sixteenth century the river Ciron, which then flowed into the Garonne at Cérons, was diverted by the Benedictine monks to flow out between Preignac and Barsac. This major operation involved re-attaching the island of Burgade to dry land and a gradual transference of that part of Cérons further downstream. Today the village of Preignac (population 2,096) has grown in comparison to its neighbouring communes, with a number of shops, a petrol station and two bars, one of which is owned by the French *boules* champion and features many trophies. There are three restaurants, *Auberge de Boutoc, Les Erables* and *Restaurant du Cap*, situated on the river and serving good, honest, local food.

The large church on the main road is a classified historic monument. A stone tomb decorated with Renaissance sculptures carries an epitaph to Pierre Sauvage whom Charles IX, passing through Preignac, ennobled and endowed with the titles of Armajan and Lamothe.

The commune is situated 5km north-west of Langon and covers 1,326 hectares of which approximately 600 are under vine. The soil here is very varied. In the north, north-east and east it is alluvial. In the south-east it is light clay and gravel. In the south and south-west it is heavy clay and gravel. In the west it is sand and gravel. The subsoil throughout is clay and gravel.

In the 1855 classification there was one *premier cru*, Château Suduiraut, and one *deuxième cru*, Château de Malle.

6. The village of Preignac from the air

49

Barsac

The village of Barsac (population 2,019) is mainly residential, with a few shops and bars, and no restaurants other than the hotel-restaurant Château de Rolland on the outskirts of the village. Set in the front part of a vineyard — not their own — it has a unique position, although a little too near the main Bordeaux road. The château is run down and in need of substantial renovation. The restaurant produces reasonable food.

The church of St Michel de Rieufret, whilst of no great architectural merit, has its history and traditions which survive today. Three old wooden chests in the sacristy are conserved from the time when they once used to receive the vows and offerings of pilgrims. By the fifth century this was a well-known pilgrimage and by the end of the eleventh century it was the most frequented holy place in the Gironde area.

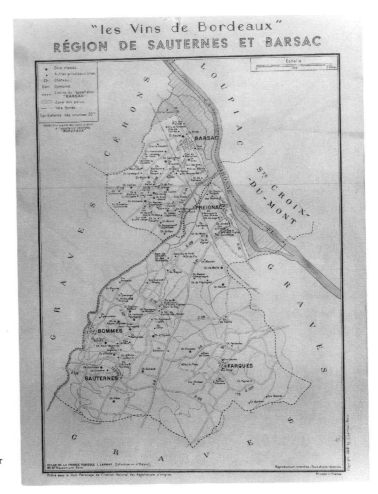

7. Map of the five communes (Sauternes, Bommes, Farques, Preignac, Barsac) showing the major properties producing appellation controlee Sauternes

Legend has it that the numerous pilgrims who came to call on the saints for help and protection went around the altars nine times, sliding underneath those of the Virgin Mary and St John. This custom can be traced back to Italy, to the Lombard sanctuary of Monte Sant'Angelo in Puglia, where it was customary for children to pass under the altar.

The commune is situated on the left bank of the river Ciron 38km south-east of Bordeaux and is not as hilly as the other Sauternes communes. Almost all of the properties are surrounded by walls of stone which were extracted from the subsoil when the ground was originally broken up to plant vines. The area has 1,429 hectares with 700 under vine, planted on a clay and limestone soil with some sand towards the south-west. The subsoil is predominantly limestone.

The 1855 classification listed two *premier crus*, Château Climens and Château Coutet, and five *deuxièmes crus*, Château Caillou, Château de Myrat, Château Doisy (now divided into Château Doisy-Daëne, Château Doisy-Dubroca and Château Doisy-Védrines), Château Broustet-Nairac (now separate properties) and Château Suau.

The *appellation contrôlée* allows the wines of Barsac to use either the *appellation* Sauternes or Barsac on the label.

The following is the Barsac output from 1982 to 1986:

> 1982 — 14,794 hectolitres
> 1983 — 14,461 hectolitres
> 1984 — 13,809 hectolitres
> 1985 — 14,186 hectolitres
> 1986 — 15,076 hectolitres

In earlier times on the high part of Barsac, called Haut-Barsac, wines were often produced which were high in alcohol and virtually dry. The wines now produced have a pronounced appley bouquet and barley-sugar flavour with a sharper acidity than the wines of the Sauternes communes. They are generally lighter in style when young but in years of concentrated botrytis the wines are of great depth and longevity.

Premier Grand Cru

Château Yquem   (Sauternes)

This unique property produces what is arguably the most
famous wine in the world and its best vintages come as close to
perfection as any man-made article can.

No-one knows how Yquem got its name and its origins are
uncertain, though philologists think that it is a corruption of
the old German 'aig-helm' meaning 'have-helmet'. Eyquem is
a not uncommon family name in the Bordeaux area. Château
Yquem and the name Lur-Saluces — these (with the d' which
distinguishes the wine from the property) and the year are the
only words on the splendidly simple main label — first came
together in 1785 when Françoise-Josephine de Sauvage, whose
family had been at Yquem since the sixteenth century, married
Louis-Amédée de Lur-Saluces, godson of Louis XV, at the
château. Two years later the American ambassador, and future
President, Thomas Jefferson was so impressed by the wine that
he ordered 30 bottles for George Washington at the White
House and ten dozen cases for himself at the Embassy. Nor
was he the only famous name to be associated with d'Yquem.
We know that in 1802 a consignment was made to Napoleon
Bonaparte, usually known as a Burgundy man. In 1859 the
Grand Duke Constantine, brother of the Tsar, tasted the 1847
vintage, said to have been picked particularly late and therefore
unusually rich, and offered the then staggering price of 20,000
gold francs for one *tonneau*, which opened a new chapter in
d'Yquem's international reputation. Nearer to our own time
Joseph Stalin was so enamoured of the wine that he begged
Comte Bertrand to send cuttings of the vines so that the
Russians might make their own Château d'Yquem!

When the Revolution came the State took over Yquem but
the Contesse, now widowed, fought hard to get the property
back, succeeded and lived there until her death in 1851. Her son
Antoine-Marie bought Coutet and Filhot into the family by his
marriage. His son, Romain Bertrand, the first owner to run the

estate himself, devised the great drainage scheme, though he did not live to see it completed. His son Amédée took over in 1867 and was eventually succeeded by his nephew Bertrand, one of the great characters of Bordeaux, guiding Yquem through two World Wars and acting as a kind of dynamic ambassador both for his property and for Sauternes as a whole. Two years before his death in 1970 he handed over to his nephew Alexandre, the present Mayor of Sauternes, who has proved himself a worthy successor.

One's first impression on visiting Yquem is that it cannot be true. The building itself, a mixture of imposing medieval castle and simple farmhouse architecture, with its fifteenth-century round towers, its sixteenth-century well in the courtyard and further sixteenth- and seventeenth-century building, is placed at the summit of the highest piece of land in the area with splendid views of its own woodland and vineyards and those of its neighbours. The impression created by its appearance and atmosphere is sustained at every point of one's investigation of the whole process of d'Yquem's evolution, from the planting and grafting of the vines to the bottling of the wine — not to mention the ultimate experience of savouring it in its maturity.

Although Comte Alexandre and his wife live in Bordeaux they entertain guests at the Château from time to time and it is always well kept up. The Comte, like his predecessor, is very much involved in the making of d'Yquem and is part of the three-man team who make all the big decisions, the others being Guy Latrille, *maître du chai* since 1970, and Pierre Meslier, *régisseur* since 1963. 'Guy Latrille commands Pierre Meslier and Pierre Meslier commands me' says the Comte.

Forty-eight *vignerons* live and work full-time at Yquem (they also work at Château de Fargues), which is a genuine year-round community. There are resident carpenters, mechanics, masons and a blacksmith, for there are still two horses for ploughing the steeper slopes. Many of this community were born at Yquem and some families have lived and worked here for several generations. Each family has a house with its own tiny smallholding and livestock, and every *vigneron* has a monthly ration of 56 litres of red wine, produced from three hectares of cabernet and merlot grown specially for this purpose and vinified in a small *chai* in the yard. The community has its own grocery co-operative in a room in the Château which a baker visits daily and a butcher and fishmonger regularly. In addition about 80 experienced pickers are brought in for the harvest when the whole combined force — apart from those needed in the *chai* to cope with the grapes as they arrive — takes to the vineyard together.

What are the reasons for d'Yquem's uniqueness? First the soil. Sloping down from its apex at the Château it has a topsoil of pebbles mixed with whitish sand and clay, rarely more than

30 cm deep, ideal for drainage and helping aeration. Also the pebbles, being light in colour, reflect and store the sun's heat to the benefit of the lower-hanging bunches. The subsoil is different from that of any other property, clay mixed with smooth, round stones and limestone fragments. It is a geological mystery why the current, which eroded most of the surface strata of the Tertiary formation clay and marl, spared this area of clay beneath Yquem. Elsewhere under the topsoil one finds tough marl or limestone. Clay, of course, can cause drainage problems but towards the end of the nineteenth century 100 kilometres of terracotta drain-pipes were laid down to alleviate these. Whenever, after some 45 years, old vines, usually in lots of 2–3 hectares, are uprooted, the pipes beneath are checked and, if necessary, repaired.

The sandiness of the area in general and of Yquem's topsoil in particular discouraged the phylloxera louse and the famous vintages of 1899 and 1900 were made entirely from ungrafted vines. The 1921, an even more renowned vintage, was probably the first to be made mainly from vines with American root-stocks.

The property is thought to have the perfect setting and microclimate for the proliferation of botrytis. To these natural advantages (and the artificially aided drainage) are added the strictest precautions against diluting the potential excellence of the wine. The pruning is drastically severe, the use of manure is minimal, and older, smaller-producing vines predominate, the average age being about 25 years. As a result the Yquem vineyards look less luxuriant than those of their neighbours but the grapes ripen earlier and better. The harvest usually starts a few days before other properties and a full week earlier than the sister château, Fargues, where the treatment of the vines is identical; in this case it is the differences in soil structure that are significant. Another important factor is the progressive genetic refinement of the two grape varieties (there is no muscadelle at Yquem), by reproduction from cuttings taken from selected high-quality vines on the property.

Next there is the meticulous testing of the sugar content of the grape juice by glucometer and the almost fanatical care of the actual selection in the repeated *tries*. The aim is to achieve a must weight for each pressing of between 19.8° and 20.5° Baumé which will leave 4.8 to 7% residual sugar (80–120 grams per litre) after fermentation has stopped naturally.

Finally, the wine is never chaptalised; all the barrels are of new, high-quality oak (usually Limousin, sometimes Slovenian from northern Yugoslavia) every year. Only a very robust and concentrated wine could benefit from the flavours and tannins that new oak contributes but it suits Yquem perfectly. The selection of the barrels to be used in the final *assemblage*, by tasting and laboratory analyses, is as rigorous as all the other stages and any deemed unworthy of becoming a part of d'Yquem for that year will be sold to be raised by the buyers and used in shippers' blends of generic Sauternes or Bordeaux A.C.

The estate covers 173 hectares, 103 under vine and the rest meadow and pine-woods. Only 90 are actually contributing to the wine at any one time, the rest lying fallow after uprooting or supporting young vines. The soil used to have to rest for several years and nitrogenous crops had to be planted and ploughed in. Now it is disinfected against fragments of rotting roots, then manured and left fallow for two years to achieve biological balance. New vines are in production six years after the old ones are pulled up. The average annual production is some 66,000 bottles. Recently part of an adjacent property (Château Pajot) was purchased, some 13 hectares, of which 8 are entitled to the *appellation* and have similar soil to Yquem; when that is in full production the vineyard area will be 109 hectares and average production should be increased by about 11,000 bottles.

The proportion of grape varieties is 80% sémillon, 20% sauvignon. Originally the sauvignon vines were planted at intervals along the rows of sémillon but since the Second World War they have been planted in separate patches. They are picked on different days and vinified separately.

When there is sufficient botrytis in the vineyard (usually in the second half of September) the army of pickers, mostly women, equipped with their wooden panniers and special small, sharp-pointed pruning-shears, start on the first *trie*, selecting only *grains rôtis* in perfect condition. The number of *tries* can be as few as three, as in 1976 when the third was carried out against time and at the risk of excessive botrytis which could lead to a heavy and unbalanced wine and the dangers of volatile acidity; or as many as eleven in 1974 when in fact no wine was considered good enough to go out under the d'Yquem label. As we have seen, at any stage rain or hail could wipe out the whole of the remaining harvest; but with the recent installation of an 18 by 12ft cryoextractor they should now be protected at least against the former.

The vinification process, as one would expect, is classically traditional. The grapes are emptied into a *fouloir*, a huge wooden funnel with interlocking rollers from which they emerge, lightly crushed, into a basket with slatted sides and a solid top and bottom, in which they are pressed. The basket is taken on a trolley along rails in the floor to one of the three old-fashioned vertical presses, much gentler than the modern horizontal ones. There is, however, one modern pneumatic horizontal press, gentle but very expensive, which is used only in emergencies. Trolley and basket are lifted to meet the press and a hole in the trolley floor is unplugged to let the juice escape. After about an hour and a half 200km of pressure per sq. cm are registered on the dial, the juice has all flowed into a 900-litre vat installed below and a cake about half the size of the basket remains. Trolley and basket are then wheeled to the crumbler or *émietteur*, a wooden drum with jagged enamel teeth projecting from its inside walls which break up the cake. The cake is forked into this and emerges to be put in another basket to be pressed again. There are three pressings, the third, though tiny in quantity, producing the richest in sugar and extract. If the first pressing is 19° Beaumé the third will be around 25°. The final cake of pips and skins goes, by law, to a government distillery. A normal maximum for a day's picking is about nine barrels of must, though in difficult years it can be as little as one and in the exceptional harvest of 1976 it rose to 36 so that the cellar crew were working 24 hours a day.

The must is then pumped from the underground vat into new oak barrels for the fermentation. They are left some twelve litres short of capacity to allow for the first, violent stage of the ferment. This is conducted at about 20°C, the *chai* being heated to this temperature if necessary, for anything from two to six weeks according to the amount of botrycine in the must. It stops naturally when the alcohol level is about 14°, leaving residual sugar, or *liqueur*, of about 6°. After the fermentation the wine spends the rest of its three and a half year maturation time in these barrels, being racked every three months and regularly topped up (twice a week) from barrels set aside for this purpose and then broken down into ever smaller hermetically sealed containers. Each barrel is marked with the date of picking and its potential alcohol. Because of the staggered nature of the harvest there may be casks at varying stages of fermentation in the *chai* for as long as three months. Yquem have recently started to cool the wine after fermentation to encourage the precipitation of tartrate crystals (what the former *maître du chai*, Roger Bureau, used to call 'butterflies in the wine') which would occasionally form after the wine had been bottled.

We have mentioned the importance of high-quality new oak to Yquem. One remarkable statistic is that over the maturation period some 20% of the wine will be lost through evaporation thanks to the porosity of the wood; but because the molecules of water are much smaller than those of alcohol they pass more easily through the dense fibres of the new oak, so that despite the greater volatility of alcohol most of the loss is water and the wine is actually concentrated by this process.

The *assemblage*, or putting together of the casks which will constitute the d'Yquem of that year, takes place over a period of some eighteen months starting in the spring following the vintage. After exhaustive tastings and analyses the proprietor, *régisseur* and *maître du chai* will make a joint decision on the selection. Some barrels always have to be excluded. Of those chosen forty at a time are racked into the same large underground vat that received the pressings and a very light dose of sulphur is added as an anti-oxidant. Another complication is that the sauvignon casks usually ferment out at about 15° with very little residual sugar so these must be balanced by an average sémillon Baumé reading of 21° to achieve the optimum 20° overall. If the sémillon average is on the low side then some will have to go into the dry Ygrec or be sold to be used in shippers' blends. In some years there is no d'Yquem: recent examples are 1952, 1972 and 1974. It is generally agreed that the 1963 vintage should not have gone out under the d'Yquem label.

In the second winter the wine is fined and this process may be repeated in the following year. Gelatine, albumen or bentonite is used; each year tests are made with half-bottle samples to see which is best suited to the particular vintage, or they may be used in combination. After fining the wine is left on the resultant lees for two to three weeks before being racked. It is bottled in March of the fourth year after, 40 barrels at a time being transferred into a wooden vat and passed through a fine sieve before bottling.

Recently a huge extension has been made to the cellars. A new maturation *chai* has been excavated, 2,000 metres square and 7 metres deep and air-conditioned, which can hold the first, second and third year barrels. The existing *chai* is now used for the fermentation. An escalator has been built leading down to a viewing platform from which, through plate-glass, visitors can observe the vista of the new *chai*.

D'Yquem can never be tasted from the cask by visitors, however distinguished, nor is it sold until it has been bottled. Between 60,000 and 70,000 bottles, of several vintages, are released each year, two Bordeaux broking firms being called in to arrange the details of sale with shippers and *négociants*.

All this dedication to excellence gives d'Yquem, year in year out, greater extract, a more complex flavour, and, perhaps most notably, a richer texture and greater length than any other Sauternes, though some may rival it occasionally. The greatest vintages are said to have been 1847, 1869 (still perfect after a hundred years), 1899, 1900 and the famous 1921; since then the best have been 1928, 1929, 1937, 1945, 1947, 1949, 1955, 1959, 1967, 1971, 1975, 1976 and 1982; no doubt 1983, 1986 and 1988 will merit inclusion in this series.

Since 1959 the Château has produced in addition a dry wine, 'Ygrec', with a confusingly similar label, in most but not all years. Its bouquet is rich, slightly honeyed and generally suggestive of Sauternes but it is dry, though quite rich on the palate. It is made from 50% sémillon and 50% sauvignon and average production is about 30,000 bottles.

Premiers Crus

Château Climens (Barsac)

This famous property takes its name, according to the present owner, M Lucien Lurton, from one Jehan Climens who, in the sixteenth century, was entitled to levy duties on ships going up the river Garonne; as a receipt he gave them a cypress branch, a practice reflected in the name sometimes used, as in 1984, for a second wine 'Les Cypres de Climens'.

It seems probable that the estate was part of the then much larger Château Coutet, the leading Barsac property, some time in the eighteenth century. In the nineteenth Climens belonged to the Lacoste family and was known as Climenz-Lacoste; it was recorded in 1824 as one of the first growths of Barsac, together with Coutet, Doisy and Caillou. In 1871 Alfred Ribet bought the estate; he was the owner of a Bommes second growth, Château Pexoto, soon to be absorbed into Château Rabaud. In the 1880s he sold it to Henri Gounouilhou at a time when the vineyard was devastated by the phylloxera disaster; his wife already owned the neighbouring Doisy-Dubroca and the two properties remained in the family until both were sold in 1971 to M Lurton who also owns Brane-Cantenac, Durfort-Vivens, Desmirail, Villegeorge, Bouscaut and a share of Clos-Fourtet.

The house is a rather ordinary building with a tower at each end. It has not been lived in for many years but Brigitte Lurton, Lucien's daughter, has taken an increasing interest in the property in recent years and the château has been redecorated and is used for entertaining.

At 20 metres above sea-level the 35-hectare vineyard is the highest in Barsac. The soil is red sand and fine gravel on a fissured limestone base and drains very well. The vineyard is planted with 98% sémillon and 2% sauvignon. The average production over the last ten years has been 14 hectolitres per hectare. There are from two to five *tries* according to the quantity and uniformity of the botrytis. There are only two pressings and the wine is fermented in oak barrels, the temperature being controlled at around 20°C by the natural coolness of the *chai*; it usually takes about three weeks for the yeasts to stop working and then a little SO₂ is added. The wine is assembled in the January following the vintage and then aged in wood (a third of the barrels are new each year) for about two years. During this time it is racked every three months and filtered before bottling, usually in June or the end of September. The wine is never chaptalised. The director is M Maurice Garros and the *maître du chai* M Christian Broustaut with Mme Janin, who has been there for many years, still acting in a supervisory capacity.

The style of Climens is unusually full and luscious for a Barsac and during this century it has maintained a very high standard of wine-making. It is one of the very few properties which has been judged by many to have rivalled or even surpassed Yquem in certain years, such as 1929 and 1947. It also often makes surprisingly good wine in poor years or years when there is little botrytis like 1964, 1972 and 1977, although these wines naturally have a shorter life than the great vintages. The outstanding wines of recent years have been 1971, 1975, 1976, 1983 and 1986. From 1984 wine considered not good enough to be sold under the Château label but too good to be mere Sauternes has been bottled as 'Les Cyprès de Climens'.

The wine is never sold *en primeur* but through *négociants* in Bordeaux. As at Yquem the wine cannot be tasted until it has been bottled.

Clos Haut-Peyraguey (Bommes)

This was part of Château Peyraguey until 1879 when the property was divided and this, the higher part (some 50–72 metres), received its present name. It was owned by Mlle Charlotte La Tremouille. It was bought by the Pauly family in 1914 and Jacques Pauly, who also owns Château Haut-Bommes, is the co-proprietor and *gérant*.

There are 15 hectares of vines, 83% sémillon, 15% sauvignon and 2% muscadelle; the average age of the vines is 30 years. The soil is sandy gravel on a clay subsoil. Some 2,000 cases are produced on average at about 18 hectolitres per hectare.

After pressing and *débourbage* the must, lightly chaptalised when M Pauly feels it necessary, is fermented in cement vats at 19–20°C for 2–8 weeks, the fermentation being stopped with SO₂ and chilling. The wine is then matured for about 21 months in barrels, 20% of which are new each year. The wines are assembled in the February following the vintage and filtered before bottling.

The wines are rather light and insubstantial for a first growth. Of the two most recent generally fine vintages the 1983 was disappointing and the 1986 had a grassy, medicinal taste and lacked depth.

About 40% is exported to various European countries, the USA and Japan.

Château Coutet (Barsac)

This is one of the oldest properties in the area. Its square tower and round, turreted towers and chapel date from the fourteenth and fifteenth centuries and the remainder from the sixteenth.

In 1643 Charles de Guérin, a councillor of the Bordeaux Parlement, purchased the estate from M de Sourdis. In 1695 his nephew, Jean de Pichard, took it over. By 1733 it had passed to the de Gasq family (relations of the de Guérins) but returned in 1765 to the Pichards who were big agricultural landowners. In 1785 Thomas Jefferson rated the *cru* Pichard as a first-class Barsac. In 1788 a Pichard cousin, Gabriel Barthélèmy Romain de Filhot (President of the Bordeaux Parlement), took over and although he was guillotined in the Revolution the property stayed in the Filhot family and was run by his widow until 1810. In that year the Lur–Saluces family took over when the Filhot daughter, Marie Geneviève, married the Marquis Amédée de Lur–Saluces. In 1922 the property was sold to the Société Immobilière des Grands Crus de France but in 1929 was bought by M Guy, an industrialist from Lyons. One of his daughters was widowed at an early age and subsequently married M Rolland, a priest who was tutor to her children. When she died in 1977 the estate was sold to M Baly, an industrialist from Strasbourg. After the terrible frost of 1956 70% of the vineyard had to be uprooted and replanted. The *maître du chai* is M Claude Pascaud, son of the *régisseur* of Château Suduiraut.

The estate is 46 hectares of clay/limestone soil on a limestone rock subsoil and produces about 7,000 cases from a *cépage* of 75% sémillon, 23% sauvignon and 2% muscadelle at 17–19 hectolitres per hectare. The number of *tries* varies from six to ten. There are two pressings, in hydraulic vertical presses, and often an overnight *débourbage*; then the must is fermented in barrels at 15° to 18°C for 20 to 30 days. The wine is aged in barrels, 20% new each year, regularly racked and filtered before bottling about 18–20 months after the vintage. It is rarely chaptalised. A little dry white wine is also made, 'vin sec de Coutet', which is entitled to the Graves *appellation* as it is partly made from grapes grown in neighbouring Pujols-sur-Ciron. About 84% of Coutet is exported, the UK, Australia and

1 The owner, Comte Alexandre de Lur-Saluces, at his *premier grand cru* château, Yquem (Sauternes)

2 *Premier cru* Château Coutet (Barsac)

Switzerland being the biggest markets.

Coutet is, with Climens, traditionally one of the two great wines of Barsac, yet they are quite unalike in style and character. Coutet is definitely ligher and less rich, some would say with more finesse. Certainly in the Rolland–Guy era it was one of the very best properties in the whole area, the 1949, 1955, 1959, 1962, 1971, 1975 and 1976 all being excellent. Since the most recent change of ownership the 1981 has been the most impressive vintage; the others have been disappointing and even the 1983 and the 1986 seemed very light and forward, especially for such generally successful vintages. The development of this wine will be watched with interest.

In 1943 M Rolland started a special *crème de tête* made from a selection of his very richest grapes in honour of his wife, which he called *Cuvée Madame*. Two or three casks were made in certain years — 1949, 1959, 1971, 1975 for example. M Baly has decided to continue this tradition and has so far made two vintages, 1981 and 1986, from grapes with 22–24° Beaumé. The grapes are very lightly pressed and fermented and aged in new oak barrels for about two and a half years. Robert Parker ranks the 1971 and 1981 Cuvées Madames with d'Yquem 1921 as the three greatest sweet white Bordeaux he has tasted.

Château Guiraud   (Sauternes)

This property, classed as a first growth in 1855 under the name of Château Bayle, is the only Sauternes estate besides Yquem to be so classified.

In the mid-eighteenth century Marie-Catherine-Thérèse de Mons married the son of Montesquieu, Jean Baptiste de Secondat and was given the Maison de Bayle. After her death it reverted to her brother Joseph, *chevalier* and member of the Bordeaux Jurat, known as the Chevalier de Mons. In 1759 he left it to his nephew who sold it in 1766 to Pierre Guiraud, a Bordeaux *négociant*, to whose family it belonged for the next 80 years. In 1846 the property was purchased by a group of investors led by M J. B. Depons. It changed hands several times in the middle years of the century, one owner being a well-known Parisian banker, Félix Solar, in 1858. In 1861 Pierre Schröder of the famous *négociant* family bought the property but sold it in 1867 to the Bernard family. Two Bernard daughters later married into the wealthy Maxwell family who ran the estate under the name of Les Héritiers Bernard before selling it to M Paul Rival in 1932. He owned Guiraud for nearly 50 years before selling it in 1981 to Hamilton Narby, a Canadian who was determined to make impeccable Sauternes.

In the latter years of M Rival's reign the expense of

maintaining this large property (118 hectares, with 83 under vine), had become a problem and some corners were being cut. For example the wine, after being fermented in oak casks, was matured in cement vats. The Narby family have restored the house and spared no expense to ensure that Guiraud once more produces wine as good as any but Yquem. M Xavier Plantey is now the *gérant* and M Roland Dubile *maître du chai*. In 1988 Hamilton Narby left Guiraud but his family still own the property.

The soil is 80% sandy gravel and 20% clay/gravel. Sixty-two hectares are devoted to Guiraud (62% sémillon, 37% sauvignon and 1% muscadelle), with an average production of 10,000 cases; 9 hectares to Bordeaux *blanc* 'G de Guiraud' (38% sémillon, 62% sauvignon), 4,000 cases; a Bordeaux *rouge*, 'Le Dauphin' is also made, from 50% cabernet sauvignon, 10% cabernet franc and 40% merlot. This is an unusually high proportion of sauvignon which perhaps gives Guiraud a certain individual freshness, though the 1983 is undoubtedly wonderfully rich and creamy. The harvesting policy of the new régime is impressively thorough. In their laboratory three oenologists chart the evolution of the vineyard from early September and monitor the progress of botrytis throughout, and the harvesters are ready to spring into action when the results indicate they should. Nothing is left to chance. In 1983 and 1986, both years that produced wines of the very highest standard, the weather conditions were very different. 1983 had a long Indian summer, too dry for botrytis, which did not arrive until very late. Guiraud made 11 *tries* finishing on 28th November. In 1986 September was hot and muggy, the botrytis proliferated and most of the harvest was in by mid-October after four *tries*. Yet the quality of the wine was very similar. Some of the initial tests done by the Institut d'Oenologie de Bordeaux leading to the perfection of the cryoextraction process took place at Guiraud in collaboration with their laboratory staff and equipment, which indicates that Mr. Narby, though dedicated to the traditional methods of ensuring excellence, was prepared to enlist science to help break new ground if the result was even finer Sauternes.

The average yield is 14 hectolitres per hectare. The vines are replaced after about 45 years. After pressing there is a short *débourbage*, and the must is fermented in temperature-controlled Inox vats for about 21 days between 18°C and 24°C according to the concentration of the must. The fermentation is stopped by chilling the wine to −4°C. It is then matured for just over two years in oak barrels, 70% of which are new each year, before being bottled in the February of its third winter. The wine is never chaptalised.

Much of the wine is exported, the main customers outside France being Belgium, Holland, West Germany, Scandinavia, the UK, the USA and Japan. Recent opening prices have been

(1978) 50FF, (1979) 55FF, (1980) 48FF, (1981) 60FF, (1982) 65FF, (1983) 90FF, (1984) 100FF, (1985) 135FF, (1986) 100FF.

Guiraud is certainly once again one of that small group who can make wine which approaches the standards set by Yquem.

Château Lafaurie-Peyraguey (Bommes)

Originally called Château Peyraguey, this is a very attractive old château; the porch and towers date from the thirteenth century and the main dwelling was reconstructed in the seventeenth. The estate is set upon a series of hillocks east-north-east of Château Yquem. It was named in the eighteenth century by President de Pichard, proprietor of Lafite; after the Revolution it was sold as a national property to M Lafaurie, a distinguished wine-grower, who did much to establish the name and fame of the growth. After he died it passed in 1860 to M Saint-Rieul-Dupouy who had married his widow and who in turn sold it to the Comte Duchâtel. In 1879 the main part, including the château and *chai*, came to MM Farinel and Grédy, then to M Frédéric Grédy, who later bought and added the neighbouring estate of Barrail Peyraguey, while a smaller part including some of the higher land, henceforth known as Clos Haut-Peyraguey, went to M Grillon. The famous wine firm of Cordier acquired the property in 1913 and have run it ever since.

There are 26 hectares under vine: 98% sémillon, 2% sauvignon — a considerable reduction of sauvignon over the last 20 years or so. The average yield is about 3,000 cases at 13 hectolitres per hectare.

In 1967 modern horizontal presses were installed and instead of the traditional oak barrel *élevage* the wine did most of its maturation time in glass-lined metal vats, covered with a layer of nitrogen, before being transferred to barrels for the last few months before bottling. Yields were also on the high side. All this led to the production of a lightish wine, often quite elegant but rather insubstantial and lacking in depth for a growth which had long been one of the very best. Fortunately this policy was reversed in the late 1970s. The cellars were renovated and air-conditioned; vertical presses are used again. The must is fermented in barrels at 18–20°C; fermentation usually stops naturally but some SO_2 is added to make sure. Then the wine is racked, left for a month, fined, left again for a month, filtered and matured in oak barrels, half of them new each year. It is racked regularly and before bottling it is chilled to precipitate the tartrates and filtered once again. The wines have improved and filled out as a result, especially since the arrival in 1982 of M Michel Laporte as *maître du chai*, succeeding M Pierre Patashon who had held the post for 42 years. The 1982 was very good for the year and the 1983 was one of the best wines of an outstanding vintage. In some years a second wine, 'L.P. du Château Lafaurie-Peyraguey', A.C. Sauternes, is made.

Château La Tour-Blanche   (Bommes)

Château La Tour-Blanche, so called because of its isolated tower, was placed at the head of the *premiers crus* in the 1855 classification with only Château Yquem classed as its superior. It had a great reputation in the nineteenth century, as its many Paris gold medals testify. The building stands on a hillock on the right bank of the river Ciron, and the soil of the vineyard is mainly gravel near the top of the slope, becoming sandier on the plain, with more clay nearer the river. Mme Veuve Focke was the proprietor in 1860 and some time in the latter part of the century the property was acquired by M Osiris of Bordeaux. In 1906 he made a will leaving the estate to the French Government, with the proviso that the State was to provide there a free practical education in viticulture and vinification. He also stipulated that his name should appear on the label, as it does to this day. He died the following year and the château and the vineyard have been State-owned ever since, being now administered by the Department of Agriculture. It was run as a part-time school until 1962, but now has 70 to 80 students living in, taking a full-time course for two years and also working in the vineyards. In the courtyard there is a statue of Ulysse Gayon as an *homage de reconnaissance* to the man who discovered the copper powder used against diseases of the vine.

The director of the school, M Jean-Pierre Jausserand, is responsible for the making of La Tour-Blanche. The *maître du chai* is M Fauré and the *chef d'exploitation* M Reberat.

There are 31 hectares under vine, 27 of them A.C. Sauternes: 78% sémillon, 19% sauvignon and 3% muscadelle. The average age of the vines is 40 years and the average yield is 13 hectolitres per hectare. There is a second A.C. Sauternes wine, 'Madamoiselle de St-Marque' (until recently known as 'Château St-Marc'), and two white A.C. Bordeaux, one sweetish and one dry, 'Osiris' and 'Chevalier de Thinoy'. Some red wine is also made under the label 'Cru de Cinques'.

From four to seven *tries* are made, the grapes are pressed in a pneumatic horizontal press for two to two-and-a-half hours and after *débourbage* the must is fermented at 22° for two to three weeks in stainless steel tanks, the ferment being stopped by chilling. It is then racked into oak barrels, 35–50% new each year, and matured, fined regularly and filtered twice before being bottled after 18 months to two years. The *assemblage* usually takes place after the fermentation. M Jausserand tells us that the wine is never chaptalised.

Despite the low yield and apparently meticulous wine-making techniques the current reputation of the wine hardly matches its standing as the leading *premier cru* at the time of the 1855 classification. The wines have often seemed rather light and undistinguished. However we feel that the standard has improved in the last few years, perhaps as a result of M Jausserand's dedication and expertise since his appointment. The 1986, in particular, shows much promise.

Château Rabaud-Promis   (Bommes)

This estate was originally the larger part of Château Rabeaud, which retained its name after the marriage in 1660 of Marie Petronne de Rabeaud to M Arnaud de Cazeau. Their descendants held it until 1819, when M Pierre-Hubert de Cazeau, Mayor of Bommes, sold it to M Gabriel Deymies. M Henri Drouilhet de Sigalas purchased the property in 1864, but in 1903 sold the larger portion, about two-thirds, to M Adrien Promis, and thus it became known by the present château name. The château was built in the reign of Louis XVI, and is situated on a small hill with an impressive view of the surrounding vineyards, and was designed by Victor Louis, the famous architect of the Grand Théatre of Bordeaux. The properties were reunited in 1929 and divided again in 1952. Some time before this the estate absorbed the second-growth vineyard of Château Pexoto. The most recent owners have been M Ginestet, and, since 1950, M R. L. Lanneluc, whose grandson, M Philippe Dejean, is the *maître du chai*.

Of the 45 hectares 33 are under vine: 80% sémillon, 18% sauvignon and 2% muscadelle. The average yield is 18 hectolitres per hectare and 3–7 *tries* are made. There have been some important modifications to the vinification process since 1982. The grapes are now pressed very slowly without being crushed first. The juice is left for 36 hours in a tank at low temperature to clear. The must is then put into a temperature-controlled 50-hectolitre Inox tank to begin the fermentation, which takes two to three weeks at 18–20°C. It is then chilled again and SO_2 is added. The first year of the two-and-a-half-year maturation period is spent in Inox vats and the remainder in oak barrels, half of which are new for each vintage, the wine being racked every three months.

For many years since the second division from its sister property the wine has been very disappointing for a first growth; not just light but sometimes musty and stale-tasting. Since the replacement of the old cement vats with stainless steel tanks and the reintroduction of oak casking for part of the maturation things have improved somewhat, and recently a pneumatic press has been installed.

A second wine, 'Château Jauga', is made from barrels not considered up to the standard required for Rabaud-Promis.

Château Rayne-Vigneau   (Bommes)

This large estate with its handsome turreted château — sadly no longer connected with the vineyard — was first owned in the seventeenth century by Etienne de Vigneau, who sold it in 1682 to Hyacinthe Sauvage. In 1742 it was acquired by the Duffour family who sold it in 1817 to M Joseph-Marie Dert. In 1834 it was purchased by the widow of Baron de Rayne, a member of the de Pontac family, though it was not until 1892 that it added the prefix 'Rayne' to its title of Vigneau. It remained in the hands of this family until 1961 when the vineyard, but not the château, was sold to a Bordeaux wine-merchant, M Raoux. Ten years later he in turn sold it to Mestrezat, the *négociant* company. This company, the present proprietors, are known as the Société Civile de Château Rayne-Vigneau, and their major shareholders are the de La Beaumelle and Merlaut families. The Vicomte de Roton, of the de Pontac family, still lives in the château.

The château enjoyed a great reputation in the nineteenth century and has made much good wine in the twentieth. There is the famous story of the tasting by a mixed panel of French and German experts at the 1867 Paris International Exhibition when a number of leading Sauternes were judged 'blind' against some of the great sweet wines of the Rhine and Mosel. The 1861 Rayne-Vigneau was voted the outstanding wine by

9. *Premier cru* Château Rayne-Vigneau (Bommes)

French and German judges alike. The estate is also famous for the remarkable quantity of semi-precious stones found in its soil, including agates, amethysts, opals, jade, onyx and white sapphires.

During the de Pontac era Rayne-Vigneau made fine wine but in the 1960s both the vineyard and the *chai* became very run down. The new owners had to replant extensively, with sauvignon, as the I.N.A.O. would at that time only authorise the planting of sauvignon. In the early years of the new régime quantity and financial viability were the main concerns and the wines, even in good years like 1975 and 1976, were disappointing. But in the early 1980s there was something of a revolution. M Jean Merlaut joined Mestrezat and now has responsibility not only for Rayne-Vigneau but also for Châteaux Grand-Puy-Ducasse in the Médoc and Tourteau-Cholet in the Graves. In 1982 Patrick Eymery joined from Château Guiraud as *régisseur* and under this dynamic partnership there have been many improvements including the revolutionary process of cryoextraction, described in detail in an earlier chapter, which could change the whole Sauternes situation.

There are 80 hectares, 72 under vine: 75% sémillon, 25% sauvignon, with an average yield of 15–20 hectolitres per hectare. The number of *tries* varies from four to ten. After three pressings in a new Swiss Buscher pneumatic press there is a one- to two-day *débourbage*, then the must ferments at about 20° in stainless steel tanks until fermentation stops naturally, usually after three weeks. The wine is matured in new and one-year-old barrels of Trancy or Limousin oak with the usual rackings and fining and bottled after about two years. The *assemblage* takes place at the beginning of the maturation period. M Merlaut is concerned about the shortage of good-quality oak and is about to embark on some experiments at Rayne-Vigneau.

A dry white wine, 'le Sec de Rayne-Vigneau', is produced from younger vines, 70% sauvignon; it is fermented and matured entirely in stainless steel and bottled in the March following the vintage. In some years a second *vin liquoreux*, 'Clos l'Abeilly', is also made.

The signs here are distinctly encouraging. The 1985 had good botrytis characteristics and the 1986 looks like being the best wine from this property since 1962. One hopes that the cryoextractor has ensured a botrytised 1987.

Château Rieussec (Fargues)

Before the Revolution the estate which was to become Château Rieussec, on the borders of Fargues and Sauternes adjoining

Yquem, belonged to a Carmelite house in Langon. It was taken over by the State and sold to a M Mareilhac. By the 1820s it is mentioned in the works of Jullien and Franck as a second growth. In 1846 four hectares of the vineyard were acquired by the estate of Château Pexoto, then a *deuxième cru*, which was later absorbed by Château Rabaud; this wine was then sold as Pexoto-Rieussec. In the same year the main estate was sold to M Maille or Maye. However in 1872 the proprietor of Rieussec, M Charles Crepin, bought back the four hectares and henceforth had the sole right to call his wine Rieussec. He was succeeded in 1892 by M Paul Defolie who did much to improve the *chai* and vineyards as well as acquiring in 1895 the neighbouring estate of Louison. Subsequent owners have been M Bannil (1907), M Gasqueton, Mr. P. F. Berry (an American, who with his brother-in-law the Viscomte de Bouzit took over during the Second World War), M Baluresque (1957–1971) and M Albert Vuillier, a great advocate of traditional methods. M Vuillier was also the first owner for many years to live in the château. In 1984 M Vuillier sold Rieussec to the Domaines des Barons Rothschild, owners of Châteaux Lafite and Duhart-Milon in Pauillac, though he stayed on as *président-directeur général* of the Société Anonyme de Château Rieussec, of which Rothschilds are the majority shareholders. He left the following year and now the *directeur* is M Charles Chevalier, brought in from Lafite, and the *régisseur* M Bertrand Latestère. No major changes in methods of viticulture or vinification have yet been divulged and the products of the new régime will be watched with interest by Sauternes-lovers. The 1985 was disappointing but the 1986 promises to be very good indeed; it is far more closed and less forward than a comparable Vuillier vintage at the same stage.

There are 65 hectares under vine (80% sémillon, 18% sauvignon and 2% muscadelle) producing about 4,500 cases at 13–18 hectolitres per hectare from gravel soil on a gravel and clay subsoil. The vineyard is said to have a special microclimate (like Yquem) which enables the grapes to ripen rather earlier than those of its neighbours. The number of *tries* varies from two to seven. The grapes are pressed (up to six times) and after *débourbage* the must is fermented in stainless steel tanks for two to eight weeks at 22°C. This usually stops naturally but some SO_2 is added to make sure. The wine is then matured in oak barrels (half of them new each year) and regularly racked, then filtered and chilled to precipitate tartrates before bottling some 22 months after the vintage. *Assemblage* usually takes place after eight months.

Rieussec has always been considered one of that small group of properties than can make outstanding Sauternes, and one of the most consistent of them. Until fairly recently it was regarded as one of the lighter and more elegant of the best wines of the area, though naturally rich and long-flavoured in good years like 1959 and 1962; indeed it has sometimes been described as Barsac-like. However since M Vuillier took over in 1971 the style has become fuller, heavier and more forward, sometimes with a distinctly roasted or raisiny taste. Whether this is a good thing or not is a matter of opinion and strong ones have been voiced both ways. Certainly M Vuillier's wines have less finesse but they also have a decadent lusciousness of flavour and texture and considerable length. It may be that in his desire to produce as rich and characterful a wine as possible — in 1975 and especially 1976 for example — M Vuillier went for what some would consider just too much concentration in his picking. Apparently in 1976 the yield was as low as 2.6 hectolitres per hectare — about half a glass of wine from each vine. At all events the wine, whether one considers it the epitome of Sauternes luxuriance or somewhat overblown and unbalanced, does not seem likely to be a long laster. The 1983, despite its forwardness and rather dark colour, is generally considered to be one of the most impressive wines of this fine vintage.

Château Sigalas-Rabaud   (Bommes)

This estate was the smaller part of the original Château Rabaud and took its present name after the division in 1903 when M Henri Drouilhet de Sigalas sold the rest to M Promis keeping the part he thought the best for himself. As already described they came together again in 1929 but have been separate estates since 1952. The late wife of the present proprietor and *directeur*, the Marquis de Lambert des Granges, was the great-granddaughter of the M Sigalas mentioned above. The *maître du chai* is M Jean-Louis Vimeney.

There are 15 hectares of vines (90% sémillon and 10% sauvignon), average age 35 years. Production is about 2,000 cases. The grapes are pressed three times in a small hydraulic vertical press. Fermentation takes place in stainless steel vats; it lasts two weeks or more and is terminated by chilling and the addition of SO_2. The wine is also matured largely in tanks, though it does spend some time in barrels, with regular racking before being filtered and bottled about 18 months after the vintage.

Despite this somewhat unconventional *élevage* the wines are highly regarded. Distinguished commentators have found them light, fresh and well balanced. We can only say that we have been disappointed with the wines that we have tasted, though we liked the 1976 in its youth. The 1986 was most unimpressive, being short, hollow and lacking in botrytis.

Château Suduiraut   (Preignac)

Preignac's only *premier cru* is one of the loveliest estates in the whole area. It is very near the boundary with Sauternes, Bommes and Fargues and due north of Yquem. Before the Revolution it belonged to the Suduiraud family and the original building was burnt to the ground, presumably after some quarrel, by order of the Duc d'Epernon, Governor of Acquitaine, some time in the seventeenth century. The present imposing building has courtyards and gardens said to have been landscaped by Le Nôtre, the designer of the gardens of Versailles. In the early 1800s a daughter of the family married a M du Roy and for a time it was known as 'Cru du Roy' (the label still bears the additional title 'Ancien Cru du Roy'). Shortly afterwards a neighbouring property, Castelnau, was incorporated into the estate. Subsequent owners were M Guillot (proprietor at the time of the 1855 classification), his heirs the brothers Guillot (1860–1873), M Henri Rabourdin, Mme Petit de Forest, M Girodon Pralong and M Emile Petit de Forest, a well-known engineer. In 1940 it was purchased by M Leopold Fonquernie, a wealthy industrialist, who, as soon as he could, set about a rigorous programme of improvement in both viticulture and wine-making, for the property had become rather run down in the 1920s and 1930s. Soon Suduiraut was again among the leaders, starting with a good 1945 and going through to an excellent 1967. There was something of a lapse in the early 1970s: from 1968 the wine was matured in plastic-lined cement tanks; but in 1978 Pierre Pascaud took over and at least partial oak-casking was resumed. M Fonquernie's daughters are now in charge, Mme de Bachey being director and Mme de Frouin commercial director, but M Pascaud is responsible for the wine and M Claude Laporte is the *maître du chai*.

There are 80 hectares of vines on the 200-hectare estate (80% sémillon, 20% sauvignon). It is claimed that Suduiraut, like

10. Large casks at *premier cru* Château Suduiraut (Preignac)

70

Yquem and Rieussec, has its own microclimate which
encourages rather earlier ripening of the grapes. Certainly M
Pascaud often picks earlier than other properties, though the
success of this policy must depend on the incidence of botrytis.
Though the 1982 was particularly good for the year the 1985
was disappointing and, more surprisingly, so were even the
1983 and 1986. The wine is sometimes chaptalised. The output
varies from 4,000 cases in 1975 and 3,000 in 1976 to an alleged
15,000 in 1983. There are usually four or five *tries*. Both vertical
and horizontal presses are used and after *débourbage* the must is
fermented in 500-litre stainless steel tanks at 18–22°C and
matured first in tanks and then, for the last year, in barrels,
30% of which are new each year. It is filtered before bottling
after about two and a half years. The *assemblage* is done six
months before bottling.

The most successful vintages of Suduiraut are undoubtedly
very good indeed, producing rich, elegant, well-balanced
wines of great length. Recently (in 1982 and 1985) a *crème de tête*
has been made from specially selected grapes particularly
concentrated by botrytis. The 1982 was made from one day's
picking (22° Beaumé) and is said by Clive Coates to be
magnificent.

Deuxièmes Crus

Château d'Arche   (Sauternes)

This is one of the oldest estates in the area — the main building dates from 1530 — and was originally known as Cru de Bran-Eyre. It takes its name from a famous eighteenth-century owner, the Comte d'Arche (1727–1789), one-time President of the Parlement of Bordeaux. After the Revolution it was split up into some 30 parts and twenty years later only a sixth of it was left. By 1848 there were four owners, the families Pentalier, Lafaurie, Vimeney and Dubourg. In 1924 M Bastit St Martin married Mlle Dubourg; in 1930 he bought out the Pentalier, and in 1960 the Lafaurie. In recent years, up to 1981, this estate was run by his son, and had been producing adequate but rather undistinguished wines; but in that year it was acquired by M Pierre Perromat, formerly chairman of the I.N.A.O., who was determined to produce the very finest Sauternes possible. Output has been cut and both viticulture and vinification tightened up to this end. The wines of the new régime, starting with an excellent 1983, look promising: the 1984 and 1985 are lightish but well balanced and good for the vintages and the 1986 shows great promise. The *maître du chai* is M Serge Banchereau who has been there for sixteen years.

There are 30 hectares under vine (75% sémillon, 23% sauvignon, 2% muscadelle) producing some 4,500 cases at 12–15 hectolitres per hectare. There are 5–8 pickings. The grapes are pressed three times in hydraulic presses and the must is fermented in water-cooled stainless steel vats for 15 days or more at 18–21°. A preliminary *assemblage* is made immediately after fermentation and the final one after 18 months. The wine is matured, with regular rackings, in oak barrels (half of them new each year) for a further two years. There is every reason to believe that the style and quality of d'Arche will maintain its recent improvement. The second wine, 'd'Arche-Lafaurie', and the occasional *crème de tête* which were formerly produced have both been discontinued.

3 Hamilton Narby at *premier cru* Château Guiraud (Sauternes) whose former greatness he did so much to restore

4 Progression of botrytis on the Sémillon grape.
A Initial botrytis infection, resulting in a discoloration of
the skin.   **B** Spores attacking the grape, showing first
stages of dehydration (beginning to 'weep').   **C** Grapes
showing partial infection – not yet ready for picking.
D Grapes in advanced stage of botrytis infection – some
grapes in the bunch ready for picking.

B

C

D

Château Broustet   (Barsac)

This property was joined to its neighbour, Château Nairac, in the mid-nineteenth century, the estate being known as Château Broustet-Nérac. Both properties were owned by M Capdeville. Later Broustet had close associations with Château de Myrat, when Mme H. Moller owned both properties. Its present owner is M Eric Fournier, the son-in-law of the owner of Doisy-Védrines. His great-grandfather acquired the estate, then only ten hectares, in 1889, primarily to install a large cooperage and storage area. There the Bordeaux Chamber of Commerce asked him to make a model of the *barrique bordelaise* to serve as the official pattern for coopers. The estate descended to Eric Fournier via his great-uncle, father, mother and brother. The family also owns Château Canon in St-Emilion.

There are 16 hectares under vine (63% sémillon, 25% sauvignon, 12% muscadelle). The average age of the vines is forty years. About 2,000 cases are produced at an average yield of 10–15 hectolitres per hectare. There are usually five or six pickings. A propos, one of the authors remembers having lunch at Château Canon in 1980 with Eric Fournier and his grandmother. Mme Fournier recalled a vintage in the first years of this century, when she was a girl, saying that if one drop of juice was found in the bottom of a basket, woe betide that picker for having selected a not sufficiently shrivelled grape. There are four pressings in the horizontal press and after the *débourbage* the must is fermented in small (2,500-litre) stainless steel tanks, for easier temperature control and so that there are more lots from which to make the eventual *assemblage*. After a slow fermentation for a month or so the wine is chilled and SO_2 added. It is filtered, then matured in oak barrels (40% new each year) with the usual regular rackings, and filtered again before bottling after two years.

The wine-making is careful and conscientious, as is the selection both in the *chai* and the vineyard — picking went on into November in 1985. Yet recent vintages have seemed disappointingly thin and light although perfectly respectable. The 1985 was good for the year.

Château Caillou   (Barsac)

Château Caillou, which takes its name from the abundance of limestone rock in its subsoil, was bought in 1907 by M Joseph Ballan from the Sarraute family and sold to the grandfather of the present owner in 1909, when the vineyard was only three hectares. The house is a rather quaint little twin-towered nineteenth-century building and there is an enormous stone wine bottle in the front garden.

The *directeur* is M J. Bernard Bravo, *régisseur* Mme Marie José Pierre and the *maîtres du chai* MM Marc Lubert and Jean Hubert de Tocqueville. There are 13 hectares of vines (90% sémillon, 10% sauvignon), average age 22 years, which produce about 4,000 cases a year with rather a high yield of 20 hectolitres per hectare. After pressing and *débourbage* the wine is fermented for upwards of 15 days in stainless steel tanks at a controlled temperature of 20–22°C, then matured for three years — one of the longest maturation periods — in oak barrels a third of which are new. It is racked three times in the first year and twice in the second and third — far less than the norm — before being filtered and bottled.

The collection of old vintages is one of the most remarkable in the area. The oldest on sale is the famous 1921 but the private stock goes back to 1908. Some of these certainly bear witness to Caillou's ability to age well in good years. The 1975 and 1976 were perhaps disappointingly light for their vintages, but certainly from 1981 the wines have been of an encouragingly high standard showing all the richness, together with appley acidity, of classic Barsac. M Bravo, who is personally involved in every stage of the wine-making, also owns Château Petit Mayne in Barsac. He makes two red wines, 'Cru du Clocher (A.C. Bordeaux)' and 'Graves Rouges du Château Caillou' at Illats. It is something of a tradition at Caillou to make a special *crème de tête* in good years, now called 'Private Cuvée'. It is made from a special selection of botrytis-affected grapes and recent vintages have been 1981, 1983, 1985 and 1986. It is usually a wine of considerable extract and complexity.

Much of the wine is sold to private customers by mail order and to visitors to the property. Some 70% is said to end up abroad, Belgium being traditionally the biggest customer.

Château Doisy-Daëne   (Barsac)

Château Doisy, originally an undivided property belonging to a single family, was split up into three parts some time in the nineteenth century. Château Doisy-Gravas (as it was first called) was purchased in 1880 by the Dubroca family, one of whom married a Mlle Climens. Château Doisy-Védrines was owned first by Mme Teysonneau, who dropped the 'Doisy'. Château Doisy-Daëne's first proprietor was an Englishman, Mr. Daëne. When he died in 1863 the property came to M Dejean of the firm of Cazalet et Cie. In 1924 it was sold by a M Debens to the father of the present owner, M Pierre Dubourdieu, who has not only done much to maintain the standard of the sweet wine, but has made a reputation for his dry wines too. He also owns Château Cantegril in Barsac.

M Dubourdieu, whose son Denis is now the oenologist, is a

highly original and independent-minded wine-maker and surely one of the best in the whole of the Sauternais. He claims to be more interested in dry wines than sweet and he makes far more — about 20,000 cases as against 4,000–7,000 of the sweet — from his 15 hectares.

Whatever his views on sweet wine, M Dubourdieu certainly makes a fine, if unconventional, one. Indeed his vinification methods are unique. For a start the *cépage* is 100% sémillon; then although three to five pickings are usual he often picks at a lower sugar level than other leading properties. The grapes are pressed five times in modern horizontal presses and fermented in stainless steel tanks in the air-conditioned *chai* at 18–22°C for about 20 days. This is terminated by chilling the wine to 2°C for two to three weeks before it is racked, lightly sulphured and — very unusually — centrifuged: this is an expensive process but one which M Dubourdieu believes gives the wine optimum clarity, finesse and concentration. The wine is bottled after 18–26 months, spending a year to 18 months in barrels (about a third of which are new) and the rest in tanks. There are usually three cold (sterilised) filtrations and the wine is racked every four months. The *assemblage* takes place in the March following the vintage.

The thinking behind this highly individual vinification technique is to reduce drastically the amount of sulphur needed to stabilise and protect the wine against oxidation by minimising the contact with air. The result is an apparently quite light wine which can be drunk with pleasure at an early stage in its development, but which has good extract in years when botrytis is abundant and has a surprising capacity for ageing. A feature of Doisy-Daëne even in less good years is its elegance and balance. Not surprisingly the 1983 and 1986 are particularly impressive.

M Dubourdieu now makes two versions of his 'Sec', one of them oak-aged. The grapes (predominantly sémillon and sauvignon with some muscadelle and a little riesling and chardonnay) are macerated, the grape-skins being left in the must for 24–36 hours to allow the enzymes to liberate the juice by severing the pectin of the cells which enclose it. It is clarified by running cold water through the must and then centrifuging it. The traditional 'Sec' is an interesting fruity wine with a hint of Sauternes richness but fresh and attractive in the mouth. M Dubourdieu also makes a good red wine, A.C. Graves, from his 23 hectares in that district.

Château Doisy-Dubroca   (Barsac)

This property, first called Doisy-Gravas, is the smallest part of the original Doisy estate. It was purchased in 1880 by the

Dubroca family and became associated with Château Climens through the marriage of one of the family to a Mlle Climens. About sixty years ago it was bought by M Gounouilhou together with Château Climens and since 1971 both have been the property of M Lucien Lurton, the owner of Climens and a number of other well-known estates in the Gironde.

The vineyard, approximately 3.5 hectares, is sited between Climens and Coutet and produces on average 400 cases a year. The *cépage* is 100% sémillon. The wine is vinified at Climens and in exactly the same way as its distinguished neighbour. Differences of soil and siting mean that it is less weighty and complex than Climens but the property makes consistently good wine which can be drunk with pleasure when quite young and has the capacity to develop well in the bottle. The wine is distributed exclusively by the firm of Louis Dubroca, which seems appropriate.

Château Doisy-Védrines   (Barsac)

As we have said, this was originally part of the single Doisy estate. The house, built around 1500, was originally a windmill, lived in by the Védrines family. For some years the property was run by Mme Castéja on behalf of her husband, who was a *négociant* with his family's company in Bordeaux; he has now retired and has taken over as *directeur* of Doisy-Védrines. M Castéja's family owned the house as far back as 1830. It was comprehensively restored in the early 1970s.

There are some 30 hectares under vine, 20 of them A.C. Sauternes (80% sémillon, 20% sauvignon) producing on average 2,500 cases at 18 hectolitres per hectare. Vinification methods are fairly traditional here, although the temperature of the fermentation is strictly controlled at 18–20°C and it is stopped by being chilled at −4°C and very lightly sulphured. The wine is matured in oak barrels a third of which are new each year, with the usual rackings before being bottled after two years. A very high proportion of the wine is exported. About 600 cases of a red wine, 'Château Latour-Védrines', are made from cabernet sauvignon, cabernet franc and merlot.

The wine is consistently good, the style being rather fuller and more luscious than its sister Doisys though not necessarily superior. The wines seem to have been even better over the last few years, the 1985 being attractive in a lighter style and the 1983 and especially the 1986 showing classic Barsac characteristics.

Château Filhot   (Sauternes)

This is the largest estate in the area and one of the most

handsome. The fine château was first acquired by the Filhot family in 1709 but was then called the Maison Noble de Verdoulet. They replanted the vineyard which had been devastated by the great frost of 1705. Gabriel Barthélèmy de Filhot, President of the Bordeaux Parlement, bought Château Coutet in 1788 (the labels are strikingly alike today). The wine of Filhot had a great reputation by now and in the same year Thomas Jefferson, in his notes on Bordeaux wines, ranked it as second only to d'Yquem among Sauternes. After the Revolution, in which Gabriel was guillotined, one of his daughters inherited the estate. In 1827 she married the Marquis de Lur-Saluces and in 1830 the neighbouring property of Château Pineau du Rey was added to the estate. In the 1855 classification Filhot was given the official status of a *deuxième cru*, but both wines were often sold under the title 'Vins de Sauternes' or later 'Château Sauternes' by the Lur-Saluces family. After the vineyards had been ravaged by phylloxera most of the Pineau vines were not replaced; a small part remains and it is from this that the dry wine of Filhot ('Château du Rey' or 'Pineau du Rey') is produced; of the château only a single seventeenth-century tower is left.

In 1935 Comte Bertrand de Lur-Saluces, the proprietor of Yquem, sold the Filhot estate to his sister, who had married Comte Etienne Durieu de Lacarelle. Over the previous 80 years the vineyard area had shrunk from 120 to a mere 20 hectares and the Comte set about restoring the property and extending the vineyard area. Since 1974 his wife's nephew, Comte Henri de Vaucelles, has been the proprietor. The *maître du chai* is M Pierre Capbern.

There are now 60 hectares under vine with an unusually high percentage of sauvignon (40%), 55% sémillon and 5% muscadelle. Yields are rather high at 23 hectolitres per hectare and 9–12,000 cases. *Tries* vary from two to six. The grapes ripen rather later at Filhot, which is the most southerly estate of the area, and said to be particularly prone to frosts. There are usually three pressings. Chaptalisation is used when it is considered necessary and the must is fermented in fibreglass tanks for about 14 days at 22°C. This is terminated by chilling the must. Up to 1985 the wine was matured in fibreglass tanks, too, but now the Comte has purchased some barrels and intends to give future vintages some wood-ageing. It will be interesting to see the effects of this move. The wine is bottled after two and a half years.

The maturation in vat, the large percentage of sauvignon and, perhaps, the rather high yield tend to make Filhot a light, fruity, less lusciously sweet wine, which often lacks the depth and complexity one expects of a top property. This is partly a question of style rather than quality and indeed the wines can be elegant and well balanced; but too often they have seemed to us rather one-dimensional and unremarkable. The 1976 is an exception and clearly the best Filhot we have tasted. The 1979 and 1981 were pleasant enough but the 1983 was disappointingly slight and short for the vintage.

Château Lamothe   (Sauternes)

This was the last of the *deuxième crus* in the order of the 1855 classification. It is on the site of a Roman fortress, and was originally called Lamothe Dassault. In the nineteenth century its owners included Jean-François de Borie (1814), Jacques Dowling (an Englishman), Simon and Jean Baptiste, MM Deiz, de La Porte and Massieux, and the Dubedat and Espagnet families. In 1905 it was purchased by M Joseph Bergey. The next owners were the Bastit St Martin family who also owned Château d'Arche; in 1961 M Bastit St Martin sold most of the property to the present proprietors, M and Mme Jean Despujols, but retained part of the vineyard, producing wine under the label of 'Château Lamothe-Bergey'. In 1981 he sold this to MM Philippe and Jacques Guignard. The Despujols' *maître du chai* and oenologist at Lamothe is M Bouise.

There are eight hectares of vines (70% sémillon, 15% sauvignon, 15% muscadelle). The yield of 20–25 hectolitres per hectare is one of the highest admitted in the area and about 2,000 cases are made. There are five pressings and after the *débourbage* the must is fermented in plastic-lined cement tanks for 3–4 weeks at 18–20°C. Though they have employed wood maturation in the past there are currently no barrels and the wine is aged in fibreglass vats, being fined four times, filtered twice and bottled two years after the vintage.

The style of the wine is generally light and uncomplicated, ready to drink quite early in its life, though the 1975 and 1976 have shown some distinction. The 1985 was disappointing and, in particular, the 1986 lacked the weight and concentration one would expect from a classed growth in this vintage. The design of the label of Château Lamothe is changed from time to time.

Château Lamothe-Guignard   (Sauternes)

This part of the original Lamothe estate, previously known, under M Bastit St Martin, as Lamothe-Bergey, was purchased from him by Philippe and Jacques Guignard in 1981; they also own Château Roquetaillade de la Grange in Graves and their family are the owners of Château de Rolland in Barsac.

There are 15 hectares of vines (90% sémillon, 5%

sauvignon, 5% muscadelle). The average age is 30 years but they have been doing a good deal of replanting recently. About 2,000 cases are made with a yield of 12–14 hectolitres per hectare. Four or five *tries* are made. The grapes are pressed four times and the must is fermented for three to ten weeks in small stainless steel tanks at 22–24°C. After racking the wine spends the winter in the tanks and is transferred to oak barrels (a quarter of them new each year) in the spring where they are matured for 12–15 months before being filtered and bottled.

The early vintages of this 'new' property have been promising. The 1981 was pleasant and quite elegant; the 1984 and 1985 were rather light; but the 1983 and 1986 had pleasingly lemony characteristics with fair depth, though they seemed rather forward. Further developments will be watched with interest.

Château de Malle (Preignac)

The only *deuxième cru* of Preignac has the most impressive building of the whole area and it is an official historic monument. It was built by the Lur–Saluces family in the early seventeenth century and has a courtyard in front, round towers on each side, and a splendid Italian formal garden at the rear. Inside there is an imposing panelled hall with a marble floor and in one of the towers a beautiful chapel. De Malle has retained its connection with the Lur–Saluces family, numbering several Comtes among its owners, and is now the property of the Comtesse de Bournazel. Her husband, who died in 1985, was a cousin of Comte Alexandre de Lur–Saluces, proprietor of Château Yquem. When he took over in 1956, 16.5 hectares had just been destroyed by the great frost of that year; but he spent a great deal of time and money restoring the château, the vineyard and the *chai*.

11. *Deuxième cru* Château de Malle (Preignac)

79

The *chef de culture* is M Pascal Sterna and the *maître du chai* M Alain Pivonet. The whole estate covers 200 hectares, 46 of which are under vine, 19 of them in Graves, thus entitling the red and dry white wines to be sold as A.C. Graves rather than merely Bordeaux. The *cépage* for the 27 hectares of A.C. Sauternes is 70% sémillon, 28% sauvignon and 2% muscadelle, producing from 1,250 to 3,500 cases with a highish yield of 20–25 hectolitres per hectare.

There are three to eight pickings. After destalking the grapes are pressed in an automatic press two or three times and the must is fermented in temperature-controlled stainless steel tanks for 15–30 days at 19–21°C. The wine is then matured, filtered, fined and assembled in tanks about nine months after the vintage, and completes its maturation in oak barrels (a quarter of them new each year) with regular rackings before being sterile-filtered and then bottled. The maturation period may vary from 18 months to three years according to the vintage.

Over the last 30 years Malle has established a reputation for making elegant, attractive Sauternes of the lighter style which can be enjoyed quite young. That is not to say that the better vintages are not capable of ageing, however, for the 1971, 1975 and 1976 have lasted and developed well. If anything the wines have perhaps been even better in the 1980s, though still on the light side and rather quick to develop. The 1983 and 1986 are, not surprisingly, the most impressive.

A second wine, 'Château de Ste Helène', A.C. Sauternes, is made from young vines; the estate also produces two dry whites, 'M de Malle', wood-aged A.C. Graves, and 'Chevalier de Malle', A.C. Bordeaux made from sauvignon; and two reds, 'Châteaux Tours de Malle' (wood-aged) and 'de Cadaillon', both A.C. Graves and made from 80% cabernet sauvignon and 20% merlot.

Château de Myrat (Barsac)

This is the property of the de Pontac family. It was owned by M Perrot in 1845 and subsequently by M Henri Moller, who also acquired Château Broustet, and later by his widow when it was known as Myrat-Broustet. In 1893 MM Flaugorgues et Cie bought it, selling it to M P. Martineau whence it came to the de Pontacs.

In 1976 Comte Maximilien de Pontac decided that making fine sweet wine was no longer an economic proposition and all the vines were uprooted. And so ten years ago we said that it was sad to write of the demise of a classed growth. The Comte, who continued to live in the mid-eighteenth-century building, died in April 1988 and his heirs quickly decided to replant the

vineyard. They had to move swiftly to give official notice of
their decision, for according to the old law the rights of
replanting a vineyard last for precisely twelve years and those
twelve years were up on 5th August 1988. (In 1980 the law was
changed and the time reduced to six years but this fortunately
was not retrospective.) In July arrangements were completed
and Château de Myrat, at least in theory, rose from its ashes.
Of course there is an immense amount of work to be done:
clearing, digging, planting and grafting in the vineyard
(though the fact that the soil has lain fallow for so long will be
no bad thing) and the re-equipping of the *chai*. It will cost
upwards of two million francs to set up the new vineyard and
probably another five million or so before the first vintage
which should be 1991.

Nevertheless this is tremendous news and we congratulate
M Xavier de Pontac, who will run the vineyard, and his
brother Jacques, who will look after the financial side of the
operation, and wish them every success. All lovers of
Sauternes will rejoice at this resurrection which is surely the
most spectacular and tangible piece of evidence of the
renaissance of interest in the great sweet wines of Bordeaux
which we mentioned in the preface.

The 22-hectare vineyard will have a *cépage* of 90% sémillon
and 5% each of sauvignon and muscadelle, similar to the old
proportions except that formerly there was no sauvignon.

Of the few vintages of de Myrat that we have come across all
have been tasted when they were at least 40 years old and have
lasted remarkably well. They include the 1909, 1928, 1948 and
best of all the 1922 in half-bottle, tasted, appropriately, in the
year of the resurrection. It was beautifully balanced, still quite
rich and only just beginning to dry out.

Château Nairac   (Barsac)

This beautiful château was built by Mollie, a pupil of the
famous architect Victor Louis, for M Elysée Nairac in the
1770s to replace a former mansion on the family estate.

In the Revolution many of the family fled, first to Holland
then to Mauritius. In the early nineteenth century the
Capdeville family bought the property. They also owned the
neighbouring Château Broustet and the wine was often sold as
Broustet-Nairac (or Nérac as it appears in the 1855
classification). M Brunet, owner of Château Piada, married
one of the Capdeville daughters and took over Nairac in the
1860s but, after the phylloxera disaster, decided to grow grapes
for red wine and Sauternes was not made for some time. The
next owner was M Charles Perpezat, who replanted the
vineyard and re-established the making of traditional

Sauternes with considerable success at the beginning of this century. The family remained at Nairac until 1966 when they sold it to Dr. Jean Gabriolle Seynat. The château had not been lived in for some time and the wine was not as highly regarded as formerly. Over the next five years the property became increasingly run down until in 1971 it embarked on a new and exciting chapter in its history.

In 1967 Tom Heeter, a young American ex-law student who had decided that wine was his true vocation, started work in a New York wine shop. Three years later he went to Bordeaux to extend his knowledge and, admiring the wines of Château Giscours in Margaux, went to work for the proprietor, M Pierre Tari. Within a year he and Nicole, the daughter of the house, were married and in 1972 they purchased Château Nairac for about 800,000 francs and immediately dedicated themselves to the production of the very highest quality of Barsac. They employed positively Yquem-like perfectionism in every aspect of viticulture and vinification, from the severest pruning and most rigorous selection to the use of new oak barrels each year for both fermenting and maturation — and the legendary oenologist Professor Emile Peynaud was called in to advise. Despite little initial help from the elements the results were impressive from the start. The 1972 and 1974 were good for those poor vintages and the 1973 was outstanding, probably the best Barsac of the year. They also renovated the château, which had not been lived in for about 60 years, and moved in themselves in 1974.

There are 15 hectares under vine (90% sémillon, 6% sauvignon, 4% muscadelle), producing about 2,000 cases. In fact the sauvignon content of the wine will be appreciably higher than this figure because, as in a number of properties, it is picked earlier when hardly shrivelled by botrytis so the grapes will contain far more juice than the sémillon *grains rôtis*. Some 25 pickers are employed and they may go out as many as eleven times. Each picking is rigorously inspected when it arrives at the *chai*, to eliminate any risk of infection. The grapes are pressed very gently in a hydraulic press. For the overnight *débourbage* a little SO_2 is added to prevent oxidation and some phosphate of ammonia and thiamin (vitamin B1) which inhibits oxydase and greatly reduces the amount of SO_2 needed. Fermentation in oak barrels is conducted slowly at 16–18°C and stops of its own accord at about 14°; cooling is rarely necessary. Tom Heeter, who has experimented with various kinds of oak over the years, eventually decided that it was preferable to have half the barrels new each year rather than all of them. The wine is racked monthly for the first three months, then three or four times a year during the two to three years of its maturation. It is lightly filtered before bottling.

The result of this dedication and meticulous attention to

detail is a very impressive wine indeed. It is luscious, powerful and well structured, in some ways more like a fine Sauternes than a Barsac. Both the 1975 and the 1976 were splendid wines, the latter being particularly rich, concentrated and complex. Of the most recent vintages the 1980 and the 1982 were very good for their years, the 1983 was outstanding and the 1986 very promising indeed. We feel that in very concentrated vintages the 100% new oak casking is effective but in years when there is less extract the wines can seem excessively oaky. The new policy of 50% new oak seems sensible.

Tom Heeter and Nicole Tari are no longer together and, starting with the 1987 vintage, Nicole is in charge. No doubt she will keep up the very high standards of wine-making that have made Nairac one of the best properties of the region over the last fifteen years. We have already spoken of her impassioned advocacy of Sauternes as an accompaniment to good food.

Château Romer-du-Hayot   (Fargues)

The first known owner of this estate, which adjoins de Malle on the edge of Fargues, was M de Montalier in about 1810. It was then called Château Montalier-Romer. He sold it in 1833 to the Comte August de la Myre-Mory, who was married to yet another member of the Lur-Saluces family. In 1881, on the death of the Comtesse, the estate was split up among her five children. In 1937 Mme du Hayot purchased two thirds of the property which amounted to about 12 hectares. Her son, M André du Hayot of Barsac, owns one part and makes and markets the wine for the whole estate, producing approximately 1,200 cases a year. The other part belonged to M Roger Fargues whose father had owned it since 1911. Not long before his death in 1977 M Fargues leased his part to M du Hayot who has since worked the whole vineyard selling the whole vintage as 'Château Romer-du-Hayot'. M Fargues' son has inherited his father's portion and continues to lease it to M du Hayot.

There are 24 hectares of vines (60% sémillon, 25% sauvignon, 15% muscadelle) producing some 4,000 cases at the highish yield of 20–25 hectolitres per hectare. There are 3–5 *tries* and the grapes are taken to M du Hayot's other property, Château Guiteronde in Barsac, where all the vinification takes place. After five pressings and *débourbage* the juice is fermented for 3–5 weeks in stainless steel and epoxy-resin tanks at 20°C. No wood is used at the moment but M du Hayot had plans to extend the cellars and *chai* to accommodate barrels in 1988. The wine is matured in tanks with five rackings in the first year and three in the second and filtered before bottling.

Not surprisingly the wines are on the light side. Some writers have thought quite highly of those of recent years but we have found them consistently disappointing — light, 'eggy' and lacking in richness. Of the two recent generally outstanding vintages the 1983 lacked centre and depth and had a grassy taste and the 1986 when tasted recently from the cask seemed to have an artificial sweetness and to be somewhat lacking in botrytis. It will be interesting to see what effect the wood-ageing has.

Château Suau   (Barsac)

The last of the classified growths of Barsac is yet another estate with Lur-Saluces connections, for we know that the family owned it in 1840. It passed then to Mme Marion in 1845 and to M Jean Marion in 1868. The next owner was a Mme Chaine, who sold it to M Emile Garros, the manager of the estates of the Marquis de Lur-Saluces, in 1895. The château itself still belongs to the Garros family, but the present owner, Mme Pouchappadesse, sold the vineyard to M Biarnès of Illats, who owns a number of properties in the area.

There are 6.5 hectares of vines (85% sémillon, 15% sauvignon) producing 1,500 cases at the high yield of 25 hectolitres per hectare. After 3–4 pressings and *débourbage* the juice is fermented in stainless steel tanks at 18–20°C for 12–15 days. Fermentation is controlled and stopped by refrigeration. The wine is matured entirely in tanks and bottled after 12–18 . months.

We have not been very impressed with the Suau vintages we have tasted. Even those of good years have been disappointing. The 1976 was dull, rather sickly sweet with little character. The 1983 had an odd, boiled sweets nose and lacked style or richness and the 1986 was open and forward with little botrytis apparent and a kind of false sweetness. Most seem to lack richness and finesse though Robert Parker has found some merit in the 1975 and 1980.

THE OTHER PROPERTIES OF SAUTERNES

Château Barjuneau
Owner M André Lahiteau-Mensencau
3 hectares

Château de Commarque
Owner Dr Nigel Reay-Jones
At one time owned by M de Souza who was more interested in his horses than his vines. The last vintage was in 1972, after which wine-making was abandoned. In 1981 Geoffrey Kenyon-May acquired the Château and converted it into an hotel/restaurant and started to replant the vineyard. He sold it to the present owner in 1987.
12 hectares (3 hectares under vine)
85% sémillon, 15% sauvignon

Château Lafon (*contigu* Yquem)
Owner M Pierre Dufour, who also owns Château Cherchy in the Graves. It has been in his family for three generations.
Situated west of Lafaurie-Peyraguey and south of Yquem at the foot of their vineyards. Also produces wine under the labels of 'Château Grand Mayne' and 'Château le Mayne'.
8 hectares (5.16 under vine) producing 129 hectolitres of wine.
95% sémillon, 5% sauvignon

Château Lafon-Laroze
Purchased in 1980 by Château Raymond-Lafon and is now part of their estate. It was only a house with no vineyard.

Château Lamaringue
Owners Rémy and Roland Sessacq who also own Château Lousteau Vieil in Ste-Croix-du-Mont and Clos Lamourasse in the Graves, producing red wine.
2 hectares being replanted
80% sémillon, 20% sauvignon

Château Pajot (*enclave* Yquem)
Formerly called Domaine de Bellevue
Purchased in 1985 from M Jacobs by Château Yquem and it is now part of their vineyards.
8 hectares

Château Raymond-Lafon
Owner M Pierre Meslier
This property was established in the nineteenth century by M Raymond Lafon. The château is an English-style mansion close to Château Lafon, just north of Yquem. At the end of the century it came into the hands of M Louis Pontallier whose family retained the property until 1952, when they sold it to Dr. Bourdier. In 1972 it was purchased by M Pierre Meslier, who in 1963 had moved from Châteaux Prieuré-Lichine and Lascombes to become *gérant* of Château Yquem. When he bought it there were just three and a half hectares under vine; over the years he has added to it bit by bit and there are now 20 hectares, 18 in production. As much of the acquired land was already planted the average age of the vines is about 40 years. It is a real family estate with Pierre Meslier supervising, one son, Charles-Henri, making the wine, another, Jean-Pierre, marketing it while Mme Francine Meslier looks after the property and receives visitors.

The *cépage* is identical with that of Yquem (80% sémillon, 20% sauvignon) and so is the miserly yield of 9 hectolitres per hectare, for M Meslier aims for perfection. The 35 pickers make anything from four to eleven *tries* and the wine is made exactly as at Yquem. Needless to say there is no chaptalisation. M Meslier has gradually built up the percentage of new casks from about 10% to 100%. The selection, both of grapes and of lots for the final *assemblage*, is as rigorous as at Yquem itself. About 2,000 cases are produced, some 30% being sold in France; the USA, the UK and West Germany are the main foreign customers.

This kind of perfectionism is certainly reflected in the quality of the wine, and, starting with the 1975, a series of excellent vintages has been made; even the 1978, when there was virtually no botrytis, had beautiful balance, texture and body and was considered by Robert Parker to be the best Sauternes of that year. The 1983 looks like being magnificent. The only doubt is whether M Meslier's decision to use 100% new oak and a full three years of wood-ageing, for a wine that is less massive than d'Yquem, is a wise one. Time will tell.

Château Terrefort
Owners MM Guy Perissé and J. Frouin

3 hectares

Château Trillon
Formerly called Château Trillon-Dube

Owner M Jean-Claude Guicheney

19.86 hectares under vine producing 496 hectolitres of wine.

80% sémillon, 10% sauvignon, 10% muscadelle

Cru Haut-Piquant
Owner M Pierre Carreyre who also owns property in Landiras.

2.59 hectares under vine producing 64 hectolitres of wine.

Cru Lamothe
Owner M Marc Saint Marc

0.68 hectares under vine producing 2 hectolitres of wine.

Cru L'Aubépin
Owner M Jean Laporte

3.75 hectares under vine producing 90 hectolitres of wine.

Domaine de Barjuneau Chauvin
Owners MM Etienne and Philippe Fouquet in whose family it has been since 1938.

A modern property, well maintained, set amongst the vines.

6.24 hectares under vine producing 156 hectolitres of wine.

85% sémillon, 10% sauvignon, 5% muscadelle

Domaine de Caplane (*contigu* Yquem)
Owner M Arthur-Jean Dubernet-Trijasson

13.18 hectares under vine producing 329 hectolitres of wine; 50% is sold in bulk.

80% sémillon, 10% sauvignon, 10% muscadelle

Domaine du Coy
Owner M Roger Biarnès of Château Navarro (Illats) and Château Suau. All the wine is produced at Château Navarro.

7.5 hectares under vine

80% sémillon, 15% sauvignon, 5% muscadelle

Domaine des Jouanous
Owner M Guy Ducos

1.3 hectares under vine producing 33 hectolitres of wine, which is sold in bulk.

Domaine de Lamothe
Owner M Jean Coignet

3.92 hectares under vine producing 98 hectolitres of wine.

Domaine de Laraude
Owner M Marcel Carreyre, who also owns property in Landiras.

2 hectares

Domaine de Terrefort
Owner M Bernard Fage

1.25 hectares under vine producing 31 hectolitres of wine.

Clos Le Parent
Owners Domaines Dubourg who also own Château du Tich in Ste-Croix-du-Mont.

Chai du Roy
Owner M Pierre Tauzin

Other owners:
Simone Ducourneau

0.5 hectares under vine producing 13 hectolitres of wine which is sold in bulk.

Arlette and Joaquim Lopez

3.09 hectares under vine producing 77 hectolitres of wine which is sold in bulk.

Jean-Francois Massieu

Small vineyard near Château Yquem.

THE OTHER PROPERTIES OF BOMMES

Château Augey
Owner Madelaine Ricaud

Farmed by Pierre Meslier, owner of Château Raymond-Lafon.

10 hectares under vine producing generic Sauternes which is vinified at Château Raymond-Lafon.

Château Béchereau
Owner M Franck Deloubes

This property is well maintained with a new *chai* situated by the edge of the river Ciron.

12 hectares (9.5 under vine) producing 238 hectolitres of wine.

75% sémillon, 20% sauvignon, 5% muscadelle

Château Béchereau-Bommes
Owner M René Philipperie

4 hectares (0.28 under vine) producing 7 hectolitres of wine.

Château Bergeron
Formerly called Cru Bergeron
Owner Bernard Laurans

This small, attractive farmhouse is well maintained and set back in the vines.

7 hectares (6.88 under vine) producing 172 hectolitres of wine.

83% sémillon, 7% sauvignon, 10% muscadelle

Château Cameron
Owner M Paul Lanneluc, who owns one third of Château Rabaud-Promis, and is a well-known vineyard photographer. The Château has been in his family since 1927.
It is farmed by M Pierre Guinabert. Wine is also produced under the name of 'Domaine Raymond-Louis'.

12 hectares (8.43 under vine) producing 210 hectolitres of wine.
100% sémillon

Château Caplane
Owner M Guy David

8.51 hectares under vine producing 292 hectolitres of wine.

Château Haut-Bommes
Owners Pauly Frères, who also own Clos Haut-Peyraguey.

7 hectares

80% sémillon, 17% sauvignon, 3% muscadelle

Château Jean Galant
Owner M Roberte Ducos

8 hectares (5.78 under vine) producing 144 hectolitres of wine.

Château Lamourette
Owner M Paul Léglise

8 hectares (7.47 under vine) producing 187 hectolitres of wine.

90% sémillon, 5% sauvignon, 5% muscadelle

Château Le Sourd Beteille
Owner M Marcel Aymard

1.8 hectares under vine producing 46 hectolitres of wine.

Château Mauras
Owners Société Civile de la Rive Gauche
Manager Jean-Luc Dualé for Société Viticole de France

The old estate of Château Mauras was purchased on 28th Frimaire (the third month of the French Republican calendar) in the year II from Mme Cameron, wife of M de Baritauly, by M Marc-Pierre-Marie

Emerigon, Chairman of the High Court of Bordeaux. He sold it in 1847 to M Henri-Maximilien de Pontac, in whose hands it was to remain until 1882. It then passed into the ownership of the family of M Albert Bertin from whose heirs it was purchased in 1925 by M Roger Bouin. It is a large and imposing property with a gated entrance and vines running either side of the château. The soil is chalky and the rock subsoil underlying the whole vineyard sometimes reaches surface level.

24 hectares (12.81 under vine) producing 320 hectolitres of wine.

65% sémillon, 30% sauvignon, 5% muscadelle

Cru Baboye
Owner M Yves Desqueyroux who also owns Château Chercy in Pujols-sur-Ciron.

2 hectares

Cru Bataille
Owner M Gilbert Dubedat

0.42 hectares under vine producing 5 hectolitres of wine.

Cru L'Agnet la Carrière
Owners Raymond and Jean-Marie Mallard who also own Château de Naudonnet-Plaisance at Escoussans.

2 hectares

Cru La Maringue
Owner M Joseph Daulan

0.41 hectares under vine producing 10 hectolitres of wine.

Cru L'Aubépin
Owner M Edgar Clavière

2 hectares

Cru Le Rousseau
Owner Marie-Louis Gour

2 hectares (1 under vine) producing 25 hectolitres of wine.

Cru Le Tachon
Owner M Jean-Pierre Ducla

4 hectares (2.32 under vine) producing 58 hectolitres of wine.

Cru de L'Hermitage
Owner M Michel Courbin, who also owns property of the same name in Budos.

3.5 hectares under vine producing 89 hectolitres of wine.

Cru du Mahon
Owners Courbin Frères

1 hectare

Cru Richard Barbe
Owner G. F. A. Château de Carles in Barsac

2 hectares

Cru Terrefort
Owner M Rene Dumé

6 hectares (5.12 under vine) producing 126 hectolitres of wine.

Domaine de Carbonnieu
Owners MM Marc and Alain Charrier in whose family it has been since 1947. It is a single-storey modern farmhouse.

10.75 hectares (10.29 under vine) producing 258 hectolitres of wine.

80% sémillon, 10% sauvignon, 10% muscadelle

Domaine Duperneau
Owner M Hector Lassauvageux

4 hectares (3.5 under vine) producing 87 hectolitres of wine.

60% sémillon, 20% sauvignon, 20% muscadelle

Domaine Janonier
Owner M Yvon Pouyaud

3 hectares (2.76 under vine) producing 68 hectolitres of wine sold mainly in bulk.

50% sémillon, 25% sauvignon, 25% muscadelle

Domaine de La Bouchette
Since the death of M Jean Jordeau in 1979, in whose family it has been

since 1923, the property is now owned by his 5 children.

2.5 hectares under vine

La Chapelle-St-Aubin
Owner since 1973 M Jean-Louis Dubos

It is a well kept, ivy-covered property and was an ancient monastery. Wine is also produced under the label of 'La Chapelle St Antoine'.

6 hectares (4.46 under vine) producing 112 hectolitres of wine.

75% sémillon, 15% sauvignon, 10% muscadelle

Domaine de La Gauche
Previously called Domaine de La Gueritte under which name some wine is labelled. Also produces wine under the label of 'Cru Haut-Lagueritte'.

Owner since 1981 M Jean Baro

2.22 hectares under vine producing 56 hectolitres of wine.

60% sémillon, 20% sauvignon, 20% muscadelle

Domaine du Pajot
Owner M Alain Arnaud and has been in his family for two generations.

16 hectares (3.38 under vine) producing 21 hectolitres of wine.

80% sémillon, 15% muscadelle, 5% sauvignon

Domaine Puydomine
Owner M Pierre Fraigneau

2 hectares

Other owners:

Nicole Lucbert

1.92 hectares producing 48 hectolitres of wine, which is sold in bulk.

Henriette Perretti

0.35 hectares producing 9 hectolitres of wine, which is sold in bulk.

Jean-Louis Peyri

2.62 hectares producing 6.6 hectolitres of wine.

THE *OTHER PROPERTIES* OF *FARGUES*

Château Barbier
Tenanted by MM Jean Médeville et
Fils who also own Château Fayau in
Cadillac, Château du Juge in Haux,
Château Greteau, Château Pessan in
Graves. The part of the property that
is Château Boyrein in Graves
produces dry white and red wines.
The part in Fargues produces sweet
white wine.

8 hectares, 5.75 under vine

90% sémillon, 10% sauvignon

Château Beauséjour
Owner M Francis Espagnet, who
also owns Château Montagne in Ste-
Croix-du-Mont.

Château Boissonneau
Owner Marie Dubourg

1.58 hectares producing 35
hectolitres of wine.

Château de Fargues
Owner Comte Alexandre de Lur-
Saluces of Château Yquem and has
been in his family since 1472.

This estate is located on the perimeter
of Fargues. The derelict castle,
perched high on a hill, dominates the
commune. The courtyard buildings
now house a recently refurbished *chai*
containing one- to two-year-old
barrels. The wine produced here is of
the highest quality and long lived.

The estate covers more than 175
hectares, with only 11.3 under vine.
It is planted with 80% sémillon and
20% sauvignon grapes producing
177 hectolitres of wine.

Château Mayne-des-Carmes
Owner M Michel Charbonneaux

15 hectares

Château Partarrieu
Owner Jacqueline Tuyttens-Laville

17.84 hectares producing 446
hectolitres of wine. Wine is also
produced under the label of 'Château
L'Ermitage'.

100% sémillon

Château Peillon-Claverie
Owner Odile Tachon

30 hectares (5.92 under vine)
producing 148 hectolitres of wine.

90% sémillon, 10% sauvignon

Château Peyron
Owner Vve Roger Chaumès. The
property has been in the family since
1953.

9 hectares (6.66 under vine)
producing 166 hectolitres of wine, all
of which is sold in bulk.

90% sémillon, 9% sauvignon, 1%
muscadelle

Château Thibaut
This property is split into two parts:

Owner M Julien Latourneau

4.43 hectares under vine producing
111 hectolitres of wine.

Owner M Jacques Latourneau

5.32 hectares under vine producing
133 hectolitres of wine.

Cru Clavaries
Formerly Château Claveries

Owner M Jean Bordenave

8 hectares (0.24 under vine)
producing 6 hectolitres of wine.

Cru Mothes
Owner Serge Bedouret

2.6 hectares (2.3 under vine)
producing 57 hectolitres of wine.

70% sémillon, 15% sauvignon, 15% muscadelle

Cru Mounic
Owner M Jean Pierre Manceau
2 hectares

Cru Pouteau
Owner M Marcelle Gouze
2.65 hectares producing 66 hectolitres of wine.

Cru Pouteau
Owner Raymond Tastet
0.92 hectares under vine producing 23 hectolitres of wine, which is all sold in bulk.
70% sémillon, 20% sauvignon, 10% muscadelle

Cru Pugneau
Owner M Jean-André-Guy Labarde
3.29 hectares producing 83 hectolitres of wine.
60% sémillon, 20% sauvignon, 20% muscadelle

Cru Soula
Owner M Henri Latapy
7 hectares (1.28 under vine) producing 33 hectolitres of wine.

Cru Thibaut
Owners Société Calvie Magni
4.27 hectares producing 106 hectolitres of wine.

Clos Barreau
Owner M Jean-Pierre Caubit
4.26 hectares producing 12 hectolitres of wine.

Domaine Baylieu
Owner M Denis Sarraute

8 hectares (5.67 under vine) producing 141 hectolitres of wine.
70% sémillon, 15% sauvignon, 15% muscadelle

Domaine de Coye
Owner Georges Clauzure

Domaine de Fillau
Owner M Amédée Labarbe; in the family since 1911.
10.5 hectares (4.20 under vine) producing 105 hectolitres of wine.
75% sémillon, 20% sauvignon, 5% muscadelle

Clos Fontaine
Owner M Claude Saint Marc
16 hectares (9.21 under vine) producing 230 hectolitres of wine.

Domaine du Haut-Claverie
Owners Sendrey Frères. The property has been in this family's possession for four generations.
14 hectares (10.06 under vine) producing 252 hectolitres of wine, most of which is sold in bulk to *négociants*. There are also 3 hectares which produce red and dry white wine.
85% sémillon, 10% sauvignon, 5% muscadelle

Domaine de La Côte
Owner M Marc Lassère
The property has been in the family since 1925. It is a small, single-storey family house.
4.7 hectares (3.78 under vine) producing 94 hectolitres of wine.
85% sémillon, 14% sauvignon, 1% muscadelle

Clos Les Tuileries
Owner M Christian Delmouny
1 hectare (0.35 under vine) producing 9 hectolitres of wine.

Clos du Pape
Owner Mme Saint-Belliès
10 hectares

Domaine de Peyre
Owner Alice Bernard
1 hectare

Clos Pilotte
Owner M Guy Dupeyron
6 hectares producing 150 hectolitres of wine.
80% sémillon, 10% sauvignon, 10% muscadelle

Domaine de Pouteau
Owner M Hubert Ferchi
3.14 hectares producing 78 hectolitres of wine.
80% sémillon, 10% sauvignon, 10% muscadelle

Domaine de Quincarnon
Owner since 1957 Marc Bridet, who also owns Château Cazebonne in St-Pierre-de-Mons.
11 hectares (5 under vine)
60% sémillon, 25% sauvignon, 15% muscadelle

Domaine de Rougement
Owner Dominique Turtaut

Domaine de Thibaut
Owner M Jean Daney; tenanted by Henri Dulac who is the director of Château Les Queyrats in St-Pierre-de-Mons.
15 hectares

THE OTHER PROPERTIES OF PREIGNAC

Château d'Argilas-le-Pape

Owner since November 1984 Mme Yvon Breignaud; in the family since 1947.

5 hectares (1.81 under vine) producing 45 hectolitres of wine.

Château d'Armajan-des-Ormes

Owners since 1953 MM Michel and Jacques Perromat

An imposing, large château set back in the vineyards bordering Preignac and Barsac. Wine is also produced under the label of 'Château des Ormes'.

9.45 hectares under vine producing 236 hectolitres of wine.

60% sémillon, 30% sauvignon, 10% muscadelle

Château des Arrieux

Owner M Hubert Lacombe

6 hectares (5.49 under vine) producing 137 hectolitres of wine.

70% sémillon, 15% sauvignon, 15% muscadelle

Château Bastor-Lamontagne

Owners since 1936 Crédit Foncier de France, who also own Château St-Robert (Pujols-sur-Ciron).

Régisseur M Michel Garat (since 1987); *maître de chai* M Jean Bayejo (previously with Château Suduiraut).

The property was owned in the eighteenth century by M Bastor, a councillor in the Parlement in Bordeaux. He joined with François de Lamontagne and the estate then passed to the Larrieu family. From there it went to an uncle, M Eugène Larrieu, and then to a Colonel René Mileret who was killed in 1918 in Argonne. It is mentioned in old records as Château Lamontagne, a *deuxième cru* Preignac.

83 hectares (38.14 under vine) producing 951 hectolitres of wine.

77% sémillon, 18% sauvignon, 5% muscadelle

Château Briatte

Owner A. Roudes

This is a modern, single-storey farmhouse.

10 hectares (9.27 under vine) producing 232 hectolitres of wine.

90% sémillon, 5% sauvignon, 5% muscadelle

Château Comet-Magey

Owner Yvette Barbe-Fontan

This is a small farmhouse with a *chai* opposite the vineyards of Château Suduiraut.

5 hectares (4.64 under vine) producing 116 hectolitres of wine.

85% sémillon, 10% sauvignon, 5% muscadelle

Château Gilette

Owner M Christian Médeville who also owns the nearby Château Les Justices and a good Graves property, Château Respide-Médeville.

This estate, just outside the village of Preignac, dates from the eighteenth century. It was purchased by the Médeville family from M de La Motte, a councillor of the Bordeaux Parlement, and has been run by them ever since.

It seems an understatement to say that the methods of production of the present proprietor, M Christian Médeville, are unique. The background is conventional enough, with strict attention being paid to traditional detail. There are 4.5 hectares of vines (83% sémillon, 15% sauvignon, 2% muscadelle), average age 30 years, and a tiny yield of 10 hectolitres per hectare produces 400–900 cases. The grapes are pressed up to six times, then after *débourbage* at 8–10°C and a light sulphuring the juice is fermented in stainless steel tanks at 14–18°C. When the alcohol reaches 14° the ferment is stopped by lowering the temperature to 10°C. The wine is then racked and blended before being put into small epoxy-lined cement tanks for 12 to 25 *years* before filtering and bottling! Each picking is vinified separately and often two wines will be made — a 'doux' or 'demi-doux' and a *crème de tête* from the most botrytised pickings. The aim of this astonishing 'buried alive' technique is to preserve the fresh fruit aromas and flavours of the wine, which M Médeville believes are apt to be lost in the more conventional wood-casking and the exposure to air which that and repeated rackings involves. The wines are usually released about four years after bottling. This means of course that the wine is fully mature when it becomes available for purchase which, to put it mildly, is most unusual for a quality wine. The wines are certainly remarkable: the 1955 tasted in 1986 was soft in the mouth, luscious and delicately peachy, with good acidity and a hint of marmalade at the finish. Its cost in the UK then was £37. It is of course debatable whether this unique method of conditioning is preferable to conventional practices. David Peppercorn in 1985 had the unusual opportunity to taste the 1959 and the 1955, bottled in 1981, alongside the 1950 and the 1949, bottled a mere six or seven years after the vintage. He felt that the early-bottled wines had distinctly more complexity than the two that had been vatted for so long, though of course this was not a direct comparison of the same vintages.

M Médeville has a splendid stock of Gilette vintages going back to the 1930s and dreams of a time when the next generation will be able to boast a collection of a century of Gilettes. This urge seems to have been inherited from his father René and his grandfather for he has a nineteenth-century price-list which mentions a diploma of honour for a collection of wines dating from 1819 to 1886!

M Médeville is now experimenting with oak barrels for fermentation and part of the maturation period, both at Gilette and Les Justices, but is worried that the oak will alter the style of his wines. It will be interesting to see how things develop.

Château Gimbalet
Owner M Jean Lahiteau who also owns Château Laribotte.

5 hectares

Château du Haire
Owner M Jean Guy Cartier

6 hectares (5.04 under vine) producing 126 hectolitres of wine.

75% sémillon, 15% sauvignon, 10% muscadelle

Château Haut-Bergeron
Owner Robert Lamothe who also owns Château Farluret (Barsac).

This is an old, small property opposite Château Haut-Mayne.

19.5 hectares (10.5 under vine) producing 263 hectolitres of wine.

90% semillon, 5% sauvignon, 5% muscadelle

Château Haut-Fontebride
Formerly called Château Fontebride-Boutoc.

Owner M André Juyon

5 hectares

Château du Juge
Owner Mme Françoise Guix de Pinos. Mme Guix de Pinos has owned this property since 1965, and it has been in her family since 1876.

5 hectares (3.93 under vine) producing 98 hectolitres of wine.

80% sémillon, 20% sauvignon

Château La Chartreuse
This is not a separate property but is part of Château St-Amand. The wine is marketed exclusively for Maison Sichel.

Château La Garenne
Owner M Christian Ferbos

6 hectares under vine producing 108 hectolitres of wine.

90% sémillon, 5% sauvignon, 5% muscadelle

Château La Gravière
Owners Société Daney Frères

5 hectares (4.39 under vine) producing 110 hectolitres of wine.

Château Lange
Owner M Daniel Picot

This property is set back amongst the vines and is a fine, turreted château.

12 hectares (7.2 under vine) producing 180 hectolitres of wine.

70% sémillon, 20% sauvignon, 10% muscadelle

Château Laribotte
Owner M Jean Lahiteau who also owns Château Gimbalet.

14.5 hectares (11.8 under vine) producing 280 hectolitres of wine.

80% sémillon, 15% sauvignon, 5% muscadelle

Château Larose-Monteil
Owner M Georges Cambefort

9 hectares (8.54 under vine) producing 210 hectolitres of wine.

80% sémillon, 10% sauvignon, 10% muscadelle

Château Laville
Owners since 1971 Yvette Barbe and Roberte Maille; it has been in the family since 1960. They also produce red wine under the labels of 'Château Mahon-Laville' and 'Château Ferrière' (sold to *négociants*).

This is a large, well-kept château, set in its own vineyards.

23 hectares (15.85 under vine) producing 395 hectolitres of wine.

80% sémillon, 15% sauvignon, 5% muscadelle

Château Le Mayne
Formerly called Château du Maine.

Owner M Bernard Roumazeilles

10 hectares (8.76 under vine) producing 219 hectolitres of wine.

Château Le Pape
Owner M Jean-Louis Daney

2.79 hectares under vine producing 69 hectolitres of wine.

Château Les Justices
Owner Christian Médeville, who also owns Château Gilette (see above)

This rather larger estate, a little less than a mile from Château Gilette, has also been the property of the Médeville family since the eighteenth century and Christian Médeville makes the wine here too.

There are 8.5 hectares of vines with a significantly higher proportion of muscadelle (80% sémillon, 13% sauvignon, 7% muscadelle), producing about 1,800 cases with a yield of around 18 hectolitres per hectare. Methods of vinification have been identical to those used at Gilette except that the wines are bottled after four years in the vats instead of twenty or more. Since the 1985 vintage some barrel-ageing has been introduced (25% new each year); the intention is to increase this over the next few years. The wines will be bottled after two to three years.

It is a wine of less extract and complexity than Gilette but nevertheless of good quality and very consistent.

Château Le Roc
Owner Marie-Louise Claverie

3 hectares (2.24 under vine) producing 57 hectolitres of wine.

Château Les Ramparts
Owner M Jean Baup

Also known as Domaine de Lamothe-Vigneau. The property originally belonged to the Busio family and is situated in the hamlet of Lamothe.

8 hectares (6.36 under vine) producing 159 hectolitres of wine.

Château Leyret
Owner M Gilbert Colomb

1.87 hectares under vine producing 46 hectolitres of wine.

Château Montalier
Owner Mme Marie-Françoise Latrille, who also owns Domaine de Lionne at Illats.

Château Monteil
Formerly called Cru Monteil.
Owner Mme Evelyne Le Diascorn

Wine is also produced under the label of 'Château Haut-Violet'.

9 hectares (8.60 under vine) producing 215 hectolitres of wine.

Château du Pick
This is a small, old but well kept property situated in the hamlet of Lamothe, bordering the autoroute. In the nineteenth century it was part of Château Bastor-Lamontagne. In 1980 it was divided into two:
Owner M Lea Pothier

10.23 hectares under vine producing 255 hectolitres of wine.

Owner M Jacques Huillet

8.90 hectares under vine producing 233 hectolitres of wine.

Château Pleytegeat
Owner M André du Hayot who also owns Château Guiteronde, where all the wine is made, and *deuxième cru* Château Romer-du-Hayot in Barsac.

10 hectares

Château Rouaud
Owners Philippe and Sylvain Guignan, who also own 6 hectares of vineyard at St-Macaire.

0.33 hectares under vine producing 8 hectolitres of wine.

Château Rouquette
Owner M Hubert Dufour

7 hectares (6.38 under vine) producing 159 hectolitres of wine.

Château Sahuc-Les-Tour
Owner M Philippe Poujardieu

Very imposing; a lovely old property.

15 hectares (11.85 under vine) producing 298 hectolitres of wine.

Château St-Amand
Owner M Louis Ricard (Grand Maître de la Commanderie de Sauternes et Barsac); 9.6 hectares are owned by Anne-Mary Facchetti-Ricard.

This beautifully kept estate dates back to the ninth century, when it was the residence of St Amand, at that time Bishop of Bordeaux. It has been in the family for many generations. Wine is also produced under the label of 'Château La Chartreuse'. This estate produces consistently fine wines.

21 hectares (18.84 under vine) producing 670 hectolitres of wine.
80% sémillon, 20% sauvignon

Château Solon
Owner M Michel Canot who also owns Château Padouen (Barsac).

A very attractive property by the side of a lake set amongst the vines, next to Château St-Amand.

4 hectares

Château de Veyres
Owner Mme Camille Serres

12 hectares (11.93 under vine) producing 297 hectolitres of wine.

Château Violet
Owner Société Civile Baro

A small, fairly modern country farmhouse.

12 hectares (11.37 under vine) producing 284 hectolitres of wine.

Château Voigny
Owners Bon Frères (0.13 hectare is owned personally by Hubert Bon; producing 3 hectolitres of wine).

Bon Frères also produce wines under the labels of 'Château les Rochers' and 'Château L'Ariste'. This château is situated in the centre of Preignac. The property is badly run down, with vineyards at the rear.

24 hectares (19.54 under vine) producing 488 hectolitres of wine.
80% sémillon, 15% sauvignon, 5% muscadelle

Cru d'Arche-Pugneau
Owners MM Jean-Pierre and Francis Daney. This old and imposing property has been in the family since 1923.

13 hectares under vine producing 266 hectolitres of wine.
75% sémillon, 20% sauvignon, 5% muscadelle

Cru d'Arrançon
Owner M Jean Taudin

5 hectares (3.43 under vine) producing 86 hectolitres of wine.
70% semillon, 15% sauvignon, 15% muscadelle

Cru d'Arrançon-Boutoc
Owner M Raymond Dumé

3 hectares (1.75 under vine) producing 44 hectolitres of wine.

Cru Bas-Peyraguey
Owner M Jean Dumé

4 hectares (3.25 under vine) producing 81 hectolitres of wine.

Cru Bel-Air
Owner Rose Capdeville

3 hectares (1.11 under vine) producing 27 hectolitres of wine.

Cru Bordessoule
Owner Christian Coulaud

1.05 hectares under vine producing 25 hectolitres of wine.

Cru Bordessoule
Owner Elaine Bou

3.14 hectares under vine producing 78 hectolitres of wine.

Cru Boutoc

Owner M Christophe Claverie
This was originally a large estate but was split up into ten parts with different owners.

5 hectares (2.67 under vine) producing 67 hectolitres of wine.

Cru Bouyréou

Owner Henriette Sabatier

1 hectare (0.77 under vine) producing 64 hectolitres of wine.

Cru de La Cave

Owner Vve Marguerite Escudey

3 hectares (2.54 under vine) producing 64 hectolitres of wine.

Cru Lalot

Owner Edouard Ricaud, who is in the process of selling it.

6 hectares

Cru La Piastre

Owner M Jean Perret

0.30 hectares under vine producing 7 hectolitres of wine.

Cru Le Haire

Owner Mme Jeanine Jacoby

6 hectares (3.67 under vine) producing 92 hectolitres of wine.

Cru Mahon

Owner M Michel Escudey

3 hectares (1.88 under vine) producing 36 hectolitres of wine.

Cru Mauvin

Owner M Christian Capdarest

7 hectares (6.68 under vine) producing 167 hectolitres of wine.

Cru Monteil

Owner Pierrette Duzan

2 hectares under vine producing 50 hectolitres of wine. Also produces wine under the label of 'Domaine Le Besin'.

90% sémillon, 7% sauvignon, 3% muscadelle

Cru Montjoie

Owner M Albert Sabalot

2 hectares

Cru Navarre

Owner M Bernard Deyres

0.96 hectares under vine producing 24 hectolitres of wine.

Cru Peyraguey

Owner M Hubert Mussotte. The property has been in this family's possession for generations.

7 hectares (6 under vine) producing 125 hectolitres of wine.

75% sémillon, 25% sauvignon

Cru Peyraguey

Owners Joël and Denise Duchamp

2.5 hectares under vine producing 50 hectolitres of wine.

80% sémillon, 20% sauvignon

Cru de Piquey

Owner M Claude Larrue

1.34 hectares under vine producing 33 hectolitres of wine.

Cru Rousset-Peyraguey

Owners Jean and Elie Dejean

6 hectares (5.34 under vine) producing 133 hectolitres of wine.

Cru Trinquine

Owner M Jean-Louis Larrue

2.29 hectares under vine producing 57 hectolitres of wine.

Clos Bourgelat

Owner M Dominique Lafosse

0.57 hectares under vine producing 14 hectolitres of wine.

Domaine de Couite

Owner M Claude Deloubes in whose family it has been since 1930.

1.60 hectares (1.41 under vine) producing 35 hectolitres of wine.

33% sémillon, 33% sauvignon, 33% muscadelle

Domaine de Guilhem-du-Rey

Owner M Jean Lalanne

7 hectares (0.45 under vine) producing 9 hectolitres of wine.

Domaine de Jeanton

Owner M Pierre-Paul Bou

3.5 hectares

Domaine de La Chapelle

Owner Yvan Fontagnol

3.05 hectares (1.14 under vine) producing 28 hectolitres of wine. A little red wine is also produced.

Domaine de La Forêt

Owner M Roger Bessières

0.83 under vine producing 20 hectolitres of wine.

Domaine de Monteils

Owner M Jean-Claude Cousin who also produces wine under the label of 'Château Haut-Violet'.

8.04 hectares producing 201 hectolitres of wine.

90% sémillon, 5% sauvignon, 5% muscadelle

Clos du Moulin Neuf

Owner M Jean-Pierre Lados

2 hectares (1.25 under vine) producing 31 hectolitres of wine.

Clos de Moynet

Owner M Jacques Pallas

0.46 hectares under vine producing 11 hectolitres of wine.

Clos du Pavillon

Owner Mme Juliette Lacomme

0.39 hectares under vine producing 10 hectolitres of wine.

33% sémillon, 33% sauvignon, 33% muscadelle

Clos des Rocs

Owner M Pierre Betus

1.05 hectares under vine producing 25 hectolitres of wine.

Other owners:

M Jean Bayejo (*maître de chai* at Château Bastor-Lamontagne)
0.25 hectares under vine producing 6 hectolitres of wine.

M Rolland Caubit
3.61 hectares under vine producing 90 hectolitres of wine.

Pierrette Deyzieux
0.45 hectares under vine producing 12 hectolitres of wine.

Simone Petit
0.54 hectares under vine producing 4 hectolitres of wine.

THE OTHER PROPERTIES OF BARSAC

Château Baulac-Dodijos
Owner M Jean Barbe. This château
has been in the family for
generations.

6 hectares

Château Bouyot
Director M Bertrand-Jammy
Fonbeney. The château has been in
his family since 1936. In January 1986
a company was formed to hold it,
Des Vignobles Barraud.

It also produces wine under the label
of 'Château Barraud'. The property
is set back off the road and is well
kept and very attractive.

13.5 hectares

95% sémillon, 3% sauvignon, 2%
muscadelle

Château Camperos
Owner since 1955 M André du Hayot

This superb, very well maintained
twin-towered château is situated on
the edge of Barsac, opposite Château
Broustet. All the wine is now made at
Château Guiteronde which M du
Hayot also owns.

3 hectares

90% sémillon, 10% sauvignon

Château Cantegril
Owners M and Mme Pierre
Dubourdieu, who also own
Château Doisy-Daëne.

Château Cantegril is situated where
an old fortified château of the same
name once stood, and played an
important military role in the Middle
Ages. It belonged to the Duc
d'Epernon, then to the Seigneurs de
Cantegril, one of whom married a
Myrat and had the present Château
de Myrat built on part of the
Cantegril estate. In 1854 the Château

Cantegril was detached from
Château de Myrat, as was confirmed
by a judgement given by the Civil
Court on 24th December 1862. The
estate is enclosed by walls.

22.5 hectares (22 under vine)
producing 450 hectolitres of wine.

70% sémillon, 25% sauvignon, 5%
muscadelle

Château de Carles
Owner G. F. A. Château de Carles;
tenanted by M Michel Pascaud.

12 hectares (9 under vine)

90% sémillon, 10% sauvignon

Château Chante L'Oiseau
Owner M Philippe Meynard

3.5 hectares under vine

50% sémillon, 40% sauvignon, 10%
muscadelle

Château Closiot
Owner M Hector Soizeau, in whose
family it has been since 1934.

9 hectares (8 under vine)

95% sémillon, 3% sauvignon, 2%
muscadelle

Château Coustet
Owners MM Roger and Jean-Pierre
Roux

7 hectares

Château Dudon
Owner Evelyne Allien (Héritier
Herteman) in whose family it has
been since the nineteenth century.

A small single-storey farmhouse set
in the trees.

8.69 hectares

83% sémillon, 15% sauvignon, 2%
muscadelle

Château Farluret
Owners M et Mme Robert Lamothe, who also own Château Haut-Bergeron (Preignac).

This single-storey well maintained property which is attached to the *chai* has been owned by this family for two generations.

8.5 hectares

90% sémillon, 5% sauvignon, 5% muscadelle

Château du Grand-Carretey
Owner M Vincent Labouille, who also owns Château de Crabitan in Ste-Croix-du-Mont and Château La Peloue in Barsac.

15 hectares

75% sémillon, 10% sauvignon, 15% muscadelle

Château Gravas
Owner M Pierre Bernard, who also owns Château Duc d'Arnauton (Graves).

The property is situated opposite Château Climens and is large and well maintained, set back in the vines. The family have owned it since 1850. The estate produces consistently fine wines, and also wine under the label of 'Château Simon-Carrety'.

11 hectares under vine

80% sémillon, 10% sauvignon, 10% muscadelle

Château Grillon
Owner Odile Roumazeilles-Cameleyre

11 hectares

75% sémillon, 15% muscadelle, 10% sauvignon

Château Guiteronde
Owner since 1964 M André du Hayot, who also owns Château Romer-du-Hayot, Château Camperos and Château Pebayle. All the wine is vinified at Château Guiteronde, which dates back to the nineteenth century and is a large, imposing ivy-covered château, very well maintained. Wine is also produced under the label of 'Château Brassens-Guiteronde'.

35 hectares

80% sémillon, 20% sauvignon

Château Hallet
Owners Denise and Michel Ballan

15 hectares

Château Haut-Mayne
Owner M Jean Bernard Bravo (who also owns *deuxième cru* Château Caillou).

3.5 hectares (3 under vine)

95% sémillon, 5% sauvignon

Château Jany
Owner M Huguette Estrade, whose family have owned the property since 1900. Tenanted by M Bernard Turtaut.

3.5 hectares under vine.

70% sémillon, 20% sauvignon, 10% muscadelle

Château Jean Laive
Owner Mme André Gajac

Situated on the road to Château Caillou, this single-storey bungalow/farmhouse is set in its own vines.

Château La Bouade
Owner Violette Pauly

25 hectares

Château Laclotte
Formerly called Château La Clotte et Cazalis.

Owner Vve Lacoste

It is a very old turreted building set back from the road.

5 hectares

Château La Peloue
Owner M Vincent Labouille, who also owns Château de Crabitan in Ste-Croix-du-Mont and Château du Grand-Carretey in Barsac.

5 hectares

Château Lapinesse
Owner since 1986 M Henri Guinabert, who also owns Château Villefranche.

4.13 hectares under vine; the wine is all sold in bulk.

85% sémillon, 10% sauvignon, 5% muscadelle

Château Latrezotte
Owner Mme Marie-Pierre Bacourès

10 hectares, 6.77 under vine

60% sémillon, 10% sauvignon, 30% muscadelle

Château Le Jaouquet
Owner M André Chastagner

Château Le Tucau
Owner M Bernard Leppert, who is also the owner of Château Hillot in Illats.

Situated on the outskirts of Barsac on the road to Cadillac, a run down farmhouse set among the vines.

7 hectares

Château Liot
Owner M Jerry David in whose family this has been for generations. M David also owns Château Poncet (Premiers Côtes de Bordeaux), Château Pinsas which produces red wine and Château St-Jean-des-Graves which produces dry white wine. This is a large, well maintained, imposing turreted château.

25 hectares (21 under vine)

80% sémillon, 15% sauvignon, 5% muscadelle

Château de Lucques
Owner M Michel Boyer, who also owns Château Haut-Mayne in Cérons, Château du Cros in Loupiac and Château Lépine in Ste-Croix-du-Mont.

22 hectares under vine producing red wine only.

Château de Luziès
Owner M Michel Perromat

10 hectares

Château Massereau
Owner since 1986 M Pierre Brasseur.

This property was built in the fourteenth century along the river Ciron. A dry white wine is also produced.

13.8 hectares (6.04 under vine)

95% sémillon, 2.5% sauvignon, 2.5% muscadelle

Château du Mayne
Owner M Jean Sanders, who also owns Château Haut-Bailly (Médoc) and Château de Courbon, producing a dry white wine, and also uses the label 'Cru Mayne Pompon'. A beautifully kept property, which has been in the family since 1937.

13 hectares (7 under vine) producing 100–200 hectolitres of wine.

70% sémillon, 30% sauvignon

Château Menota
Owner M Noel Labat

This is a very large, sixteenth-century walled estate situated next to Château Climens and also incorporating Château Menatte. The property was owned in the sixteenth century by François de Pignéguy, a lawyer and President of the Bordeaux Parlement. It was also owned, in the nineteenth century, by Mme Teyssonneau, whose family own Doisy-Védrines. Also produces wines under the label of 'Château Menatte'.

25 hectares

50% sémillon, 50% sauvignon producing wine which is slightly drier than the average Barsac.

Château Montalivet
Owner M Pierre Doubourdieu who also owns *deuxième cru* Château Doisy-Daëne and Château Cantegril.

Château Mont-Joye
Owner M Franck Glaunès, who also produces wine under the labels of 'Château Mercier' and 'Château Jacques-Le-Haut'.

20 hectares under vine

60% sémillon, 20% sauvignon, 20% muscadelle

Château Padouen
Formerly called Château Padouen-Terre-Noble.

Owner M Michel Canot, who also owns Château Solon in Preignac.

A well kept, imposing property built in 1703.

14.5 hectares (10 under vine)

80% sémillon, 15% sauvignon, 5% muscadelle

Château Pascaud-Villefranche
Owner M Pierre Pascaud, in whose family it has been for four generations.

7.89 hectares under vine

85% sémillon, 10% sauvignon, 5% muscadelle

Château Pebayle
Owner since 1980 M André du Hayot, who is also the owner of *deuxième cru* Château Romer-du-Hayot, Château Camperos and Château Guiteronde where all the wine is made.

The estate is bordered by an unusual Roman wall.

7 hectares

60% sémillon, 25% sauvignon, 15% muscadelle

Château Pernaud
Owner Mme Isabelle Regelsperger-Jacolin, in whose family it has been since 1908.

This estate belonged in the eighteenth century to the Lur-Saluces of Yquem. The turreted house with adjoining *chai* is opposite Château Doisy-Védrines. Wine is also produced under the label of 'Château Pey-Arnaud'.

16.5 hectares (14.35 under vine) producing 300 hectolitres of wine.

70% sémillon, 25% sauvignon, 5% muscadelle

Château Piada
Owner since 1940 M Jean Lalande

This large estate, adjoining Coutet, set back off the road amongst the vines, was once in the hands of the Lur-Saluces family. The property is one of the oldest in the Sauternais: there are documents relating to the estate dating from 1217 now in the Tower of London. Red wine is produced under Château Piada's label and a dry white wine and a sweet wine as 'Clos du Roy'.

14 hectares (6.66 under vine)

95% sémillon, 5% sauvignon

Château Piaut
Owner M René Minville

Château Piot-David
Owner M Jean-Luc David, who also owns Château Poncet (Premières Côtes de Bordeaux). The property was originally called Château Piot but in 1911 it was divided. 3 hectares were sold to M Jean Dufour and are now part of Château Simon. The remaining 17 hectares are now Château Piot-David.

17 hectares (6.8 under vine)

80% sémillon, 20% sauvignon

Château Prost
Owner M Jean Perromat

This lies opposite Château Nairac. The imposing seventeenth-century building, in walled vineyards, was partly rebuilt in the early twentieth century.

11 hectares under vine

65% sémillon, 20% sauvignon, 15% muscadelle

Château Raspide
Owner M Louis Pourquey

5 hectares

Château de Rolland
Owner since 1971 M Jean-Pierre Guignard, who also owns Château de Gensac (Pujols-sur-Ciron) and Château de Roquetaillade in Mazères (Clos des Moines). His sons own Château Lamothe-Guignard (second-growth Sauternes).

This beautifully kept and imposing château bordering the Ciron is one of the oldest in the area, dating back to 1462 when it was owned by the family de Rolland du Pont. It was replanted in 1942 with sémillon, sauvignon and muscadelle, having previously been planted with red grapes. It is situated on Route Nationale 113 coming into Barsac and has in its grounds a hotel and restaurant which is not owned by M Guignard. Wine is also produced under the label of 'Château Arnaudas'.

20 hectares (18 under vine)

60% sémillon, 20% sauvignon, 20% muscadelle

Château Roumieu
Owner G. F. A Bernadet, in which family it has been since 1918. The director is Olivia Bernadet. In 1937 the family installed the first horizontal press in Sauternes.

10 hectares (7 under vine)

80% sémillon, 15% sauvignon, 5% muscadelle

Château Roumieu
Owner since 1983 Mme Cathérine Craveia-Goyaud; it has been in the family for generations.

Large farmhouse with *chai* attached, bordering Château Climens.

14 hectares under vine

95% sémillon, 5% sauvignon

Château Roumieu-Lacoste
This was previously part of Château Roumieu. The owners are Bouchet Dubourdieu et Fils, and it has been in this family for 300 years. The director is Hervé Dubourdieu.

Lying opposite Château Climens, it has a beautiful old single-storey farmhouse.

18 hectares (12 under vine)

84% sémillon, 13% muscadelle, 3% sauvignon

Château St-Marc
Owner M Didier Laulan, who also manages Château Brochon in the

Graves, producing dry white and red wines.

Wine is also produced under the label of 'Château Hournalas' and a red wine is produced under the label of 'Château de Roux'. It is a well kept property, set amongst the vines.

18 hectares under vine

70% sémillon, 20% sauvignon, 10% muscadelle

Château Simon
Owner Mme Dufour in whose family it has been for three generations.

They produce a dry white and red wine. Wine is also produced under the label of 'Château Grand-Mayne'. It is a well kept family house.

33 hectares (12 under vine)

90% sémillon, 9% sauvignon, 1% muscadelle

Château Terre-Noble
Wine produced under the 'Château Terre-Noble' label is the choice of the finest *crus* in the district blended together.

Château Villefranche
Owner M Henri Guinabert

Well maintained single-storey ivy-covered house. A red wine is also produced.

7 hectares under vine

85% sémillon, 10% sauvignon, 5% muscadelle

Cru Janguet
Owner M Bertrand Turtaut

5 hectares

Cru La Bouade
Owner M Pierre-Etienne Tauzin

4 hectares

Cru St-Michel
Owners Pommade heirs

Clos Lardit
Owner M Georges Danglade

4.3 hectares under vine

80% semillon, 15% sauvignon, 5% muscadelle

Clos Mayne-Lamouroux
Owner M René Désert, who also owns Domaine de Mareuil in Pujols-sur-Ciron.

2 hectares

Clos des Princes
Owner M François Mussotte

7 hectares

Other owners:

Pierre Commet

0.26 hectares under vine

One third sémillon, one third sauvignon, one third muscadelle

THE CRUS OF CÉRONS

In the eighteenth century the flourishing port of Cérons was exporting locally produced wine and wheat, as well as oak barrels which were the livelihood of many workers. In the nineteenth century Cérons underwent a profound period of change. Cooperage became less important whilst the exploitation of Cérons stone was on the increase. The port of Cérons served for a long time as a major export route for this stone to Bordeaux.

Today the small, attractive town of Cérons, situated 35km south-east of Bordeaux, with a population of 1,300, has approximately 800 hectares under vine: of this some 500 hectares produce dry white, 200 hectares produce red wine under the Graves and Graves Supérieur *appellations* and 100 hectares produce sweet wine under the *appellation contrôlée* Cérons. The soil is siliceous gravel and pebbles with a little sand to the west with a subsoil of limestone and some gravel in the west and central vineyards.

The town centre still has a communal washing-area and a number of restaurants, namely *La Grappe d'Or*, which also has rooms, *Grillobois* on the main road and *Chez Mimi*. The surrounding wooded countryside is extremely attractive, full of acacia trees; it is very popular with the local hunters.

The *appellation contrôlée* states that A.C. Cérons, which also covers Illats and Podensac, applies to sweet wines where the must has a minimum of 212 grams per litre of natural sugar, and that the wine is a minimum of 12.5° alcohol. Also that the yield must not exceed 40 hectolitres per hectare, while allowing 6,500–7,500 vines per hectare to be planted. Pruning is the same as in Sauternes and Barsac.

The wines are generally inclined to be semi-sweet and only in favourable years are they rich, with a honeyed bouquet and well balanced fruit. They tend to be somewhat lighter in style than the wines of Sauternes and Barsac.

Château Balestey
Owners MM Pierre and Louis Chaumel

13.89 hectares under vine owned by Pierre Chaumel

13.78 hectares under vine owned by Louis Chaumel

Château de Bessanes
Owner M Jean Perromat, who also owns Châteaux Ferbos, Mayne-Binet and de Cérons, and in Barsac Château Luziès. The estate also produces dry white and red wines.

Château de Cérons

Owner since 1958 M Jean Perromat, who is the mayor of Cérons and whose brother, Pierre Perromat, owns the Sauternes *deuxième cru* Château d'Arche.

In the seventeenth century this magnificent property was the residence of the Marquis de Calvimont. A dry white wine and red wine is also produced under the label of 'Château de Calvimont'.

74.24 hectares under vine in all the owner's estates.

Grand Enclos du Château de Cérons

Owners Lataste Frères

This property consists of the Grand Enclos, the most extensive part of the old Château de Cérons, a magnificent property which used to belong to the Marquis de Calvimont, Mayor of Cérons. During the First Empire, when the national highway from Bordeaux to Spain was built, the property was cut in two. Then the Marquis de Calvimont sold the property in three lots. The Grand Enclos was acquired in 1875 by the Lataste family who also produce dry white wine under the label of 'Château Lamouroux'.

23.60 hectares under vine

12. Map of the commune of Cérons, showing the major wine-producing properties

Château Ferbos

Owner M Jean Perromat, who also owns Château de Bessanes (see above) and Château de Cérons. The vineyard of Château Ferbos, which covers nearly 5 hectares, is one half of the former Enclos de Lalannette Ferbos, which M Audian, the owner of the Château, sold as a whole to the family in 1829.

Château Ferbos-Lalannette

Owner Georges Constantin

0.20 hectares under vine

Château Haut-Mayne

Owner M Michel Boyer, who also owns Château du Cros in Loupiac.

11 hectares producing red and dry white wines only.

Château Huradin

Owner M Yves Ricaud; in the family for three generations.

The château produces dry and sweet wine. The red wine is produced under the label of 'Domaine du Salut'.

13.11 hectares under vine

80% sémillon, 20% sauvignon

Château La Salette

Owner Edith Frechaut, who also owns Château de Tuileries in Virelade Graves.

3.7 hectares under vine

Château de L'Emigré

Owner M Gérard Despujols, who also owns Château Coulac in Ste-Croix-du-Mont.

The château was built in the nineteenth century and has been in the family since 1830. Originally the land was used as the hunting ground of the Duc d'Epernon. This property produces only dry white and red wines.

Château du Mayne

Owners GAEC Vignobles Moulin à Vent.

25.25 hectares under vine

Château Mayne-Binet

Owner M Jean Perromat who also owns Châteaux de Bessanes, Ferbos, and de Cérons (see above).

This château is an imposing old property in need of renovation set on the Haut-Cérons plateau. There is a predominance of sauvignon vines planted on very pebbly soil. The estate also produces red and dry white wine.

Château de Méric

Owner M Marc Broussignac

0.46 hectares under vine

Château du Peyrat

Owner M André Cambillau

8.92 hectares under vine

Château Sylvain

Owner M Alain Pargade

6.88 hectares under vine

Cru des Grands-Chênes

Owners MM Michel and Dominique Expert

4.33 hectares under vine belonging to M Michel Expert

3.02 hectares under vine belonging to M Dominique Expert

Cru du Moulin

Owners Andres Frères

1.12 hectares under vine

Cru du Moulin

Owner Charles Duron

3.13 hectares under vine

Cru du Moulin-à-Vent

Owner Bernard Marcau

0.96 hectares under vine

Cru de Peyroutin

Owner J.-Pierre Gardelle

1.46 hectares under vine

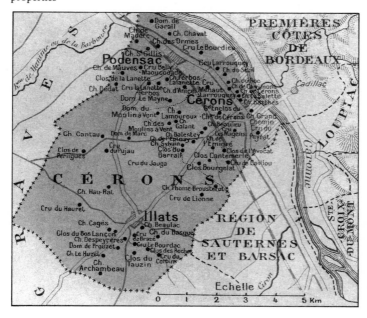

Cru de Pineau
Owner M Philippe Expert
7.91 hectares under vine

Cru Voltaire
Owners MM Henry and Yvan Priam
1.34 hectares under vine

Clos du Barrail
Owners MM Guy and Claude Uteau
who also own Château de Madère in
Podensac.
32.64 hectares under vine

Clos Bourgelat
Owner M Dominique La Fosse, in
whose family it has been for six
generations. They also own
vineyards in Preignac.
It is a large imposing property set in
the vineyards.
10.98 hectares (9.95 under vine)
80% sémillon, 20% sauvignon

Domaine de Freyron
Owners MM Lavignac and Masset
2 hectares under vine

Clos de L'Avocat
Owner M Michel Ricaud
14.81 hectares under vine

Clos de Moulins-à-Vent
Owner M André Ducasse
7.87 hectares under vine

Domaine du Moulin-à-Vent
Owner Mme Vve Expert-Labilotte
9.01 hectares under vine

Domaine du Salut
Owner Yves-Pierre Ricaud
13.11 hectares under vine

Domaine de Salvané
Owners G. F. A. de Salvané
7.77 hectares under vine

Proprietors selling their wine in bulk:
Roger Barrière
2.56 hectares under vine

Jean-Pierre Berdoulai
0.40 hectares under vine

J-Marie Cambillau
8.04 hectares under vine

Pierre Courouge
0.34 hectares under vine

S.D.F. Decorsy
3.68 hectares under vine

Dominique Dugoua
4.91 hectares under vine

André Dupeyrot
0.23 hectares under vine

Claude Duverges
0.44 hectares under vine

Aubin Egelmont
0.29 hectares under vine

Jean-Gilbert Expert
1.55 hectares under vine

René Expert
0.19 hectares under vine

Charles Fourtaine
0.19 hectares under vine

Richard Gaillaud
0.10 hectares under vine

Julien Gans
0.11 hectares under vine

Philippe Lassus
7.45 hectares under vine

Gerard Peyrat
0.10 hectares under vine

Henri-Pierre Priam
0.83 hectares under vine

Pierre Tourre
1.58 hectares under vine

THE CRUS OF PODENSAC

The town of Podensac, with its population of 1,925, is dominated by the twelfth-century church which is a classified monument. The apse is lined with columns, the centre of one showing the martyr St Lawrence, another the Madonna with the Christchild on her knee. In the sacristy is a fifteenth-century ivory crucifix. There is a superb market in the centre of the town, where in 1615 members of the Bordeaux Parlement came to welcome Anne of Austria, the future Queen of France, and Louis XIII snatched his first glimpse of her. On the outskirts of the town, towards Illats, is a superb sixteenth-century mansion, Château de Cagès.

The area covers 834 hectares of which only 125 are under vine. It comes under the Cérons *appellation* for sweet wines, but this is produced only in exceptional years. Most of the wine produced is dry white wine with some red under the Graves and Graves Supérieur *appellations* and is grown on a gravel soil with a stony subsoil. Many growers use the co-operative at Langoiran to produce their wine whilst others sell their crop to the major growers in the area.

Château d'Anice
Tenanted by Mme Henri Lévêque (whose family also owns Cru Madérot and Château de Chantegrive).

It was the ancient feudal castle of the lords of La Chapelle, then was owned by MM Biarnès and Mendelhson. It was confiscated in 1914, then sold to M Michel Navarri in 1921 and then to Mme Médeville. All the wine, red and dry white, is made at the Château de Chantegrive.

Château Bédat
Formerly called Château Haut-Bédat
Owner M St Blancard; tenant Henri Bouche.
The wine is made at Château de Mauves.

Château de Chantegrive
Owners M and Mme Henri Lévêque, who also tenant Château d'Anice,

and own Château Mayne-Lévêque and Cru Madérot.

The house is a modern bungalow set amongst the 75 hectares under vine. The estate produces dry white and red wines under the label of 'Château Bon Dieu des Vignes'. It produces a sweet wine only in exceptional years. All the wines are produced at Château Chantegrive.

55% sémillon, 35% sauvignon, 10% muscadelle

Château Gravaillas
Owners MM Roucel and Labarrière

Château Larrouquey
Owner M André Lejeune, who also owns Domaine de Chasse-Pierre in Cadillac.

Château de Madère
Owners MM Guy and Claude

Uteau, who also own Clos du Barrail in Cérons.

Château Mayne-d'Imbert
Owner M Henri Bouche
22 hectares

Château de Mauves
Owner M Bernard Bouche
The estate had been owned by the Moreau family since 1859. It was sold to M Bouche in 1965. Only red and dry white wine are produced.
22 hectares (20 hectares under vine)
100% sémillon for the white wine; 70% cabernet sauvignon, 30% merlot for the red wine

Château du Peyrat
Owner M André Cambillau

Cru de La Maoucouade
Formerly called Cru Belly-Maoucouade.
Owner Vve Jeanine Bouchet

Cru Larrouquey
Owner M Michel Lalande

Cru Maderot
Owners M and Mme Henri Lévêque, who also tenant Château d'Anice and own Château Chantegrive, where all the wine is produced. A dry white and a red wine are produced.

Cru Menaut-Larrouqueyre
Owner M Jacques Pauly, who also owns the *premier cru* Clos Haut-Peyraguey in Bommes.

Domaine du Caillou
Owner M Roger Charançon

Clos Cantemerle
Owner M Jean-Pierre Peyronnin

Domaine de Castagnaou
Owner M Pierre Trenit
Also produces wine under the label of 'Domaine Brouillaou'.
6 hectares

Domaine Le Cossu
Owner M Pierre Dupont
15 hectares

Domaine du Mayne
Owner M Charles Fortinon who also produces wine under the label of 'Cru de Bruilleau'. All the wine is produced at the co-operative in Langoiran.
10 hectares

THE CRUS OF ILLATS

This small village, with its population of 1,009, lying 7km south of Podensac, surrounds the sixteenth-century Gothic church. The façade was altered towards the end of the ninetenth century to a more flamboyant style with delicately pointed windows and coats of arms. There is also a fine water-tower, now registered as a listed building, which was built by Le Corbusier.

The area covers 2,923 hectares of which approximately 350 are under vine. It is included in the Cérons *appellation* for sweet wines. The soil is gravel, clay and sand with a clay and gravel subsoil. The wines produced are similar in type and style to those of neighbouring Cérons. The growers produce mainly dry white and red wines.

Château Archambaud
Owners Dr Jean and M Philippe Dubourdieu
This is a well kept property set back in the vines. It produces fine wine.
7 hectares

Château d'Ardennes
Owners MM François and Bertrand Dubrey, who also own Château La Tuilerie. The Dubreys have owned this fourteenth-century château since 1968. It is an imposing building set back amongst its vines. Dry white and red wines are also produced.

Château Beaulac
Owner Mme Pommade; it is farmed by Jean Banos

Château Cantau
Owner M Daniel Ballion; tenant M Trijasson

Château Haura
Owner B. Leppert, who also owns Château Le Tucau in Barsac. The vineyards are attached to Château Hillot.
8 hectares producing sweet wine

Château Hillot
Owner B. Leppert, who produces a dry white and red wines under this label and a sweet wine from the vineyard of Château Haura. This is an eighteenth-century single-storey house adjoining the vineyards of Château Haura.
23 hectares under vine

Château La Hontasse
Owner M Jean Banos

Château Laroche
Owner M Pierre Ducau

Château La Rouille
Owner M Michel Labé

Château La Tuilerie
Owner M Bertrand Dubrey, who also owns Château d'Ardennes. Red and dry white wines are produced.
20 hectares

Château La Merle
Owner M Albert Pargade

Château Navarro
Owner M Roger Biarnès, who also

owns the vines at Château Suau (*deuxième cru*) in Barsac which are vinified at Château Navarro. Only dry white and red wines are produced under this Château's label; other wines are produced under the label of 'Domaine du Coy' and 'Moulin du Jauga'. The modern farmhouse and *chais* are set well back from the road down a long and wooded drive.

25 hectares under vine

Château Peyragué
Owner M Alain Pargade

Château des Peyrères
Owner M Jean-Claude Labat

Château du Prouzet
Owner Mme Paulette Audibert

Château Thôme-Brousterot
Owner Jeanne-Marie Babel

Cru Bel-Air
Owner Salvador Vicente

Cru de Cabiro
Owner M Michel Duron

Cru St-Roch
Owner M Louis Labat
2 hectares

Domaine des Arrouats
Owner M Georges Skaypczyk

This is a small, fairly run down farmhouse on the main road from Cérons to Illats.

Clos de Barraille
Owner M Albert Rodez

Domaine du Calac
Owner M Jacques Banos

Domaine de La Citadelle
Owner Camille Carreyre

Clos Courrèges
Owner M Dominique Dugoua

Domaine des Deux-Moulins
Owner M Roger Pastol

Domaine de Lionne
Owner Mme Marie-Françoise Latrille.

This small eighteenth-century farmhouse is set amongst the trees down a side road and has been owned by Mme Latrille since 1962. She also owns Domaine de Perliguès here and Château Montalier in Preignac. Only dry white and red wines are produced.

53 hectares

Domaine de Perliguès
Owner Mme Marie-Françoise Latrille, who also owns Domaine de Lionne and Château Montalier in Preignac. Only dry white and red wines are produced.

Clos des Pins-Francs
Owner M Jean Cluchet; farmed by Andre Laulan

Clos St-Georges
Owners Nöel and Solange Labat

THE CRUS OF STE-CROIX-DU-MONT

The village of Ste-Croix-du-Mont, set on top of a hill, is 43km south-east of Bordeaux, bordering the right bank of the river Garonne. It commands splendid views across the vineyards to Sauternes. The church with its magnificent bell-tower is situated in the main square, from which one can descend the steep slopes to a grotto cut into an ancient oyster-shell cave to taste and purchase vintages of Ste-Croix-du-Mont dating back ten years or so. These wines are produced by the Syndicat Vinicole, who select five proprietors' wines each year, and are bottled by the proprietors but with the Syndicat's label (similar to Tastevinée).

There is a population of 890, of which 100 are vine growers producing 12,000–15,000 hectolitres of wine each year. The total area is 898 hectares, of which 500 are under vine. The *appellation contrôlée* requires a minimum alcoholic strength of 13° and a maximum yield of 40 hectolitres per hectare.

The slopes are relatively steep with clay and limestone soil and a subsoil of limestone and oyster shells and other fossils of marine origin. There is some alluvial soil along a narrow strip at the foot of the hills along the river edge. The rest of the commune has a clay and limestone soil becoming clay and sand towards the north with a subsoil of limestone and a little gravel towards the centre and east of the commune.

The wines are of a lighter style compared to Sauternes/Barsac with a distinctive barley-sugar bouquet and flavour. Some properties produce exceptionally fine and long-lived wines.

Château de Baritaud
Owners Pierre and Odette Larrieu
7.08 hectares under vine

Château Bel-Air
Owner M Michel Méric
This property is built on one of the highest points in the commune.
14 hectares, 8.26 under vine
80% sémillon, 20% sauvignon

Château Bertranon
Owner M André Remaut

This is a superb eighteenth-century château.
2.54 hectares under vine

Château Bouchoc
Owner Jean-Michel Ballade who also owns Château Lescure in Cadillac. The château has been in the Ballade family for generations, but is now about to be sold. It is a single-storey building opposite the restaurant.

Château Chantegrit
Owner M Bernard Souq
5.65 hectares under vine

Château Coulac

Owner M Gerard Despujols, who also owns Château de L'Emigré in Cérons.

This is an imposing double-turreted nineteenth-century building overlooking the Garonne. A dry white, red and rosé wines are produced under the label 'Domaine des Deux Lions' and 'Château de L'Emigré' (Cérons) for red and dry white.

5.72 hectares under vine

Château de Crabitan

Owner M Vincent Labouille who also owns Château du Grand-Carretey (Barsac) and Château La Peloue (Barsac). The château has been in the family for many years. The estate also produces red, dry white and rosé wines.

35 hectares (30 under vine)

Château Crabitan-Bellevue

Owner M Bernard Solane

Château Gaillardet

Owner M Pierre Larrieu

2 hectares under vine

Château du Gallion

Owner Jocelyne Larrue

8.33 hectares under vine

Château Grand-Coustin

Owner Camille Pourgaton

6.1 hectares under vine

Château du Grand-Peyrot

Owner M Salles; tenanted by Jean-Marie Tinon, who also owns Château La Grave.

5 hectares under vine

Château Jean Lamat

Owner M Joël de Vathaire

4.56 hectares under vine

Château Laborie

Owner Roland Danies-Sauvestre

10.8 hectares under vine

Château Lafaurie

Owner M Alfred Croizet who also owns Château Lafaurie in Cadillac.

4.76 hectares under vine

13. ABOVE RIGHT View from the hill-top of Ste-Croix-du-Mont looking across the vineyards Preignac

14. RIGHT Map of the commune of Ste-Croix-du-Mont, showing the major wine-producing properties

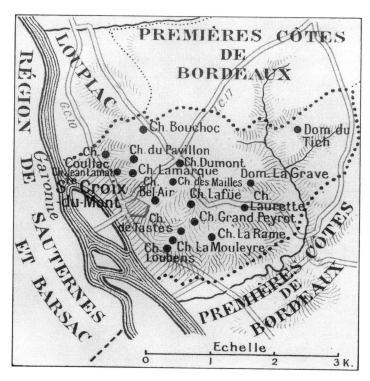

107

Château Lafue
Owner Brigitte Pons
Large, single-storey farmhouse with extensive Roman tiling, set in the vineyards.
5.1 hectares under vine

Château La Grave
Owner Jean-Marie Tinon
A rambling, modern farmhouse.
7 hectares under vine

Château La Graville
Owner M Bernard Fermis
Single-storey farmhouse with courtyard. All wine is now made under the label of 'Domaine des Grands Vignots'.
8.42 hectares under vine

Château Lamarque
Owner M Roger Bernard
Small family house built on stilts overlooking the vineyard.
14.31 hectares under vine

Château La Moulegre
Owner M Pierre Videau; tenanted by G.F.A. Château La Rame.
3 hectares under vine

Château La Peyrère
Owner Jean-Pierre Dupuy
8.16 hectares under vine

Château La Rame
Owner M Claude Armand, who also produces a dry white wine under the labels of 'Château La Caussade' and 'Domaine du Barrail' (Bordeaux Rouge).
19.9 hectares under vine
88% sémillon, 12% sauvignon

Château Laurette
Owner M François Pons, who runs Château Lafue.
There are a lot of old vines. The wine has good quality which is long lived.
18.64 hectares under vine

Château Lépine
Owner M Michel Boyer, who also owns Château du Cros in Loupiac, Château Haut-Mayne in Cérons and Château de Lucques in Barsac.
2.39 hectares under vine

Château L'Escaley
Owner M Roger Saint Marc
7.54 hectares under vine

Château Les Mailles
Owner M Robert Larrieu
A large, attractive château set back from the road.
11.68 hectares under vine

Château Les Marcottes
Owner M Gérard Cigana
10 hectares under vine

Château Loubens
Owner Société Civile du Domaine du Château Loubens.
This is an imposing and superb château situated at the top of Ste-Croix-du-Mont. The château was originally the site of an ancient fort. At the beginning of the sixteenth century it belonged to Pierre de Spens de Lancre. It has seven joined cellars, 220ft deep. In 1620 the owner was M de Lancre, Councillor of the Parlement in Bordeaux. Arnaud de Sèze is currently in charge and a dry white wine is produced under the label of 'Fleuron Blanc'. Wine is also produced under the label of 'Château Terfort'.
14.5 hectares under vine

Château Lousteau Vieil
Owners Remy and Roland Sessacq, in whose family it has been since 1843. They also own Clos Lamourasse in Graves producing red wine and Château Lamaringue in Sauternes, which is not producing any wine at present as it is being replanted. This property is situated on one of the highest points, at 390ft above sea-level.
13 hectares (11.47 under vine)
85% sémillon, 15% sauvignon

Château Médouc
Owner M François Gaussem, who also owns Domaine de Loches in Cadillac.
3.5 hectares under vine

Château du Mont
Owner M Paul Chouvac, whose family have owned it since 1945. He also produces dry white and red wine.
20 hectares (11.04 under vine)

Château Montagne
Owner M Francis Espagnet
5 hectares under vine

Château des Noyers
Owner Yvette Dieuxyssies
8.69 hectares under vine

Château Pampelune
Owner Pierre Latestève
4.35 hectares under vine

Château du Parc
Owner since 1981 Yves Bernède, whose family also owns Domaine de Verduc in Cadillac and Domaine de Massac in Loupiac.
3 hectares (1.2 under vine)
100% sémillon

Château du Pavillon
Owners M and Mme Delaville d'Arfeuille
This was originally owned by the Comtes de La Chassagne but was purchased in 1890 by the Ballan family and sold in 1978 to M Delaville, who married Mme d'Arfeuille, whose family also own Château La Pointe (Pomerol), Château La Serre (St-Emilion) and Château Les Roques (Loupiac).
11 hectares (4.63 under vine)
85% sémillon, 15% sauvignon

Château Roustit
Owner M Albert-Michel Dubourg
9.63 hectares under vine

Château de Tastes
Now the Town Hall. The former owner was Société des Domaines Prats (1927–77).
Situated on the top of Ste-Croix-du-Mont, this superb property has one of the best views of the region. The château dates back to 1230, when it was owned by Gérard de Tastes who, on 1st June 1342, was granted tax exemption on his wines by Edward III on account of their excellence. It no longer produces wine but a picture of the château appears on the generic Ste-Croix-du-Mont.

Château du Verger
Owner M Bernard Croizet, in whose family it has been for many years. A red wine is also produced.
30 hectares, 1.25 under vine for sweet wine
80% sémillon, 20% sauvignon

Château de Vertheuil
Owner Françoise Noël
10 hectares (5.84 under vine)

Cru des Arroucats
Owner Marc Buzos
3.45 hectares under vine

Cru de Gravère
Owner M Jean Reglat, who also owns Château Teste in Cadillac.
0.7 hectares under vine

Cru Mounet
Owners MM Roland and Gérard Fiat
0.73 hectares

Domaine des Arroucats
Owner Annie Lapouge, who also owns Domaine Bougan.
Small, modern, single-storey farmhouse and *chai*, adjoining Château La Graville.
7.55 hectares under vine

Domaine Bougan
Owner Annie Lapouge, who also owns Domaine des Arroucats.

Domaine du Bougat
Owner Jean-Michel Bardot
4.73 hectares under vine

Domaine des Coulinats
Owner Camille Brun, who also owns Château de Berbec in Cadillac. The property has been owned by the family since 1953. Dry white and red wines are also produced.
14 hectares (3.87 under vine)
85% sémillon, 15% sauvignon and some muscadelle

Domaine Damanieu
Owner M Yves Chassagnol
4.26 hectares under vine

Domaine du Gaël
Owner M Henri Daney
2.35 hectares under vine

Domaine de Geraudineau
Owner M Noël Ranoux. Small family house.
5.43 hectares under vine

Domaine des Graves du Tich
Owner M Jean Queyrens, who also owns Domaine de Pilet and Domaine du Pin France in Cadillac.

Clos du Haut Larrivat
Owner Robert Hazera
2.74 hectares under vine

Domaine de La Chataigneraie
Owner Jean Donnadier
1.98 hectares under vine

Clos Larrivat
Owner Vve Vimeney
2 hectares under vine

Domaine Morange
Owner M Jean Mauriac; tenanted by Frédéric Durr.

This is one of the oldest properties in the region. M Mauriac also owns Château du Comte (Cadillac) producing red wine under AC Premières Côtes and Châteaux Boisson and Larrouy producing Bordeaux Supérieur Rouge. A dry white wine is also produced.
17 hectares (11 under vine)
80% sémillon, 20% sauvignon

Domaine des Palmiers
Owner Fraigneau et fils
3.36 hectares under vine

Clos du Pin Copies
Owner M Robert Gillet, who also owns Château Le Tarey in Loupiac.

Domaine des Platanes
Owner M Bernard Mounissens
4.75 hectares under vine

Domaine de Roustit
Owner Société de fait Yves Dulac et Jean Séraphon who also own Clos de L'Ange in Cadillac and Château La Nère in Loupiac.
1.2 hectares under vine

Domaine du Tich
Owner M Jean Fonteyraud, who also owns Domaine de Grave in Cadillac.
4.04 hectares under vine

Other owners, who sell their wine in bulk:
Roger Amanieu
34.1 hectares under vine

Jean-Pierre Duluc
48.95 hectares under vine

René Frouin
2.41 hectares under vine

René Gallet
0.19 hectares under vine

C. and G. Maurio
4.13 hectares under vine

Jean Queyrens
1.98 hectares under vine

Christian Ranoux
7.65 hectares under vine

THE CRUS OF LOUPIAC

Situated on the right bank of the Garonne (opposite Sauternes and Barsac), 40km south-east of Bordeaux and 2km south-east of Cadillac, the village of Loupiac has an old church and an imposing town hall, amid modern bungalows and a few large châteaux set amongst the vines. The commune is 956 hectares of which 550 are under vine. Its history dates back to Roman times and a Roman villa, which belonged to Ausonius, was on the site of the ancient Prieuré de St Romain. Records show sales of wine from Loupiac as early as 1282–1303.

Earlier editions of Cocks et Féret referred to Loupiac as part of Entre-Deux-Mers. In 1936 the Bordeaux Court of Appeal granted Loupiac its own *appellation contrôlée*, which stipulates that a maximum of 40 hectolitres of wine per hectare is produced and that it must have a minimum of 221 grams per litre of natural sugar before chaptalisation of the must, and that the resultant wine must have a minimum strength of 13°.

The southern slopes are the western continuation of the slopes of Ste-Croix-du-Mont. The soils are quite varied with alluvial in the west and clay and limestone in the east. There is a subsoil of limestone at the bottom of the slopes and clay and gravel on the high ground. The vine planting is restricted to 5,000–7,500 per hectare.

The wines are similar to those of Ste-Croix-du-Mont with many properties also producing a dry white and red wine.

Château Barbe-Maurin
Owner M Pierre Poignet

Château de Beaupuy
Owner M Pierre Plaize de Beaupuy; the château has been in the family for many generations.
5 hectares under vine
85% sémillon, 5% sauvignon, 10% muscadelle

Château des Bois de Roche
Owner M André Laporte, who also owns Domaine Robin in Cadillac.

Château Bourdieu-Fonbielle
Owner Jean-Marie Galineau

Château Chichoye
Owners Roger and Gisèle Gallissaire

Château du Coteau
Owner M Michel Darriet, who also owns Château Arnaud-Jouan in Cadillac.

Château Couloumet
Owner M Roland Peyronnin

Château du Cros
Owner M Michel Boyer, who also owns Château de Lucques in Barsac, Château Haut-Mayne in Cérons, and Château Lépine in Ste-Croix-du-Mont.

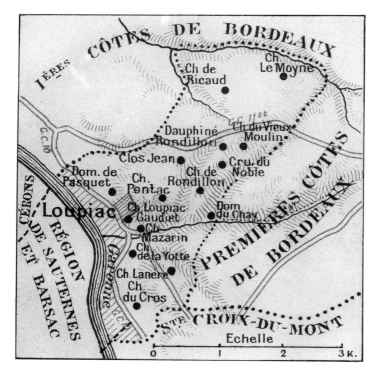

15. Map of the commune of Loupiac, showing the major wine-producing properties

The first lords of Le Cros, around 1250, were the Ségurs. In 1322 Bernard de Ségur obtained permission from Edward II to build a fort which was to become Château de Cros. It is positioned high on a hill at 100 metres above sea-level. This large and imposing château commands the finest views of the whole area. In 1921 François Thevenot, grandfather of the present owner, acquired it from the Comte de La Chassaigne. Château du Cros produces a dry white wine under the labels of 'Château du Cros', 'Château des Rochers' and 'Clos de l'Olivier'.

96 hectares (37 under vine)

50% sémillon, 30% sauvignon, 20% muscadelle

Château Dauphiné-Rondillon

Owner M Jean Darriet, who also owns Château de Roquette in Loupiac, Château Les Tourelles in Cadillac, Château Moutin in Portets and Domaine de La Maroutine in Premières Côtes de Bordeaux.

This large, modern property is situated on the plateau of Haut-Loupiac.

Château Grand-Peyruchet

Owner M Henri Gillet, who also owns Château Le Bertrande in Cadillac.

Château La Gravette

Owner M Didier Lejeune, who also owns Domaine de Chasse-Pierre in Cadillac.

Château La Nère

Owner Société Yves Dulac et Jean Séraphon, who also own Clos de L'Ange and Château Chanteloise in Cadillac and Domaine de Roustit in Ste-Croix-du-Mont.

Château de La Yotte

Owner MM de Fontainemarie and Bouffard

This is a lovely old property set back from the road.

Château Le Moyne

Owner Mme Vve David-Chaussé

Château Le Portail Rouge

Owner M Jean-Pierre Bernède

This property is divided into three parts.

Château Le Tarey

Owner M Robert Gillet

Château Loupiac-Gaudiet

Owner M Marc Ducau, who also owns Domaine de Gaudiet and Château Pontac.

Château Loupiac-Gaudiet has been in the family since 1919. The château was originally owned in the fifteenth century by Mme Combabebouse when it passed to M Bidot-Naude and then to M Reinhold-Dezeimeris. It is a beautiful, large and imposing property.

26 hectares

Château Margès-Dussaut

Owner M René Collivard

5 hectares (3.63 under vine)

Château Mazarin

Owner M Louis Courbin, who also owns Château Barthes in Cérons and Château Clarens in Cadillac.

There is a private museum of coopering artifacts, etc. The property was owned by the Meyssan family from 1534 and was named after Cardinal Mazarin, Louis XIV's Prime Minister, after he had visited the château in 1659. It was previously known as Domaine de Mouliot.

50 hectares (25 under vine)

Château du Merle

Owner Jacky Fouquet

Château Miqueu-Bel-Air

Owners Ouvrard Frères

Château de Montallier

Owner M Jacques Balan

Château Moulin-Neuf

Owner M Alain Bosviel, who also owns Domaine de St-Martin in Cadillac.

Château Pageot

Owner M Francis Guignard

Château Pontac

Owner M Marc Ducau, who also owns Château Loupiac-Gaudiet and Domaine de Gaudiet.

Château de Ricaud

Owner since 1980 M Alain Thienot.

Previous owner Mme Maurice Wells. This beautiful and imposing château is set high on a hill. The estate was originally owned by Bernard de Lamensans in the fifteenth century, then passing to the Sainte-Marie family in the next century and the de Fleurier family during the seventeenth and eighteenth centuries. The nineteenth-century owner was Charles de Bignon, the property then passing to Mme Maurice Wells's grandfather. The vineyard was completely reconstituted between 1892 and 1912 by M Wells, the father-in-law of the previous owner. The estate also produces a dry white and a red wine under the labels of 'Château Garrance' and 'Château Rahoul'. Earlier vintages have been superbly rich and long lasting, particularly the 1929. Recent vintages are of a much lighter and more commercial style.

122 hectares (70 hectares under vine)

95% sémillon, 4% sauvignon, 1% muscadelle

Château des Roches and Clos de L'Olivier

Formerly this was two properties.

Owner M Michel Boyer, who also owns Château du Cros in Loupiac and Château Lépine in Ste-Croix-du-Mont.

Château Rondillon

Owner M Lionel Bord, who also owns Clos Jean in Loupiac, where all the wine is vinified.

The property is situated at the south-west limits of Loupiac.

9 hectares under vine

65% sémillon, 30% sauvignon, 5% muscadelle

Château de Rouquette

Owner M Guy Darriet, who also owns Château Dauphiné-Rondillon and Château Les Tourelers in Cadillac, and Château Moulin, Domaine de La Marouline and two other properties in the Graves.

Château de Terrefort

Owner M François Peyrondet

Château de Tertre de Pezelin

Owners Daumec et Fils, who also own property in Cadillac.

Château de Vieux-Moulin

Owner Mme Suzanne Perromat-Dauné

This large and imposing château takes its name from the windmill at Loupiac which, for more than two centuries, turned on the highest hill in Loupiac.

18 hectares

80% sémillon, 20% sauvignon, plus a little muscadelle

Cru des Arrouillats

Owner M Roland Pouvereau

Cru de Barberousse

Owner M Michel Vignon

Cru Champon

Owner M Yvan Reglat, who also owns Château Balot in Cadillac.

Cru de La Sablière

Owners M Boucau et Frères

Cru de Montallier-Lambrot

Owner M B. Castel

Cru Mounet

Owner M Gérard Fiat, who also owns Cru Mounet in Cadillac.

Domaine de Caillives

Owner M Jean-Guy Cartier

Domaine du Chay

Owner M Jean Tourré

Domaine des Caupos

Owner Henri Daumec, who also owns property in Cadillac.

Domaine de Giron

Owner M Louis Bord

Domaine Haut-Caupos

Owner M Michel Gabas, who took over in 1979. The property has been owned by this family since 1940. A dry white wine and a red wine is also produced.

5 hectares under vine

60% sémillon, 30% sauvignon, 10% muscadelle

Clos Jean

Owner M Lionel Bord, who also owns Château Rondillon.

This property has been in the family since the nineteenth century, through six generations. It was once a hostel belonging to the Knights of Malta. Red wine is also produced.

17 hectares under vine

65% sémillon, 30% sauvignon, 5% muscadelle

Clos de La Mionomette

Owner M Bernard Bord, who also owns vineyards in Cadillac.

Domaine de Massac

Owner since 1988 Bernadette Bernède

The family have had the property since 1940. Mme Bernède also owns Château du Parc in Ste-Croix-du-Mont and Domaine de Verduc in St-Maixant.

4.8 hectares under vine

100% sémillon

Domaine Massac-La-Nère

Owner René Perez

Domaine du Noble

Owners Dejean Père et Fils

Domaine de Peytoupin

Owners Yves and Jean-Paul Cartier

Domaine de Pichat

Owner M Jean Perez

Clos du Pieuré

Owner M Jean Escudey

Domaine des Rochers

Owner Santiago Lopez

Domaine de St-Cricq

Owner M Michel Navarri, who also owns Domaine St-Cricq in Cadillac.

CADILLAC

The old town of Cadillac, which gave its name to this relatively new *appellation contrôlée*, is situated on the right bank of the Garonne, 38km south-east of Bordeaux, and is still partially fortified by the walls built in 1280 by Jean de Grailly. In the centre of the town, with its flourishing market-place, is the superb castle of the Ducs d'Epernon built between 1600 and 1650. It has been carefully restored by the Department of Historic Monuments. There is also a very imposing church with a high spire and an attractive town hall and clock-tower. The outskirts of Cadillac are slowly being built up with modern flats.

The region which now benefits from the Cadillac *appellation* previously had the 'Premières Côtes de Bordeaux' *appellation*. Then six communes, Cadillac, Omet, Béguey, Laroque, Rions and Cardan, were given the right to add the name 'Cadillac' to that of 'Premières Côtes de Bordeaux'. On 10th August 1973 (modified on 23rd December 1980) the Cadillac *appellation* was granted and extended to the wines of 22 communes (most of which still produce dry white and red wine). Those mentioned below are known to produce quality sweet white wine under the Cadillac *appellation*.

Commune	Population	Hectares under Vine
Baurech	598	160
Béguey	1,054	110
Château des Quatre Ecus (*owner* Dominique Dubroca)		
Château Birot (*owner* Jacques Boireau)		
Cadillac	2,348	350
Château Fayau (*owner* Jean Médeville)		
Château Lardiley (*owner* Marthe Lataste)		
Capian	591	500
Cardan	285	220
Donzac	144	200
Gabarnac	275	250
Haux	614	380
Château Roquefort (*owner* Michel Pion)		
Château Manos (*owner* Pierre Nioutout)		
Langoiran	2,017	350

Commune	Population	Hectares under vine
Laroque	336	100
Lestiac-sur-Garonne	545	40
Le Tourne	714	70
Monprimblanc	275	275
Omet	164	185
Paillet	792	100
Rions	1,135	375
St-Germain de Grave	169	220
St-Maixant	1,036	250
Château La-Croix-Bouey (*owner* Maxine Bouey)		
Semens	176	150
Tabanac	678	150
Verdelais	942	200
Villenave-de-Rions	216	100
Domaine du Saureau (*owner* Urbain Lacroix)		

All these communes are to claim the new Cadillac *appellation* for their sweet white wines (providing they comply with the A.C. requirements). Should the grower wish to choose the Cadillac *appellation* for his sweet white wine, he can only use *appellation* 'Bordeaux' for any other white wines produced. Alternatively, he can choose to have all his wines classified under the 'Premières Côtes de Bordeaux' *appellation*. Red wines also qualify for the 'Premières Côtes de Bordeaux' *appellation*. A.C. Cadillac can only apply to bottled wines.

The total surface area of the vineyards capable of producing white wine with the Cadillac *appellation* is approximately 2,600 hectares. The *appellation* stipulates that the must before any addition has to contain a minimum of 221 grams per litre of natural sugar and that the wine, after fermentation, must have a minimum strength of 13° and contain a minimum of 18 grams per litre of residual sugar.

The maximum output is 40 hectolitres per hectare on alluvial soil with stone, gravel and some sand with a subsoil of limestone and clay.

The style of sweet wine produced under the Cadillac A.C. is similar to those of Ste-Croix-du-Mont and Loupiac, but slightly lighter and in lower quantity as botrytis does not attack the grapes as consistently every year in this area.

GRAVES

There are a number of communes in the areas on the fringes of Sauternes and Barsac on the left side of the Garonne which are entitled to the *appellation* Graves and Graves Supérieur.

Commune	Population	Hectares under vine
Arbanats	562	100
Budos	491	150
Guillos	228	36
Landiras	1,089	175
Langon	7,000	205
Portets	2,009	460
Pujols-sur-Ciron	419	100
St-Michel-de-Rieufret	260	6
St-Pierre-de-Mons	585	300
Virelade	658	90

In certain, climatically good years they can produce sweet wines by similar methods to Sauternes and Barsac, particularly:

Domaine de Toumilot – Langon (*owner* Marc Belis)
Château Ludeman-La Côte – Langon (*owner* Pierre Chaloupin)
Château de St-Pierre – St-Pierre-de-Mons (*owner* Henri Dulac)
Château Les Queyrats – St-Pierre-de-Mons (*owner* Henri Dulac)

although most growers produce dry white and red wines.

The gravel soil is similar to the Médoc, Cérons and Sauternes areas. The depth varies according to the commune from 50 cm to more than 3 metres on a subsoil of sand, iron and clay.

TASTING NOTES AND COMMENTS ON VINTAGES

FROM 1890 TO 1986

The authors include this chapter both for general interest and as some sort of guide for prospective buyers of fine Sauternes. It can only be a rough indication for many reasons. First, of course, there can always be exceptions in any vintage and there may be wines which the authors have not come across which have dried out in a vintage which has generally lasted well, or which are beautifully preserved at the age of fifty in a lightweight year. The methods of vinification used by châteaux vary astonishingly and will affect the rate of development and longevity of the wine. Storage too may play an important part. A bottle which has spent all its life in a dark, cool cellar at a stable temperature is likely to be in a better condition than one which has changed hands several times and been subjected to various changes of temperature. Incidentally it is worth noting here that darkening colour does not necessarily indicate *maderisation* or even very great age. It can be caused simply by the effect of light on a bottle over a long period without adversely affecting the other characteristics of the wine significantly. Similarly, if a bottle is ullaged it does not necessarily mean that the wine is *maderisé* or dried out — such is the strength and extract of fine Sauternes. Finally, even among bottles of the same vintage of the same wine that have been identically cellared all their lives there may be variation in old age caused by the condition of each individual cork.

The notes, which cover almost a century of Sauternes vintages, are those of experienced tasters who have been fortunate enough to taste many fine and mature Sauternes. The notes made over the last ten years are particularly comprehensive and, with the earlier notes, make this, we hope, an important and perhaps unique reference section for Sauternes-lovers and potential buyers. Comments on wines tasted before 1960 are those of André Simon, Maurice Healey, Ian Maxwell, Charles Walter Berry and P. Morton Shand. Notes on those tasted after 1959 are those of Jeffrey Benson, Alastair Mackenzie, Dr. Christopher Davenport-Jones and Patrick Grubb MW.

116

All wines are châteaux-bottled unless otherwise stated.
L.B. = London bottled
F.B. = French bottled

1890

A good vintage. The best wines have lasted quite well. Picking started 29th September.

d'Yquem   tasted 1975
Bronze amber colour
Fine old honeyed bouquet
Dryish, strong flavoured, spirity
Lovely dry honeyed finish

d'Yquem   tasted 1987
Deep gold and brown
Lovely rich honeyed nose
Quite rich and full; slightly drying on finish

Filhot   tasted 1987
Very deep gold
Honeyed, rich bouquet
Drying but still quite a full, sweet finish

Guiraud   tasted 1983
Deep gold
Lovely old honeyed and botrytised nose
Full, rich, lovely balanced finish

Rayne-Vigneau   tasted 1985
Deep gold and brown
Marmalade with acidity
Fairly rich but quite a dry finish

Suduiraut   tasted 1986
Old Cognac colour
Crème brulée bouquet
Still rich and sweet; fading; drying on finish

1891

Mediocre wines with high acidity. Picking started 2nd October.

Filhot   tasted 1985
Very deep and brown
Mushroom bouquet
Dry, but quite drinkable

Rayne-Vigneau   tasted 1980
Deep gold and brown
Musty, leafy nose
Still quite sweet; dry finish

1892

An indifferent year generally. Some remarkable exceptions. Picking started 2nd October.

d'Yquem   tasted 1975, London
Deep amber
Old honeyed bouquet
Dried out, very powerful, immense character, dry honeyed finish

d'Yquem   tasted 1977 at the Château

Very deep amber
Nutty fruity soft nose, very slight oxidation
Very full, luscious, slight signs of age
Full of fruit, very long finish, delicious

d'Yquem   tasted 1982
Deep gold and brown
Rich and full
Slightly drying on finish

d'Yquem   tasted 1983
No change

Filhot   tasted 1986
Mid gold
Quite light and sweet
Good rich centre; dry finish

Suduiraut   tasted 1985
Deep gold and brown
Lovely old marmalade nose
Quite rich and sweet; dryish finish

1893

A very hot summer. Excellent wines the best of which are still magnificent. Picking started 14th August.

d'Yquem   tasted 1939
Deep gold
Lively and luscious

d'Yquem   tasted 1947
Dark golden colour
Remarkably fine

d'Yquem   tasted 1968
Brown/gold
Honeyed, still holding
Still residual sugar, drying finish

d'Yquem   tasted 1986
Deep gold
Superbly rich, honeyed, botrytised nose
Full, rich centre; fading on finish

Filhot   tasted 1987
Mid gold
Lovely honeyed/peachy nose
Good fruit. Drying on finish

Guiraud   tasted 1962
Colour deep golden rather than brown
Magnificent bouquet
The wine was still fresh and vivacious, fruity and well constituted but now dry at the finish
A remarkable wine for such an old Sauternes with no signs of decay

Rayne-Vigneau   tasted 1962
Wonderful colour, even better than Guiraud
Magnificent bouquet

Wine still possessed richness and sugar combined with freshness
A truly fine old Sauternes

Suduiraut   tasted 1985
Deep gold/brown
Lovely rich honeyed nose
Holding very well with rich finish

1894

Generally a poor vintage producing thin wines. Picking started 5th October.

d'Yquem   tasted 1983
Pale/mid gold and brown
Quite rich, sweet nose
Drying out but quite a rich finish

Filhot   tasted 1987
Mid gold
Lovely sweet honeyed bouquet
Quite dry but rich finish

1895

A very hot summer, producing poor-quality wines generally. Picking started 22nd September.

Guiraud   tasted 1987
Deep gold
Leafy, grassy nose
Quite sweet; dry finish

Rayne-Vigneau   tasted 1975
Deep gold/brown
Old decaying nose but still fruity
Dried out but still some fruit in centre
Pleasant finish with acidity

Rayne-Vigneau   tasted 1986
Deep gold/brown
Thin acidic nose
Still drinkable; some sweetness on finish

1896

In 1935 the wines were showing well, light with finesse. By the mid-1970s the best were still very aromatic, though beginning to dry out. Picking started 20th September.

d'Yquem   tasted 1975
Deep gold
Superb honeyed nose, slightly *maderisé*
Still a lot of fruit; dry finish

d'Yquem   tasted 1987
Deep gold
Lovely rich honeyed/peachy nose
Full and rich; slightly dry finish

Filhot   tasted 1982
Pale gold
Light, honeyed nose
Drying now but still has quite a rich finish

Rayne-Vigneau   tasted 1985

Deep gold
Rich, sweet nose
Quite full, but dry finish

1897
Mediocre wines produced. Small crop. Picking started 20th September.
Rayne-Vigneau   tasted 1982
Deep gold
Old honeyed nose with acidity
Quite sweet; dry finish

Suduiraut   tasted 1987
Very deep brown
High acidity and some fruit
Lost fruit on palate. Acidic finish

1898
Wines produced were harsh. Small crop. Picking started 23rd September.

Filhot   tasted 1988
Deep gold and brown
Old honeyed nose with high acidity
Dried out with acidic finish

Suduiraut   tasted 1986
Mid gold and brown
Light peachy nose
Soft and rich; drying on finish

1899
In 1935 the best wines of this vintage were still very good, full bodied and sweet. By the mid-1970s they were drying out, but still drinking well. Picking started 24th September.
Climens   tasted 1974
Deep gold
Nice fruity nose with acidity
Drying now but good fruit in centre

d'Yquem   tasted 1939
Still excellent but will not last much longer

d'Yquem   tasted 1985
Deep gold and brown
Rich honeyed nose with slight acidity
Quite rich in centre but drying on finish

Filhot   tasted 1987
Deep gold
Lovely *crème brulée* nose
Good rich centre and finish

Guiraud   tasted 1984
Very deep gold
Marmalade nose with acidity
Full and sweet with dry finish

Suduiraut   tasted 1935
Superb

Suduiraut   tasted 1985
Deep gold
Lovely luscious, honeyed nose
Full and rich, long finish

1900
In 1935 the best wines were still excellent. Even by the mid-1970s they were still very fine. Picking started 24th September.
d'Yquem   tasted 1942
Perfection

d'Yquem   tasted 1974
Deep gold
Rich lovely nose
Full, fruity, all there, good rich finish

d'Yquem   tasted 1988
Deep gold
Amazing concentration of botrytis
Superb richness of extract. Very long finish

Filhot   tasted 1983
Deep gold
Wonderfully honeyed nose
Long rich finish

Guiraud   tasted 1985
Very deep gold
Honeyed and sweet
Long, full, rich, luscious finish

Rayne-Vigneau   tasted 1983
Very deep gold
Superb richness with great concentration

Suduiraut   tasted 1988
Very deep gold and brown
Rich barley-sugar nose
Complex; great extract and finish

1901
An indifferent vintage producing fairly thin wines. Picking started 15th September.
Filhot   tasted 1987
Mid gold
Light with high acidity

Rayne-Vigneau   tasted 1986
Deep gold
Thin, lean nose
Dry, with high acidity on finish

1902
A poor vintage producing mediocre wines. Picking started 27th September.
Rayne-Vigneau   tasted 1986
Mid gold and brown
Quite musty and acidic
Dry, some sweetness on finish

1903
A moderate and variable vintage.

Most dried out completely now. Picking started 28th September.
Filhot   tasted 1986
Pale/mid gold
Fragrant, honeyed nose
Still sweet; drying on finish

Guiraud   tasted 1987
Deep gold
Old honeyed nose
Quite dry but sweet finish

1904
In 1935 the best wines were excellent. By the mid-1970s some still had remarkable sugar and extract. Picking started 19th September.
Climens   tasted 1930
Superb, classic

Coutet   tasted 1980
Deep gold
Lovely honeyed and delicate nose
Full and luscious; long finish

d'Yquem   tasted 1973
Deep gold
Superb nose
Good fruits, lots of body, good finish

d'Yquem   tasted 1986
Deep gold
Superb richness and botrytised nose
Full, luscious, marmalade. Long finish

Guiraud   tasted 1985
Deep gold
Lovely honeyed rich nose
Superb extract and concentration

Lafaurie-Peyraguey   tasted 1986
Deep gold
Full and rich honeyed nose
Lovely, rich and full; long finish

Rayne-Vigneau   tasted 1976
Light caramel colour
Superb honeyed nose, no signs of age
Full, enormous, luscious fruit, perfect balance

Rayne-Vigneau   tasted 1978
Very dark brown
Full, big, slight oxidation but soft
Very full, fruity, long luscious finish

1905
A vintage which produced light, rather forward wines. Most are well past their best now. Picking started 18th September.
Filhot   tasted 1986
Deep gold
Light marmalade nose
Lacks fruit. Dry finish

Rayne-Vigneau   tasted 1982
   Gold and brown
   Dry, acidic nose
   Faded but with a hint of
   marmalade

1906

In 1935 the wines were regarded as
good with plenty of natural sugar but
were beginning to show signs of
decline. By the mid-1970s
considerable variation was evident;
some were still excellent, others were
drying out and losing extract.
Picking started 17th September.
Climens   tasted 1976
   Cognac colour
   Light, slight fruit, signs of
   oxidation
   Lost most of its fruit, acidity
   showing through

Coutet   tasted 1987
   Mid gold and orange
   Light honeyed nose
   Fruit fading, but a lovely wine

d'Yquem   tasted 1930
   Brown
   Not very good

d'Yquem   tasted 1931
   Luscious, but lacking in bouquet

d'Yquem   tasted 1973
   Deep gold
   Lovely honeyed nose with acidity
   Still a lot of fruit but beginning to
   get tired, dryish finish

d'Yquem   tasted 1988
   Deep gold
   Honeyed with acidity
   Good, sweet centre but drying
   considerably

Guirard   tasted 1984
   Very deep gold
   Complex, delicate marmalade
   nose
   Still quite full and rich; slightly dry
   finish

Lafaurie-Peyraguey   tasted 1976
   Very fine, lightweight

Rayne-Vigneau   tasted 1987
   Deep gold
   Rich marmalade nose
   Holding well, drying slightly on
   finish

1907

A moderate vintage similar to 1905.
Few wines have survived. Picking
started 25th September.
Climens   tasted 1985
   Mid/deep gold
   Appley/barley-sugar nose

Quite rich in centre but drying on
finish

Lafaurie-Peyraguey   tasted 1981
   Very deep gold and brown
   Still fairly rich and high acidity
   Holding, but dry finish

1908

In 1935 the best wines were still very
good; by the mid-1970s some were
still excellent, others had declined
appreciably. Picking started 21st
September.
Climens   tasted 1930
   Fine and of great breed

Climens   tasted 1986
   Mid gold
   Lovely complex barley-sugar nose
   Superb balance

d'Yquem   tasted 1975
   Deep gold
   Superb rich honeyed nose
   Full of fruit, delicious wine, long
   rich finish

d'Yquem   tasted 1987
   Deep gold
   Superb marmalade nose
   Very full and rich. Very long
   concentrated finish

Guiraud   tasted 1967
   Full golden colour but not brown
   Lovely delicate old Sauternes nose
   Wine is very well balanced and
   preserved
   Plenty of sweetness still and no
   sign of oxidation

Lafaurie-Peyraguey   tasted 1983
   Deep gold
   Superb, rich barley-sugar nose
   Lots of fruit and richness; long
   finish

Rayne-Vigneau   tasted 1984
   Mid gold
   Superb extract of botrytis
   Rich and complex. A great wine

1909

By the mid-1970s considerable
variation was evident. Some wines
were still beautifully balanced and
complete; others were well past their
best. Picking started 26th September.
Climens   tasted 1983
   Deep gold
   Appley, barley-sugar nose
   Superbly rich; great finish

Coutet   tasted 1986
   Deep gold with orange tinge
   Delicate, complex barley-sugar
   nose
   Full and rich; long finish

de Myrat   tasted 1972
   Deep gold
   Honeyed with signs of age
   Lightweight, fruity, good finish,
   slightly drying

d'Yquem   tasted 1949
   Pale gold, perfection, honey
   bouquet
   Honeyed palate

d'Yquem   tasted 1973
   Deep gold
   Full luscious nose
   Honeyed, fruity, long luscious
   finish, excellent

d'Yquem   tasted 1985
   Deep gold
   Full, very rich marmalade nose
   Lovely complex concentration;
   long finish

Guiraud   tasted 1984
   Very deep gold
   Lovely rich burnt-sugar nose
   Full and concentrated. Long finish

Lafaurie-Peyraguey   tasted 1977
   Brown-gold; deep unctuous,
   marmalade nose
   Splendid fruit, texture and balance
   Not very glutinous, sugar drying
   out a bit
   Something of peaches in flavour
   Beginning to thin out right at the
   end and slow acidity

Rayne-Vigneau   tasted 1986
   Very deep gold
   Rich marmalade nose
   Full bodied; long finish

1910

A very poor vintage. Rarely seen
now. Picking started 10th October.
de Myrat   tasted 1984
   Deep gold and brown
   High acidity, some fruit
   Dry. Oxidation showing

Rayne-Vigneau   tasted 1986
   Deep gold
   Thin, acidic nose
   Dry with high acidity on finish

1911

Unusually variable. Some of the best
wines were in decline by the 1930s,
one or two were still attractive in the
1970s. Picking started 20th
September.
Climens   tasted 1930
   Drying out

d'Yquem   tasted 1930
   Dried out; not a fine wine

d'Yquem   tasted 1931
   Disappointing

d'Yquem   tasted 1985
  Deep gold and brown
  Acidity overpowering any
  sweetness
  Distinctly musty and medicinal
  High acidity on finish

Guiraud   tasted 1980
  Deep brown
  Slightly honeyed and musty
  Grassy with high acidity

Lafaurie-Peyraguey   tasted 1984
  Deep gold and brown
  Dry, acidic nose, with some
  sweetness
  Lost most of its fruit. Dry finish

Rayne-Vigneau   tasted 1973
  Deep gold/brown
  Signs of *maderisation*; still quite
  peachy
  Drying out but pleasant

1912
A mediocre year. Wines rarely seen
now. Picking started 26th
September.
d'Yquem   tasted 1987
  Mid gold
  Light, honeyed nose
  Showing its age with dry finish

Rayne-Vigneau   tasted 1980
  Deep brown/gold
  Good richness and acidity
  Dry but still quite sweet in the
  centre

1913
A big harvest; mostly lightish wines,
but some have lasted remarkably
well. Picking started 25th
September.
Climens   tasted 1930
  Drying out

Climens   tasted 1984
  Mid/gold
  Light acidic nose
  Has lost its fruit; dry finish

d'Yquem   tasted 1986
  Mid gold
  Light, delicate honeyed, grassy
  nose
  Quite dry but good richness
  underneath

Guiraud   tasted 1982
  Deep gold
  Light but complex
  Fine quality; rich finish

Lafaurie-Peyraguey   tasted 1977
  Deep gold/brown; well-preserved
  nose with good fruit
  Acidity slightly overpowering,

fruit in the mouth, quite good
  texture, quite sweet but the
  sweetness seems not fully
  integrated

Lafaurie-Peyraguey   tasted 1982
  Mid gold
  Delicate lightweight nose
  Honeyed fruit; light finish

La Tour-Blanche   tasted 1926
  Exceptionally fine

1914
A good vintage; some wines are still
superb, others beginning to dry out.
Picking started 20th September.
Climens   tasted 1964
  Lovely nose
  Exquisite, but drying finish

Climens   tasted 1981
  Deep gold
  Superbly rich barley-sugar nose
  Full and luscious. Long, rich finish

d'Yquem   tasted 1932
  Excellent

d'Yquem   tasted 1972
  Deep gold
  Superb, luscious nose, slight signs
  of age
  Full, superb fruit, long luscious
  finish

d'Yquem   tasted 1986
  Deep gold
  Lovely rich honeyed botrytis
  Full of richness in centre, showing
  age on the finish

Filhot   tasted 1948
  Rather light, but full of flavour
  Sweet but not extravagantly so
  Nutty and unspoilt

Filhot   tasted 1986
  Deep gold
  Lovely complex nose, good
  botrytis
  Medium rich, good long finish

Guiraud   tasted 1933
  Excellent

Lafaurie-Peyraguey   tasted 1977
  Deep gold/brown, good full
  classic old Sauternes nose
  Good texture, luscious marmalade
  flavour, lots of extract, beautifully
  integrated and balanced
  Very long finish
  Lovely but not cloying
  A very distinguished wine

Rayne-Vigneau   tasted 1985
  Deep gold and orange
  Lovely delicate honeyed nose
  Good extract, slightly drying

1915
A poor vintage. One or two
exceptions. Rarely seen now.
Picking started 22nd September.
Coutet   tasted 1986
  Deep gold and orange
  Light, delicate, old lemony nose
  Still holding, but fading fast

Guiraud   tasted 1986
  Deep gold
  Lovely old honeyed botrytised
  nose
  Quite rich; drying on finish

Lafaurie-Peyraguey (half
bottles)   tasted 1976
  Deep gold, good bouquet for age
  Medium sweet, drying finish

Rayne-Vigneau   tasted 1984
  Deep gold and brown
  Good extract marmalade nose
  Full centre, sweet; drying on finish

1916
Quite a good vintage, highly
regarded in the 1920s and 1930s;
some have lasted well into the 1970s,
others are in decline. Picking started
26th September.
Climens   tasted 1930
  Fine and of great breed

Coutet   tasted 1926
  Admirable

Coutet   tasted 1985
  Deep gold
  Lovely rich honeyed nose
  Still a great wine; long finish

d'Yquem   tasted 1930
  Very good

d'Yquem   tasted 1933
  Very good

d'Yquem   tasted 1974
  Deep gold
  Fine rich honeyed nose, some signs
  of age
  Still holding with fruit in centre,
  drying finish

d'Yquem   tasted 1987
  Deep gold
  Lovely honeyed nose
  Good concentration; slightly
  drying on finish

Guiraud   tasted 1981
  Very deep gold
  Quite rich but high acidity
  Drying out, but a pleasant bottle

Lafaurie-Peyraguey   tasted 1984
  Deep gold
  Complex barley-sugar nose
  Good rich honeyed fruit; long
  finish

1917

A vintage highly regarded in the 1920s and 1930s which produced attractive but rather lightweight wines some of which lasted well into the 1970s. Picking started 19th September.

Climens   tasted 1986
Mid gold
Light, delicate honeyed nose
Good balanced centre; drying on finish

Coutet   tasted 1926
Admirable

d'Yquem   tasted 1973
Deep gold
Light but good rich nose
Good fruit and acidity, dry finish

d'Yquem   tasted 1988
Deep gold and brown
Lovely delicate botrytised nose
Still quite rich, but drying on finish

Guiraud   tasted 1984
Deep gold
Quite full and rich
Good extract — dry finish

Lafaurie-Peyraguey   tasted 1977
Deep gold
Delicate light nose, slightly hot
Good depth of fruit, delicate finish

Millanges (Gabarnac)   tasted 1981
Pale/mid gold
Lightweight, sweet nose
Lovely rich fruit and firm finish

1918

Not a great vintage. Mostly dried out now. Picking started 24th September.

d'Yquem   tasted 1978
Pale/mid gold
Very little signs of age, light fresh nose
Dried out on palate, still very drinkable

d'Yquem   tasted 1987
Mid gold
Light honeyed nose
Still sweet, but dry finish

Rabaud-Promis   tasted 1987
Pale gold and brown
Quite rich honeyed nose
Drying with slightly bitter, coarse finish

Suduiraut   tasted 1986
Deep gold
Rich marmalade nose and acidity
Drying out but still rich in the centre

1919

Quite a good vintage but most had

dried out by the mid-1970s. Picking started 24th September.

Climens   tasted 1930
Top of its form

Climens   tasted 1987
Deep gold and brown
Superbly rich barley-sugar nose
Very full and rich. Excellent balance and finish

Coutet   tasted 1984
Deep gold
Rich old honeyed nose
Good centre, dry finish

d'Yquem   tasted 1977
Deep gold
Acidity high on nose but good depth of fruit
Dry palate with acidity

d'Yquem   tasted 1986
Deep gold with tinge of brown
Lovely marmalade botrytised nose
Full and rich in the centre; drying, with acidity on finish

Rayne-Vigneau   tasted 1983
Dark bronze
Lovely old nutty flavour
Still rich; slightly drying on finish

Rieussec   tasted 1963
Very fresh green colour. Wine almost dry, plenty of acidity but sugar gone (could be an off bottle)

Rieussec   tasted 1987
Very deep gold
Superb rich honeyed nose
Lots of extract. Very long finish

1920

A good vintage. Picking started 22nd September. Highly regarded in the 1930s; most drying out in the 1970s.

Climens   tasted 1984
Deep gold
Light, delicate honeyed nose
Good richness, but dry on finish

Coutet   tasted 1976
Deep gold
Losing fruit but still holding
Drying out but nice fruit in centre

Doisy-Dubroca (half bottles)   tasted 1982
Dried out with acidity showing predominantly

d'Yquem   tasted 1948 (must weight 16°)
Unquestionably a fine wine but outclassed by the 1921

d'Yquem   tasted 1977
Deep gold
Superb full nose, slight signs of age

d'Yquem   tasted 1987
Deep gold
Good extract but showing age
Still rich in centre but drying on finish

Guiraud   tasted 1981
Deep gold and brown
Old marmalade nose
Delicate balance, lovely richness
Slightly drying

Lafaurie-Peyraguey   tasted 1977
Deep gold, light delicate nose
Full, luscious, long, slightly burnt finish

Rayne-Vigneau   tasted 1986
Dark bronze
Old decayed nose
Slight sweetness but has become sour

1921

One of the greatest vintages. Picking started 15th September. An exceptionally hot summer. Some wines still quite outstanding, especially Château d'Yquem and Château Climens; many others still very fine but some just beginning to dry out.

Caillou   tasted 1987
Very deep and brown
Superb butterscotch nose
Deep rich burnt-caramel taste
Superb, long, excellent depth and extract

Climens   tasted 1976
Deep, rich, outstanding classic wine

Coutet   tasted 1980
Deep gold
Complex, rich, delicate
Lovely balance of richness; very long finish

de Ricaud (Loupiac)   tasted 1985
Honeyed and rich
Complex, old-style Sauternes
Slightly drying out

de Ricaud   tasted 1987
Deep rich gold
Lovely rich concentrated barley-sugar
Superb extract; very long finish

d'Yquem   tasted 1930 (must weight 19.9°)
Magnificent

d'Yquem   tasted 1932
Clear, clean, crisp
The volume of its bouquet, the perfection of its body, its incomparable beauty absolutely

wonderful, luscious, but no trace
of sugar
Unctuous but no vestige of
glycerine, God's own masterpiece
as compared to man's clever fake

d'Yquem   tasted 1948
Clean, luscious, unlikely to retain
this

d'Yquem   tasted 1976
Deep brown gold
Superb rich botrytis nose
Full, honeyed, enormous fruit,
very long finish

d'Yquem   tasted 1988
Deep gold
Very concentrated rich marmalade
Thick extract, full, very rich, very
long finish; superb

Filhot   tasted 1930
Not great

Filhot   tasted 1977
Deep gold
Light, dry, slight acidity, some
fruit and botrytis
Drying out, slight fruit in centre

Guiraud   tasted 1982
Deep gold
Old Sauternes barley-sugar nose
Still quite rich; fading on finish

Lafaurie-Peyraguey   tasted 1982
Gold and brown
Burnt-sugar nose
Very rich and full; long finish

La Tour-Blanche   tasted 1983
Deep gold with orange tinge
Good rich nose with acidity
showing
Quite lightweight; dry on finish

Montagne (Ste-Croix-du-Mont)
tasted 1981
Brown
Still sweet
Coffee flavoured; drinking well

Rabaud-Promis   tasted 1963
Rather dark golden colour
Big, tarry nose
Rich wine with plenty of sugar still

Raymond-Lafon   tasted 1985
Deep old gold
Superb extract of botrytis. Very
rich marmalade nose
Extremely thick in the mouth
Enormous concentration and
extract. Almost 'essence'. Superb

Rayne-Vigneau   tasted 1978
Cognac brown, old musty nose
with some depth
Spirity, fruit drying out, although
a lot of sugar and extract
High alcohol finish, fruit fading
fast

Rieussec   tasted 1976
Deep gold
Light but good depth, slight
oxidation
Fruit and weight; slightly dry
finish

Suduiraut   tasted 1986
Deep gold
Lovely honey extract nose
Full, rich; very long finish

1922
A big vintage. Picking started 19th
September. Mostly dried out in the
1970s but some still fine wines.
Caillou (Belgium bottled)   tasted
1979
Good fruit. Very well balanced
A very fine wine

Climens   tasted 1986
Mid/deep gold
Barley-sugar nose
Lovely complex balance and finish

Coutet   tasted 1984
Mid gold
Rich honeyed nose
Lovely extract and concentration.
Long finish

Coutet (half bottles)   tasted 1988
No change

de Myrat (half bottles)   tasted 1988
Deep gold and brown
Rich, old honeyed nose
Full, sweet, botrytised; long finish
just starting to dry

d'Yquem   tasted 1932 (must weight
16.8°)
Moderate

d'Yquem   tasted 1963
Deep golden colour
Very fine nose
Wine now quite dry at the finish
but a fine wine

d'Yquem   tasted 1976
Deep gold
Full rich deep nose, slight signs of
age
Good rich fruit, slightly dry finish

d'Yquem   tasted 1987
Deep gold
Lovely rich old botrytised nose
Rich centre, good extract; slightly
drying on finish

Filhot   tasted 1957
Fine golden colour without a hint
of *maderisation*
Fine bouquet
Beautiful full-bodied sweet wine
with no sign of decay

Guiraud   tasted 1967
Light mahogany colour
Pleasant nose
Light and finely-balanced wine
still in good condition

Lafaurie-Peyraguey   tasted 1977
Lovely deep gold
Nice young fresh fruit nose, hint of
linseed and barley-sugar
Good texture, very clear, fresh,
lovely fruit, good acidity and
balance

Rieussec   tasted 1988
Deep gold
Marmalade nose
Great concentration drying on
finish

Sigalas-Rabaud   tasted 1981
Deep brown Cognac colour
Superb rich marmalade nose
Enormously rich fruit
Long, soft, sweet finish

Sigalas-Rabaud   tasted 1987
No change

1923
A mediocre vintage. Wines rather
thin but having a lot of charm.
Picking started 1st October.
Coutet   tasted 1983
Mid deep gold
Lovely, rich honeyed nose
Full and rich. Long finish

d'Yquem   tasted 1973
Deep mahogany
Fading although still some fruit
and sugar

d'Yquem   tasted 1977
Very deep gold
Old nose and slight honey
Quite fruity but drying out

d'Yquem   tasted 1986
Deep gold
Old honeyed nose
Quite rich but drying a lot on
finish

Filhot   tasted 1981
Deep gold and brown
Light and sweet
Drying on centre and finish

Guiraud   tasted 1985
Deep gold
Lovely delicate botrytised nose
Slightly fading but a lovely rich
finish

Guiteronde (half bottles)   tasted 1982
Deep gold
Honeyed, well balanced
Very well preserved; sweet, old-
style Sauternes

La Tour-Blanche   tasted 1987
  Deep gold and brown
  Lovely rich marmalade nose
  Slightly drying, but still superb

Rabaud-Promis   tasted 1978
  Deep Cognac colour
  Dry nose complex, drying out in
  centre and dry finish with acidity

Rayne-Vigneau   tasted 1937
  Particularly good

Rayne-Vigneau (half bottle)   tasted
1977
  Remarkably light in colour still
  Nice fruit and maturity on the
  bouquet
  Absolutely no sign of oxidation
  The wine is fresh with a nice
  balanced sweetness without being
  really liquorous

1924

A great vintage. Picking started 19th
September. Most drying out
somewhat by the 1970s but one or
two (Château St-Amand among
them) quite outstanding.
Climens   tasted 1930
  Promises to be wonderful

Climens   tasted 1974
  Deep gold
  Soft smooth fruity nose, slight
  oxidation
  Luscious full slightly dry finish

Climens   tasted 1982
  Deep gold
  Lovely, full, rich, botrytised nose
  Lots of fruit in centre; slightly
  drying on finish

Doisy-Daëne   tasted 1987
  Deep gold and browning
  Light, delicate, botrytised nose
  Holding well; delicately balanced
  finish

d'Yquem   tasted 1976 (must weight
17°)
  Deep gold
  Good fruit slightly drying and
  oxidised slightly
  Drying but still just holding on

d'Yquem (magnum)   tasted 1977
  Deep gold
  Huge nose
  Full of fruit, drying out on finish

d'Yquem   tasted 1987
  Deep gold and brown
  Lovely rich marmalade nose
  Full of extract, drying on finish

Filhot   tasted 1983
  Deep gold

Lovely, delicate, botrytised nose
Full and sweet; slightly drying on
finish

Guiraud   tasted 1982
  Deep gold
  Old botrytised nose
  Quite rich centre; drying finish

Guiteronde (half bottles)   tasted 1982
  Lemony flavour on nose
  Dryish old wine

Lafaurie-Peyraguey   tasted 1973
  Deep gold
  Full botrytis nose, slight oxidation
  Drying slightly but still fruity with
  depth

La Tour-Blanche   tasted 1970
  Perfect colour
  Beautiful nose, soft, dryish, good
  balance

La Tour-Blanche   tasted 1975
  Deep gold
  Light dry austere nose with
  oxidation now showing
  Drying out, some fruit in centre

Rabaud-Promis   tasted 1929
  Excellent

Rieussec   tasted 1986
  Deep gold and brown
  Full and concentrated; lovely rich
  finish

St-Amand   tasted 1976
  Deep gold
  Full honeyed nose, slight signs of
  age
  Full, fruity a lot of depth, luscious
  finish

1925

A mediocre vintage. Picking started
3rd October. Rather light and green
wines mostly dried out now with one
or two exceptions.
Coutet   tasted 1986
  Mid gold
  Light, appley nose
  Drying, but quite sweet finish

Doisy-Dubroca   tasted 1930
  Drying out

d'Yquem   tasted 1976 (must weight
15.8°)
  Deep gold
  Honeyed nose and *maderisé*
  Still a lot of fruit although thin
  centre
  Slightly drying on finish

d'Yquem   tasted 1988
  Deep gold
  Honeyed, *crème brulée* nose
  Quite rich centre; drying on finish

Lafaurie-Peyraguey   tasted 1976
  Deep gold
  Old nose, slightly *maderisé*
  Still holding and plenty of fruit,
  good finish

Rayne-Vigneau   tasted 1980
  Mid gold
  Dry medicinal nose
  Quite sweet, leafy finish

1926

A very good vintage. Picking started
4th October. By the 1970s most were
starting to dry out, although they
were still very good wines.
Climens   tasted 1981
  Deep gold
  Lovely delicate botrytised nose
  Still rich in centre; slightly dry on
  finish

Coutet   tasted 1975
  Deep gold
  Lovely rich nose
  Perfect balance, still a lot of fruit
  Slightly drying on finish

d'Yquem   tasted 1975 (must weight
17.4°)
  Mid gold
  Good rich nose, slightly *maderisé*
  Nice fruit, slightly thin centre
  Drying on finish

d'Yquem   tasted 1988
  Mid/deep gold
  Rich botrytised old honeyed nose
  Quite sweet, but drying a lot on
  finish

Filhot   tasted 1975
  Pale gold
  Dryish nose, spirity, no acidity,
  dry finish

Filhot (half bottles)   tasted 1988
  Pale gold and tawny
  Light on fruit with high acidity
  Drying out rapidly. A drinkable
  dry wine

Lafaurie-Peyraguey   tasted 1976
  Mid gold
  Good nose
  Lovely balance
  Still good fruit

Lafaurie-Peyraguey   tasted 1982
  Very deep gold and brown
  Lovely rich, barley-sugar nose
  Very big; soft, rich fruit; very full
  finish
  Superb

Rabaud-Promis (half bottles)   tasted
1978
  Cognac colour, old nose but still
  fruity, slightly drying out
  Still holding with acidity on finish

Rayne-Vigneau   tasted 1987
  Very deep gold and brown
  Lovely rich delicate honeyed nose
  Full, superb. Chewy centre
  Very slightly drying on finish

St-Amand   tasted 1982
  Has lost most of its fruit
  Candlewax/incense flavour

1927

A poor vintage producing wines
rather high in acidity and somewhat
lacking in richness. Most have dried
out now. Picking started 25th
September.

Climens   tasted 1981
  Mid gold
  Delicate nose and acidity
  Still quite rich in centre, light dry
  finish

Coutet   tasted 1960
  Dark gold
  Maderisé but still fruity
  Still holding but dryish finish

Coutet   tasted 1977
  Dark golden brown, rather short
  nose
  Great flavour of raisins with dry
  finish

d'Yquem   tasted 1977 (must weight
15.5°)
  Deep gold
  Nice botrytis and acidity
  Slightly drying but good thick
  fruit in centre, high acidity on
  finish

Lafaurie-Peyraguey   tasted 1976
  Deep gold
  Nice nose
  Good fruit, slightly high acidity
  Nice finish

La Tour-Blanche   tasted 1977
  Dark brown/gold
  Caramel nose
  Fresh, full of fruit, drying out on
  finish

1928

Hot summer. A classic vintage.
Picking started 25th September.
Some of the best wines still superb
and will last, others beginning to dry
out a little.

Climens   tasted 1974
  Very deep yellow
  Dry, some sugar and fruit
  Lovely but faded fairly quickly

Clos Haut-Peyraguey   tasted 1976
  Light brown
  Slight oxidation on nose but good
  fruit

Slightly drying out but full of fruit,
slightly oxidised finish

Coutet   tasted 1976
  Mid gold
  Soft, full, appley
  Full, long, slight acidity, drying
  finish

d'Yquem   tasted 1977 (must weight
18.2°)
  Mid gold
  Beautiful honeyed nose
  Full, heavyweight, magnificent
  mouthful
  Full, deep extract

d'Yquem   tasted 1987
  Deep gold
  Magnificent extract — full and rich
  Superbly rich and full long finish

Filhot   tasted 1972
  Dark colour
  Very perfumed nose
  Good fruit and sugar, drying on
  finish

Guiraud   tasted 1979
  Deep gold
  Rich extract of botrytis
  Full bodied; long finish

Lafaurie-Peyraguey   tasted 1977
  Mid gold
  Perfect balance, rich nose
  Perfection — long, full, fruity,
  superb balance, years to go

Rieussec   tasted 1980
  Deep gold
  Lovely rich marmalade
  Great depth of extract. Long finish

Suduiraut   tasted 1988
  Deep gold and tawny
  Lovely orange marmalade, old
  Sauternes nose
  Very full and rich; no signs of age
  Lovely, very long orangey finish
  with botrytis

1929

Very hot summer. Another great
vintage. Picking started 26th
September. Perhaps they lack the
delicacy of the 1928s in general, but
their greater extract is probably
giving them greater staying power.

Bechereau   tasted 1987
  Very deep gold with brown
  Superb rich fruit
  Excellent balance; long marmalade
  finish

Climens   tasted 1937
  Excellent

Climens   tasted 1958
  Quite exquisite
  Rich, full, soft, perfection

Climens   tasted 1965
  Rather dark in colour (could be a
  badly stored bottle)
  Showing age but still sweet

Climens   tasted 1985
  Deep gold
  Excellent rich complex nose
  Full of extract and botrytis
  Wonderful finish — perfection

Coutet   tasted 1979
  Mid deep gold
  Light delicate rich nose
  Full and sweet; slightly fading on
  finish

Coutet (L.B. Lebegue)   tasted 1980
  Mid gold
  Volatile acidity
  Dried out on finish

de Ricaud (Loupiac)   tasted 1978
  Deep gold
  Honeyed rich nose, slight signs of
  oxidation
  Full, luscious, rich, long finish,
  slight oxidation on finish

de Ricaud (half bottles)   tasted 1982
  Very sweet and honeyed
  Well balanced
  Lots of rich fruit
  Perfection

d'Yquem   tasted 1976 (must weight
21.2°)
  Mid gold
  Full superb hot nose, full botrytis
  Superb weight and balance
  Perfection

d'Yquem   tasted 1987
  Deep gold
  Luscious, rich, botrytised
  marmalade nose
  Excellent balance; long rich finish
  Superb

Filhot   tasted 1962
  Mid gold
  Good nose and slight oxidation
  Beautiful, fruity, superb finish

Filhot   tasted 1984
  Deep gold
  Lovely delicate botrytised nose
  Rich, lovely, full finish

Guiraud   tasted 1980
  Deep gold
  Lovely complex botrytised nose
  Full and rich; long finish

Lafaurie-Peyraguey   tasted 1977
  Deep gold
  Superb honeyed nose, slightly hot
  Slightly burnt flavour with some
  acidity but masses of fruit, long
  finish

Laville (L.B.)   tasted 1978
   Deep gold
   Lovely honeyed flavour. Good
   balance
   A fine wine; slightly drying on
   finish

Rayne-Vigneau   tasted 1935
   Very good indeed, sweet and yet
   full of flavour

Rayne-Vigneau   tasted 1963
   Colour is quite remarkable, very
   deep — almost tawny
   Bouquet and quality were in no
   way affected
   Wine still very rich and sweet
   Magnificent flavour

Rieussec   tasted 1985
   Deep gold
   Superbly rich concentrated nose
   Beautiful in every way

Trillon   tasted 1984
   Mahogany
   Slightly oxidised, but still honeyed
   Good rich old Sauternes; treacly
   finish

1930

A very poor vintage. Picking started
1st October. Rarely seen. No
d'Yquem made.
Filhot   tasted 1984
   Deep gold and brown
   Acidic, musty nose
   Dried out

Guiraud   tasted 1986
   Very deep Cognac colour
   Slight richness and acidity
   Dry but still with fruit on finish

Rayne-Vigneau   tasted 1935
   Tastes of sugar only

1931

An undistinguished vintage. Picking
started 25th September. Most have
dried out now.
Climens   tasted 1935
   Quite pleasing

d'Yquem   tasted 1937 (must weight
16.6°)
   Not great

d'Yquem   tasted 1963
   Rather brown in colour but still
   very good with some sugar left,
   fruity

d'Yquem   tasted 1965
   Deep golden colour
   Still some sugar
   Remarkably well preserved for
   such a year

d'Yquem   tasted 1975
   Unusually pale gold
   Light, fresh, signs of oxidation
   Lightweight, lacks depth, drying
   finish

d'Yquem   tasted 1986
   Mid gold and brown
   Honeyed rich burnt nose
   Good balance of sweet honeyed
   fruit and acidity
   Slightly drying on finish

La Tour-Blanche   tasted 1935
   Unpleasant — high SO_2

Rayne-Vigneau   tasted 1980
   Deep and brown
   Quite honeyed with acidity
   Fairly rich centre with dry finish

Rieussec   tasted 1935
   Poor and high SO_2

1932

A very poor vintage. Picking started
15th October. Rarely seen.
Climens   tasted 1985
   Mid gold
   Thin acidic nose. Sour botrytis
   Quite musty and leafy. Dry finish

d'Yquem   tasted 1935 (must weight
15°)
   Very poor quality

d'Yquem   tasted 1977
   Deep gold
   Old *maderisé* nose
   Light, thin, hardly any fruit left
   Dry finish

1933

Quite a lightweight vintage. Picking
started 22nd September. Some have
lasted surprisingly well though
drying out now.
Climens   tasted 1935
   Excellent — not too sweet

Coutet   tasted 1986
   Deep gold
   Marmalade, appley nose
   Holding well with good finish

d'Yquem   tasted 1935 (must weight
16.3°)
   Superior but curious after-taste

d'Yquem   tasted 1977
   Mid gold
   Good honeyed nose
   Still full of fruit, long finish and
   acidity

Lafaurie-Peyraguey   tasted 1976
   Deep gold
   Still good nose, slightly *maderisé*
   Nice fruit, slightly dry finish

La Tour-Blanche   tasted 1935 (must
weight 14°)
   Not impressive

Raymond-Lafon   tasted 1984
   Deep gold and brown
   Old Madeira nose but botrytis
   underneath
   Drying fast but still a fruity finish

Rayne-Vigneau   tasted 1935
   Very good

Rayne-Vigneau   tasted 1987
   Deep gold
   Rich marmalade nose
   Rich sweet fruit with slightly
   drying finish

Rieussec   tasted 1935
   Quite good but rather coarse

1934

A good vintage. Picking started 14th
September. Many still very attractive
but beginning to dry out.
Climens   tasted 1985
   Deep gold
   Honeyed botrytised nose
   Good depth, delicate finish

Coutet   tasted 1983
   Gold and brown
   Waxy lemony/honeyed flavour
   with well-balanced acidity

Doisy-Daëne (magnum)   tasted 1965
   Colour ageing but still good
   Lovely nose, wine soft, very fruity
   and sweet
   Beginning to show a little age
   Now at its best

d'Yquem   tasted in barrel 1935 (must
weight 18°)
   Will be good

d'Yquem   tasted 1973
   Deep gold
   Superb full fruity nose, slight
   acidity
   Luscious, fruit, long soft finish,
   slightly dry on end

d'Yquem   tasted 1986
   Deep gold
   Marmalade with classic extract
   Full and rich, very slight drying on
   finish
   A lovely wine

Guiraud   tasted 1977
   Deep gold
   Good full nose, slight oxidation
   Nice full fruity, drying finish

Lafaurie-Peyraguey   tasted 1976
   Excellent appearance, classic
   Sauternes

La Tour-Blanche   tasted 1935 (must weight 12°)
  Might turn out good

Monteils   tasted 1980
  Brown Cognac colour
  Lovely rich old botrytised nose
  Superb. Full, great extract and finish

Monteils   tasted 1981
  No change

Rieussec   tasted 1980
  Deep gold and brown
  Lovely rich old marmalade nose
  Slightly drying but lovely balance

Suduiraut   tasted 1975
  Dark gold
  Sweet luscious nose
  Lovely wine, still full, good balance

1935

A mediocre vintage. Picking started 30th September. Château d'Yquem still interesting in the mid-1970s but already drying out.

d'Yquem   tasted 1970 (must weight 15.9°)
  Pale gold
  Soft and rounded
  Good fruit and balance, drying out on finish

d'Yquem   tasted 1975
  Amber gold
  Poor nose
  Dryish wine, no acidity but quite full bodied

d'Yquem   tasted 1987
  Mid gold
  Light honeyed nose
  Fairly dry, but still quite sweet

Filhot   tasted 1985
  Mid gold
  Nice *crème brulée* nose
  Still sweet centre with dry finish

Lafaurie-Peyraguey   tasted 1987
  Mid/deep gold
  Marmalade complex nose
  Quite dry with grassy finish

La Tour-Blanche   tasted 1987
  Pale gold
  Light delicate honeyed nose
  Slightly drying on finish but still quite rich in centre

1936

A poor vintage. Picking started 2nd October. Virtually all dried out by the 1970s.

d'Arche   tasted 1984
  Deep gold and brown

Light, slightly *maderisé* nose
Drying, but some fruit on finish

d'Yquem   tasted 1974 (must weight 17.7°)
  Deep gold
  Still some fruit but dry and acidity on nose
  Just holding on

d'Yquem   tasted 1988
  Mid gold
  Light, marmalade, honeyed nose
  Quite rich. Lightish finish and acidity

Filhot   tasted 1983
  Mid gold
  Light medicinal nose
  Lacks body and finish

Lafaurie-Peyraguey   tasted 1976
  Deep gold
  Maderisé nose
  Lightweight, drying out

1937

A great vintage. Picking started 20th September. Most of the best wines still showing beautifully. The best preserved of the pre-Second World War vintages.

Caillou   tasted 1982
  Deep gold and brown
  Good concentrated barley-sugar nose showing age
  Lovely complex balance. Slightly drying on finish

Climens   tasted 1967
  Deep gold
  Full bodied with sweetness

Climens   tasted 1975
  Mid gold
  Superb rich deep nose
  Excellent balance, firm delicious finish

Clos Haut-Peyraguey   tasted 1976
  Deep gold
  Lacks depth although fruity, slight oxidation
  Fruity, a lot of luscious depth, long, slightly dry finish

Coulat   tasted 1982
  Amber/gold
  Lemony
  Delicate, refined, barley-sugar
  A lovely wine

Coutet   tasted 1978
  Very deep gold
  Deep rich strong bouquet
  Slightly roasted with acidity
  Full of fruit, luscious, long, slightly burnt finish

Coutet   tasted 1982
  Bronze
  Sweet, varnishy nose
  Drying a little on finish, but long rich centre
  Well preserved

Dauphiné-Rondillon (Loupiac)   tasted 1982
  Deep gold
  Rich and full of botrytis
  Full, sweet barley-sugar; long finish

de Ricaud (Loupiac) crème de tête   tasted 1978
  Deep gold
  Beautiful full nose
  Superb balance and weight, perfection, long full finish

d'Yquem   tasted 1956 (must weight 19.1°)
  This wine no longer as fine as in June 1954
  A little darkness now evident
  Bouquet still superb
  Full flavour

d'Yquem   tasted 1959
  Deep gold
  Beautiful nose
  Lovely nectar, very long finish

d'Yquem   tasted 1961
  Exquisite
  Very fine and full, not drying up
  No sign of *maderisation*
  One of the best bottles of d'Yquem taster has had

d'Yquem   tasted 1965
  Very deep colour
  Wonderful nose
  Wine still delicious and velvety at the finish with no signs of going dry
  Still a superb wine

d'Yquem   tasted 1975
  Deep gold
  Superb honeyed nose
  Full of fruit, long rich finish

d'Yquem   tasted 1988
  Deep gold
  Superb botrytis, rich marmalade
  Excellent concentration and balanced acidity
  Wonderful honey and rich finish

Filhot   tasted 1959
  Deep gold
  Good nose, slightly oxidised
  Luscious and very beautiful, long finish

Filhot   tasted 1981
  Deep gold
  Full, rich. Lovely long old finish

Gilette   tasted 1987
   Lovely rich Cognac colour
   Superbly rich, full botrytised nose
   Classic. Full, complex. Perfection.
   A great, great wine

Guiraud   tasted 1977
   Deep gold
   Full, luscious, complex, tight nose
   Full fruit, perfect balance, no signs
   of age

Guiraud   tasted 1982
   Dark gold/Cognac colour
   Creamy mint nose
   Huge wine. Sweet with plenty of
   fruit
   Slightly unbalanced finish

Lafaurie-Peyraguey   tasted 1977
   Brown/gold
   Full, luscious, lots of botrytis
   Full, fruity, lots of residual sugar,
   no signs of age

Lafaurie-Peyraguey   tasted 1982
   Brown/bronze
   Aristocratic, old Sauternes nose. A
   perfect wine
   Superb balance of acidity and
   sweetness
   Delicate, masses of fruit, great
   depth; long finish

Rabaud   tasted 1963
   Lovely golden colour
   Superb nose
   Very fine rich wine beginning to
   lose sugar

Rabaud   tasted 1965
   Colour now rather deep
   Good nose
   Wine very well preserved, rich and
   has kept its sugar

Rayne-Vigneau   tasted 1982
   Deep gold
   Full rich old nose
   Good extract in centre
   Slightly drying on finish

Rieussec   tasted 1986
   Deep gold
   Lovely marmalade botrytised nose
   Full and rich, delicate with great
   finesse

Voigny   tasted 1983
   Star-bright yellow
   Germanic-style nose
   Light style of Sauternes
   Well balanced, appley flavour
   Reminiscent of Loire or old
   German wine

1938
A moderate vintage. Picking started
28th September. Some still
acceptable but most have dried out.

de Malle   tasted 1982
   Mid/deep gold
   Light, delicate nose
   Quite rich and full; drying on
   finish

d'Yquem   tasted 1973 (must weight
17.6°)
   Deep gold
   Lightweight, slight signs of age
   Nice fruit but drying out

d'Yquem   tasted 1987
   Deep gold
   Light, complex botrytised nose
   Delicate and sweet; dry finish

Lafaurie-Peyraguey   tasted 1976
   Deep gold
   Maderisé nose, but still fruity
   Nice balance, but light on fruit

Rayne-Vigneau   tasted 1983
   Mid gold
   Honeyed nose
   Quite rich centre; drying finish

Rieussec   tasted 1984
   Deep gold and brown
   Light marmalade
   Losing fruit with dry finish

Suduiraut   tasted 1980
   Mid/deep gold
   Leafy, medicinal nose
   Lacks depth and finish

1939
An abundant vintage producing
fairly light wines. Picking started 2nd
October. Most wines are drying out
now.
Climens   tasted 1981
   Deep gold
   Lemony nose
   Drying out. Short finish

Coutet   tasted 1976
   Deep gold, sweetness on nose but
   beginnings of *maderisation* — rather
   coarse
   Maderisé but deep 'marmalade'
   effect
   Still interesting

d'Yquem   tasted 1977 (must weight
17.8°)
   Mid gold
   Full luscious nose, slight signs of
   age
   Fruity, full, slightly drying finish

d'Yquem   tasted 1987
   Deep gold
   Good marmalade, botrytised nose
   Medium rich, showing its age
   Fading on finish

Filhot   tasted 1977
   Fine old Sauternes nose, slight

signs of age
   Beginning to dry out but still a lot
   of fruit left

Guiraud   tasted 1984
   Deep gold and brown
   Fairly rich marmalade nose
   Quite full extract, drying on finish

Lafaurie-Peyraguey   tasted 1976
   Pale gold
   Oxidised but still there

La Tour-Blanche   tasted 1976
   Pale gold
   Youthful appearance
   Slight signs of age on the nose with
   a lemon smell and good fruit
   Good fruit on palate still holding,
   slightly dry finish

Loupiac (L.B. Nathaniel
Johnston)   tasted 1980
   Mid gold
   Light and sweet; good botrytis
   Quite rich, sweet, full finish

Marquis de La Rose (F.B.
Sichel)   tasted 1980
   Mid gold
   Light botrytised nose
   Light on fruit and finish

Rabaud   tasted 1978
   Deep gold
   Lovely rich botrytis nose
   Superb rich fruit
   Slightly drying on finish

Rayne-Vigneau   tasted 1973
   Mid gold
   Beautiful nose
   Still a lot of fruit and sugar, not
   drying on finish

1940
A fair vintage, but most have dried
out now. Picking started 26th
September.
Climens   tasted 1980
   Deep gold
   Light appley, leafy nose
   Drying out — short finish

Coutet   tasted 1975
   Mid/deep gold
   Lightweight fruity nose
   Still holding but dry finish

d'Yquem   tasted 1974
   Very deep brown–gold
   Rich, old heavy bouquet, beautiful
   deep 'essence of marmalade'
   flavour
   Wonderfully oily texture,
   developing a slightly 'burnt' taste
   Stays on and on in the mouth

d'Yquem   tasted 1977
   Deep gold

Superb rich nose, slight signs of
age
Good fruit on extract, good finish,
slightly drying

d'Yquem   tasted 1986
Mid gold with tinge of brown
Soft, honeyed nose
Rich and quite full. Slightly
medicinal finish

Guiraud   tasted 1985
Deep gold
Marmalade botrytised nose
Quite rich and complex; drying on
finish

1941
A mediocre vintage. Picking started
3rd October. Virtually all dried out
now.
d'Yquem   tasted 1975 (must weight
17.6°)
Deep gold
Nice delicate nose
Losing fruit, dry finish

Filhot   tasted 1987
Mid gold
Old honeyed nose
Still fruity and sweet; dry finish

Lafaurie-Peyraguey   tasted 1986
Mid gold
Leafy nose
Dried out

La Tour-Blanche   tasted 1973
Mid gold
Thin dry nose
Dried out, but pleasant

1942
A very good vintage. Picking started
19th September. The best wines are
still very fine.
Climens   tasted 1975
Mid gold
Perfect classic nose
Sweet, full bodied, not of great
depth, a lot of finesse

Coutet   tasted 1975
Darker gold
Acidity on nose
Slightly drier than the Climens
with more acidity

Coutet   tasted 1988
Deep gold and brown
Lovely rich complex delicate
honeyed nose
Full, beautifully round. Lots of
botrytis sweetness
Subtle with great finesse

d'Arche-Lafaurie   tasted 1978
Deep yellow gold, no signs of
browning

Fine powerful bouquet of honeyed
sémillon
Outstanding balance, will last for
years
d'Yquem   tasted 1976 (must weight
20.7°)
Deep gold
Beautiful fine rich nose
Superb depth and balance, long
fruity finish

d'Yquem   tasted 1988
Deep gold
Lovely marmalade botrytised nose
Full and rich. Superb depth

Guiraud   tasted 1984
Deep gold
Lovely marmalade botrytis nose
Full and rich; superb finish

Lafaurie-Peyraguey   tasted 1975
Mid gold
Lovely nose
Superb balance of sugar and fruit

Rabaud   tasted 1978
Old gold
Superb rich nose
Good depth
Slightly drying on finish

Rieussec   tasted 1986
Deep gold and brown
Honeyed, full of botrytis
Long and rich, beautifully full
finish

Suduiraut   tasted 1983
Deep gold and brown
Lovely delicate honeyed nose
Full, complex, delicate finish

1943
An excellent vintage. Picking started
19th September. Most of the best
wines are still beautiful, rich, with
very good extract and long finish.
Caillou   tasted 1977
Dark gold, good weight
Complex, light, fruity and acidity
Luscious, fruity and acidity, long
finish

Caillou crème de tête   tasted 1982
Deep gold
Lovely old botrytised nose
Rich, full. Excellent finish

Caillou crème de tête   tasted 1984
No change

Climens   tasted 1963
Lovely colour with no hint of
darkening
Was everything a Barsac should be
— very fruity and liquorous
Not too sweet or heavy

Climens   tasted 1978
Good rich golden colour
Fine delicate Barsac nose
A superb wine — well balanced
with no signs of age

Coutet   tasted 1964
Superb nose with depth
Perfect balance, long beautiful
finish

Coutet   tasted 1978
Deep gold
Good rich botrytis, slightly appley
Full rich enormous fruit, balance
and depth
Deep extract on finish

Doisy-Daëne   tasted 1977
Deep gold
Good full nose
Luscious, good balance and acidity
Youthful finish

Doisy-Daëne   tasted 1987
Deep gold
Lovely rich *crème brulée* nose
Still very full and rich in the mouth
Very slight dryness on finish

d'Yquem   tasted 1973 (must weight
21.5°)
Deep gold
Superb rich honeyed nose
Full rich excellent wine

d'Yquem   tasted 1987
Deep gold
Superb botrytis nose
Lovely rich fruit and extract
Very long finish

Guiraud   tasted 1975
Deep gold
Good full botrytis deep nose
Long, full, fruity, a lot of weight,
slight acidity on finish

Lafon   tasted 1980
Deep gold
Delicate botrytised nose
Lovely rich extract. Long, full
finish

La Tour-Blanche   tasted 1976
Deep gold
Full botrytis nose and slight acidity
Full palate, slight dryness on finish
— superb bottle

Laurette (Ste-Croix-du-Mont)   tasted
1976
Mid gold
Light, delicate, a lot of finesse,
apricot nose
Very good balance, long fruity
finish

Rayne-Vigneau   tasted 1980
Deep gold

Marmalade nose
Rich centre; drying on finish

Rieussec   tasted 1954
Nice nose
Lacks fruit and body

Rieussec   tasted 1981
Deep gold and brown
Superb honeyed rich full nose
Classic in every way. Real perfection
Long, rich, full; beautiful

Suduiraut   tasted 1963
Lovely light colour, fine nose
Wine delicate with plenty of sugar
Very fine
At its best

1944

A mediocre vintage with some exceptions. Picking started 27th September. Most wines are now dried out.
d'Yquem   tasted 1974 (must weight 20.7°)
Deep gold
Nice fruity nose, slight signs of age
Still holding, drying finish

d'Yquem   tasted 1986
Deep gold and brown
Quite rich, old honeyed nose
Fairly full, drying on finish with acidity showing through

Lafaurie-Peyraguey   tasted 1970
Deep gold
Pleasant nose
Light, thin on fruit but pleasant

La Tour-Blanche   tasted 1975
Brown
Still quite sweet, classic style, medium weight

Rayne-Vigneau   tasted 1986
Deep gold
Lightweight, sweet nose
Still quite rich
Drying on finish

1945

A superb vintage, but crop reduced owing to frost on 2nd May. Picking started 13th September. Most of the best wines are still magnificent and will last for years.
Camperos   tasted 1985
Lemon/gold
Sweet lemony nose
Delightful; fairly sweet, lemon marmalade
Complex with very long finish

Climens   tasted 1975
Mid gold
Superb rich nose, a lot of weight
Lovely rich wine full of fruit

Coutet   tasted 1977
Mid gold
A lot of finesse, slight signs of age
Nice balance, but drying on finish

de Ricaud (Loupiac)   tasted 1986
Deep gold
Full, rich honeyed nose
Lovely balance
Lots of fruit and botrytis. Long finish

Doisy-Daëne   tasted 1982
Mid/deep gold
Sweet, fairly rich nose
Good balance. Delicate finish

d'Yquem   tasted 1976 (must weight 22.7°)
Mid gold
Superb, slightly hot, a lot of character
Full, luscious, fruity, enormous fruity finish

d'Yquem   tasted 1988
Deep gold
Superbly rich marmalade nose
Excellent concentration of botrytis
Perfection in all respects

Filhot   tasted 1980
Mid/deep gold
Complex honeyed nose
Delicate balance. Rich finish

Guiraud   tasted 1974
Mid gold/browning
Superb rich botrytis nose
Full of fruit, excellent balance

Haut-Sauternes (L.B. Hankey Bannister)   tasted 1980
Old gold
Rich, full nose
Good extract; long finish

Lafaurie-Peyraguey   tasted 1977
Mid gold
Delicate nose with perfect balance
Long, luscious, perfect balance, long finish — years to go

La Tour-Blanche   tasted 1984
Mid/deep gold
Good honeyed nose
Medium weight on palate. Fairly rich finish

Loupiac (F.B. Calvert)   tasted 1981
Deep gold
Lovely rich honeyed nose
Lots of rich fruit; long finish

Rabaud   tasted 1984
Deep gold
Light, sweet nose
Lacks the weight of a 1945; shortish finish

Rayne-Vigneau   tasted 1976
Mid/deep gold

Good rich nose, slight signs of age
Not as full as would be expected from a Sauternes of this year, but nice fruity finish

Rieussec   tasted 1983
Deep gold
Lovely marmalade botrytised nose
Lots of richness. Long finish

Sauternes (L.B. Rosenheim et Fils)   tasted 1980
Mid gold
Lovely rich botrytised nose
Long, full finish

Suduiraut   tasted 1986
Deep gold
Lovely honeyed nose
Full and rich; long finish

Voigny   tasted 1985
Bronze gold
Fresh, good lemony nose
Light style. Well preserved
Rich marmalade complex
Slightly drying and tart on finish

1946

A moderate vintage. Picking started 30th September. Most wines had dried out by the 1970s.
Coutet   tasted 1984
Mid gold
Light, leafy nose
Quite sweet, short finish

d'Yquem   tasted 1972 (must weight 18.2°)
Deep gold/brown
Dryish nose still quite fruity
Just holding on, dry finish

d'Yquem   tasted 1986
Deep gold and brown
Quite sweet, leafy nose
Fairly rich centre. Dry finish

Guiraud   tasted 1983
Deep gold
Light dry nose
Lacks fruit and finish

Lafaurie-Peyraguey   tasted 1987
Mid gold
Complex, leafy nose
Quite dry with sweet centre

1947

A very hot summer producing wines very rich in extract. Picking started 19th September. By the 1970s Château d'Yquem and Château Climens quite outstanding but some have a slightly roasted after-taste, perhaps a legacy of the extreme heat.
Broustet   tasted 1978
Deep amber/gold

Lovely botrytis acidity, earthy
moistness
Superb depth, slightly burnt finish
and drying slightly and acidity

Caillou crème de tête   tasted 1982
Mid–deep gold
Delicate with superb rich nose of
barley-sugar
Great finesse. No signs of age
Perfect balance. A full, botrytised
finish

Caillou crème de tête   tasted 1987
No change

Climens   tasted 1962
Everything a fine Barsac should be
Light clear colour
Beautiful fragrant bouquet
Wine delicate and fresh
Perfect balance and sweetness

Climens   tasted 1977
Pale gold
Full fruity nose
Perfect balance, a great wine, will
last for years

Coutet   tasted 1975
Deep gold
Hot roasted nose and slight acidity
Fruit, deep with burnt after-taste
and acidity

Coutet (magnum)   tasted 1976
Deep gold
Very perfumed nose
Sweet not cloying

Coutet   tasted 1987
Mid gold
Good rich botrytised nose
Lovely balanced finish

Coutet (L.B. Justerini &
Brooks)   tasted 1982
Mid/deep gold with brown
Marmalade nose
Lovely and rich, full centre
Slightly clumsy on finish

Doisy-Védrines   tasted 1985
Mid gold
Light delicate nose
Good, rich fruit and balanced
acidity

d'Yquem   tasted 1966 (must weight
22.5°)
Full golden colour
Glorious, soft, rich, fruity bouquet
Exquisite wine in superb condition
Very soft and unctuous without
the hardness which often comes
with age
One of the best bottles of d'Yquem
the taster has had

d'Yquem   tasted 1974
Mid gold

Full rich honeyed nose
Superb balance, rich fruity finish

d'Yquem   tasted 1988
Deep gold
Full rich roasted botrytised
marmalade nose
Lovely rich balance and extract
Long finish

Filhot   tasted 1959
Pale yellow
Lovely nose
Good fruit and sugar, rather dry
underneath, seems unbalanced

Filhot   tasted 1978
Deep gold, musty nose with
acidity
Drying out, lacks depth, herby
finish

Guiraud   tasted 1986
Deep gold
Superb rich marmalade and
botrytised nose
Excellent balance
Long concentrated finish

Lafaurie-Peyraguey   tasted 1977
Mid gold
Slightly burnt, full, fruity
Slightly roasted, good fruit and
acidity, slightly unbalanced finish

Lafaurie-Peyraguey   tasted 1986
Orange brown
Orange-peel nose
Mature with weight
Losing fruit, dry finish

Rieussec   tasted 1983
Deep gold
Lovely rich botrytised nose
Full of extract; long finish

Roumieu   tasted 1976
Deep gold
Superb richness, but drying finish

Suduiraut   tasted 1985
Mid/deep gold
Good botrytis, marmalade nose
Full and rich; lovely finish

1948

A good vintage. Picking started 28th
September. Lighter in extract than
'47 or '49, but still holding well.

Cantegril   tasted 1978
Mid gold
Light and acidity although superb
fruit underneath
Full, lightweight but long fruity
finish

Coutet   tasted 1985
Mid/deep gold
Lovely balanced botrytised nose
Light but delicate

de Myrat   tasted 1981
Mid gold
Lightweight, appley nose
Good fruit and centre, slightly
drying on finish

Doisy-Védrines   tasted 1982
Mid gold
Light, sweet nose
Lacks centre; drying finish

d'Yquem   tasted 1973 (must weight
19,9°)
Deep gold
Fat, lots of fruit
Perfection

d'Yquem   tasted 1978
Deep gold
Deep, rich, and slight acidity,
peachy honey
Full, rich; luscious full finish and
slight acidity

d'Yquem   tasted 1988
Mid gold
Lovely delicate botrytised nose
Well balanced and delicate finesse

Filhot   tasted 1953
Taste of oranges
Nice and round, light centre

Guiraud   tasted 1975
Deep gold
Fine rich nose
Delicious full-bodied nose
Fruity, big wine, long finish

Rabaud   tasted 1984
Deep gold
Good rich fruit and honeyed,
botrytised nose
Lovely, full. Lots of extract. Long
finish

Rieussec   tasted 1978
Mid gold
Fragrant, complex, light nose
Good fruit and sweetness drying
out slightly on finish

Rieussec   tasted 1979
Bronze
Slightly yeasty nose
Quite a big wine
Very rich, well balanced. Good
finish

1949

A superb vintage. Picking started
27th September. Most were
magnificent wines in the 1970s and
Château d'Yquem could develop still
further. Perhaps the finest post-War
vintage.

Brousset   tasted 1977
Mid gold
Good tight creamy nose
Good fruit and balance, light finish

Caillou   tasted 1980
    Deep, Cognac colour
    Ripe apples and showing signs of
    ageing
    Still quite rich; slightly drying on
    finish

Climens   tasted 1986
    Mid gold
    Lovely rich appley nose
    Full rich, superb extract. Long
    finish

Coutet   tasted 1952
    Very mellow, round, clean

Coutet   tasted 1953
    Delicate
    Lacks depth of balance

Coutet   tasted 1964
    Pale gold
    Delicious soft fruit, perfect balance
    Sweet but not cloying

Coutet   tasted 1964
    Lovely pale gold colour
    Very fine bouquet
    Wine just beginning to lose its
    sugar
    Extremely good, not too heavy or
    sweet, beautifully balanced

Coutet   tasted 1965
    Good colour
    Fresh clean nose
    The wine is very delicate and
    fruity, perhaps sugar is beginning
    to slip away

Coutet   tasted 1978
    Deep gold
    Full, big and a lot of botrytis, slight
    spirit on nose
    Very big, a lot of fruit and tannin,
    hot finish and alcoholic

Coutet   tasted 1982
    Deep gold
    Rich, delicate, slight burnt-sugar
    nose
    Full, rich superb long finish

d'Arche   tasted 1980
    Deep gold and brown
    Quite rich honey and barley-sugar
    Very rich in the mouth, hot and
    high alcohol
    Barley-sugar finish with acidity
    and burnt-sugar after-taste

d'Arche   tasted 1984
    Deep gold and brown
    Quite rich barley-sugar
    Lovely hot fruit, good burnt-sugar
    finish

de Malle   tasted 1984
    Deep gold and brown
    Quite rich barley-sugar, slightly
    medicinal

Fairly rich, hot, high alcohol;
    showing age on finish

Doisy-Daëne   tasted 1985
    Mid gold
    Lovely appley delicate nose
    Good balance and finish

d'Yquem   tasted 1964 (must weight
20.8°)
    Fine nose
    Full, very delicious with huge fruit
    and little acidity to balance

d'Yquem   tasted 1978
    Deep gold
    Deep complex nose with
    enormous depth of quality
    Full, tight, luscious, huge, closed,
    long way to go

d'Yquem   tasted 1987
    Deep gold
    Superbly rich botrytised,
    marmalade nose
    Full, superb extract and
    concentration
    Long, rich, perfect balance
    Excellent

Filhot   tasted 1981
    Very deep and brown
    Good rich honeyed barley-sugar
    Superbly rich, full and very long,
    luscious finish

*Gilette Grand Réserve crème de
tête*   tasted 1987
    Very deep gold and brown
    Lovely rich, old botrytised nose
    Crème brulée. Thick centre
    Slightly drying on finish which is
    attractive for such a hot year

Guiraud   tasted 1986
    Deep gold and brown
    Rich, burnt deep nose
    Quite rich and sweet; slightly
    short, drying finish

Lafaurie-Peyraguey   tasted 1985
    Very deep Cognac colour
    Light, delicate and honeyed
    Remarkably fresh. Superb balance

Le Mayne (*Cérons*)   tasted 1952
    Very smooth and clean nose
    Excellent balance

Rabaud   tasted 1975
    Deep gold
    Rich nose
    Lovely balance, delightful, fully
    developed

Rabaud   tasted 1979
    Deep Cognac colour
    Lovely fresh rich delicate barley-
    sugar
    Superb balance. Rich. Excellent
    long finish
    A stunning wine

Rabaud   tasted 1987
    Deep gold
    Superb rich barley-sugar and lots
    of botrytis
    No signs of age. Full, rich, luscious
    Perfection. Long chewy finish

Raymond-Lafon   tasted 1986
    Deep gold and brown
    Nice, rich burnt honeyed nose
    Good balance, slightly drying on
    finish

Rayne-Vigneau   tasted 1963
    Wonderful liquid-gold colour
    Big full nose
    A big wine, very robust
    Fruity but perhaps at its best
    Rather full blown

Rieussec   tasted 1952
    Beautiful nose
    Very smooth, light on fruit

Rieussec   tasted 1965
    Lovely yellow/gold colour with
    greenish tinge
    Beautiful delicate nose
    The wine has great finesse and
    superb savour
    In prime condition

Rieussec   tasted 1985
    Deep gold
    Lovely deep botrytis nose
    Full, complex. Well balanced

Suduiraut   tasted 1980
    Deep gold
    Rich marmalade
    Very full, hot; beginning to dry on
    finish

Suduiraut   tasted 1982
    Deep gold
    Lovely light delicate nose
    Delicious, rich centre
    Slightly drying on finish

1950
A good vintage. Picking started 23rd
September. Rather underrated, the
wines have lasted quite well but
many have started to dry out now.
Climens   tasted 1981
    Cognac brown
    Lovely old rich barley-sugar
    Superbly full, lovely balance
    Very slightly drying on finish

Coutet   tasted 1953
    Full nose
    Lovely balance of sugar and fruit
    Nectar!

Coutet   tasted 1966
    Light colour, attractive fresh
    bouquet
    Wine amazingly light and youthful

Quite belies its age
A fine example of a light year with fruit and freshness

Coutet   tasted 1976 (L. B. Sichel)
Mid gold
Slightly high acidity and so₂ but nice fruit
Lightweight but nice finish, generally lacks centre

d'Arche-Lafaurie   tasted 1953
Pleasant but lacks balance
Nice finish

d'Yquem   tasted 1967 (must weight 24.4°)
Deep gold
Delicate luscious nose
Full fruity long finish, slightly dry finish

d'Yquem   tasted 1977
Deep gold
Delicate luscious nose, full, fruity, long finish, slightly dry finish

d'Yquem   tasted 1987
Deep gold
Full, rich botrytised nose. Slightly leafy
Good firm centre; slightly fading on finish

Guiraud   tasted 1954
Lovely nose
Round and smooth, good balance and finish

Guiraud   tasted 1984
Deep gold
Good rich botrytised nose
Lovely balance. Fine finish

Lafaurie-Peyraguey   tasted 1976
Mid gold
Pleasant nose, not full
Fairly rich light centre, good finish

Rieussec   tasted 1954
Nice, quite big and round on nose
Short finish, nice fruit

Rieussec   tasted 1986
Deep gold
Sweet rich nose
Full-bodied centre; lightish finish

1951
A poor vintage. Picking started 9th October. Rarely seen.
Filhot   tasted 1986
Mid gold
Sweet, lightweight nose
Still fruity and sweet; drying a lot on finish

Rayne-Vigneau   tasted 1984
Deep gold

Crème brulée nose
Good depth of fruit. Dry finish

Rieussec   tasted 1953
Quite pleasant but thin

1952
A variable vintage producing some good wines. Picking started 17th September. No d'Yquem (ruined by hail).
Climens   tasted 1975
Full, round, subtle after-taste

Climens   tasted 1976
Deep gold
Old decaying nose
Lost fruit, dried out, high acidity on finish

Climens   tasted 1985
Mid gold
Light, rich sweet nose
Losing fruit but pleasant, sweet finish

Coutet   tasted 1984
Mid gold
Light, dry nose
Losing fruit. Short finish

de Rolland   tasted 1988
Deep gold and orange
Light, rich honeyed nose
Good depth of fruit and extract in centre but finishes short

Doisy-Védrines   tasted 1986
Mid gold
Sweet full nose
Good rich centre; lighter on finish

Guiraud   tasted 1976
Deep gold
Fruity but quite high acidity, slight signs of age
Drying, but still there

1953
A good year. Picking started 1st October. Most of the wines are holding well.
Climens   tasted 1976
Gold classic colour, full, luscious apple nose, full well-balanced long finish

Climens   tasted 1984
Mid gold
Lovely rich complex botrytised nose
Full, rich; long finish

Coutet   tasted 1978
Pale yellow, good fresh nose and acidity
Superb balance of sugar and fruit

Doisy-Daëne   tasted 1963
Fine, light colour

Very elegant bouquet
Wine in fine condition but some years off its best with a delicious freshness of savour

Doisy-Daëne   tasted 1965
Lovely light colour
Superb honey nose
The wine has a lovely fruity richness but at the same time is light
A truly fine Barsac of great finesse

Doisy-Daëne   tasted 1984
Very deep gold and brown
Rich, deep, fully botrytised
Thick in extract. Well balanced finish

d'Yquem   tasted 1969 (must weight 23°)
Full golden colour
Rich full nose, very liquorous
Good balance
Very fresh but probably at its best

d'Yquem   tasted 1980
Deep gold
Lovely rich barley-sugar
Very slightly fading with acidity showing through (?bottle)
Good balanced finish

d'Yquem   tasted 1988
Much richer with good extract

Filhot   tasted 1976
Mid gold
Full good fruity nose
Lightweight in mouth but fruity and long luscious finish

Filhot   tasted 1988
Deep gold and brown
Barley-sugar nose. Good botrytis
Still quite rich with lovely balance; slightly drying on finish

Gilette crème de tête (bottled 1974)   tasted 1987
Pale/mid gold with hint of brown
Lovely delicate melon/marmalade nose
Very thick in the mouth with lovely delicacy
Long, full, superb balance
A wine of great finesse and complexity

Guiraud   tasted 1954
Not fruity or big but quite round and mellow

Lafaurie-Peyraguey   tasted 1976
Mid gold
Lovely rich nose
Full and well balanced

Rieussec   tasted 1954
Nice nose, lacks depth of fruit and body

Rieussec   tasted 1972
Pleasing, soft without great depth

Rieussec   tasted 1979
Mid yellow
Strong, dryish nose
Not a very sweet wine. Lemony
flavour
Full finish

1954
A poor year largely ruined by frost.
Picking started 10th October. Most
wines thin and acidic.
Coutet   tasted 1983
Mid gold
Quite rich, appley nose
Still rich with dry finish

d'Yquem   tasted 1978
Dark gold
Nice, soft, honeyed with botrytis

d'Yquem   tasted 1986
Deep gold
Full blown, rich, botrytised nose
Rich palate in centre; slightly
drying on finish

Lafaurie-Peyraguey   tasted 1986
Deep gold
Leafy, musty nose
Dry with high acidity

1955
A fine vintage. Picking started 29th
September. Producing beautiful
wines of great depth and finesse
many of which had just started to dry
out by the late 1970s.
Climens   tasted 1965
Beautifully rich and fruity on nose
and palate, smooth and mellow.

Climens   tasted 1976
Mid gold
Superb apple nose
Big, full, luscious; perfect finish

Climens   tasted 1978
Mid gold
Soft, luscious; disappointing palate
Slightly dry finish

Coutet   tasted 1969
Good deep colour
Depth of fruit and sugar on nose
Marked glycerine in texture, long
finish

Coutet   tasted 1978
Deep gold
Great depth and delicate with
finesse, hidden fruit
Tannin and acidity, great
character, long finish
Needs two hours decanting

Doisy-Védrines   tasted 1978
Mid pale gold, lightweight nose

Signs of sulphur and lacking in
depth
Lacks body and weight, thin and
watery finish, no signs of age

d'Yquem   tasted 1966 (must weight
20.5°)
Golden
Huge powerful nose
Truly exquisite

d'Yquem   tasted 1969
Classic rich Sauternes,
characteristic on nose and palate
with very distinctive oiliness of
texture

d'Yquem   tasted 1976
Deep gold
Great sweetness, drying on finish

d'Yquem   tasted 1980
Deep gold
Good rich botrytised marmalade
nose
Rich and full, slightly drying on
finish

d'Yquem   tasted 1987
No change

Filhot   tasted 1987
Mid gold
Nice rich sweet nose
Fairly rich centre with drying
finish

Gilette crème de tête (bottled
1979)   tasted 1987
Mid/deep gold
Lovely delicate balance, rich with
finesse
Superbly delicate. Still quite
youthful
Lovely melon-tasting finish

Guiraud   tasted 1988
Mid/deep gold
Medicinal, herby nose
Fairly rich, but leafy undertones

Lafaurie-Peyraguey   tasted 1976
Mid gold
Fairly thin
Lacks depth

Lafaurie-Peyraguey   tasted 1987
Mid gold
Fairly sweet, but lacks
concentration
Quite full, but falls short

Rabaud-Promis   tasted 1978
Deep gold
Signs of oxidation on nose
Drying out but still a lot of fruit
and sugar

Rayne-Vigneau   tasted 1986
Mid gold
Sweet but light
Lacks depth. Drying on finish

Rieussec   tasted 1983
Deep gold
Good rich nose
Not as full on palate. Light finish

Suduiraut   tasted 1981
Mid gold
Good rich botrytised nose
Full-bodied, lovely rich centre and
finish

1956
A very poor vintage with crop
devastated by frost in February.
Picking started 16th October. Wine
thin and acidic.
d'Yquem   tasted 1976 (must weight
19.5°)
Dark lemon yellow
Dull nose
Dryish wine, woody and acidic.
Not a good wine

d'Yquem   tasted 1988
Deep gold with tinge of
brownness
Light marmalade nose
Quite full in centre, fading slightly
on finish

Filhot   tasted 1984
Mid gold
Quite sweet barley-sugar nose
Pleasant and fruity; dry finish

Rayne-Vigneau   tasted 1986
Deep gold
Leafy acidic nose
Dry with high acidity

1957
Small crop producing wines of
variable quality some of which are
still attractive. Picking started 3rd
October.
Coutet   tasted 1984
Mid gold
Light, sweet lemony nose
Good fruit, light finish

Doisy-Daëne   tasted 1982
Pale/mid gold
Appley sweet nose
No great depth; light finish

d'Yquem   tasted 1974 (must weight
19°)
Deep gold
Nice light fruity nose
Still a lot of fruit, high acidity on
finish

d'Yquem   tasted 1980
Mid/deep gold
Rich barley-sugar nose
Full, soft, rich finish with balanced
acidity

d'Yquem   tasted 1984
Mid gold

Deep complex marmalade nose
Great depth, rich full finish

Lafaurie-Peyraguey   tasted 1985
Mid gold
Medicinal nose
Light with short finish

Liot (L.B.)   tasted 1976
Mid gold
Slightly unclean nose, not a lot of fruit
Light, lacks depth on finish

Rieussec   tasted 1965
Full and fruity on nose and palate with hint of linseed oil, good acidity and balance

Suduiraut   tasted 1963
Very light in colour
Very fine bouquet
Distinctive, delicate flavour
A tone of great refinement and balance

Suduiraut   tasted 1986
Mid gold
Rich, good nose
Quite full; lovely balance

1958

Another small crop producing some good rich wines. Some were holding well in the 1970s, a few are beginning to dry out. Picking started 7th October.

Climens   tasted 1984
Pale gold
Lightweight, flowery nose
Not of great depth; short finish

Coutet   tasted 1968
Deeper gold
Nice appley nose
Nice fruit, slight tannin and acidity

Coutet   tasted 1976
Drying out now, firm with full body

Coutet   tasted 1982
Mid gold
Light, leafy nose
Drying with short finish

Doisy-Védrines   tasted 1984
Deep/mid gold
Honeyed, leafy nose
Light with sweet finish

d'Yquem   tasted 1974 (must weight 19.7°)
Fine, full, well balanced

d'Yquem   tasted 1978
Deep gold
Huge scent, slight *maderisé* background

Exquisite balance of acidity, sugar and fruit

d'Yquem   tasted 1987
Deep gold
Lovely marmalade, botrytised nose
Full, rich. Well balanced finish

Guiraud   tasted 1975
Mid/deep gold
Nice honeyed nose
Light but nice fruit, slight acidity on finish

Rieussec   tasted 1986
Mid gold
Medicinal sweet nose
Quite rich in the centre with short finish

Suduiraut   tasted 1962
More colour and richness than the 1957
Very fine, elegant fruity nose
Rich but finely balanced
Typical Suduiraut flavour
Should continue to develop for some time

Suduiraut   tasted 1967
Fine mature colour and nose
The wine has a lovely flavour
Very fruity but not too heavy
Probably about at its best

Suduiraut   tasted 1978
Gold
Good, sweet, rich nose
Very full, lots of extract
Slightly drying on finish

Suduiraut   tasted 1986
No change

1959

A third consecutive small crop which produced some beautiful rich wines a few of which had just started to dry out in the late 1970s. Picking started 21st September.

Broustet   tasted 1983
Mid gold
Lovely, rich delicate nose
Sweet, good extract; long finish

Caillou crème de tête   tasted 1982
Deep gold
Light, delicate, appley nose
Good fruit and depth with lovely botrytised nose

Caillou crème de tête   tasted 1987
Very deep gold
Lovely rich honeyed open nose — hot.
Very full, superb extract; long finish

Climens   tasted 1978
Mid gold
Lovely rich nose
Good fruit, lovely balance and finish

Climens   tasted 1987
Mid/deep gold
Lovely rich, appley/peachy nose
Full and rich. Superb extract and finish

Coutet   tasted 1977
Mid gold
Good rich nose with slight signs of age
Drying out, losing fruit fast, dry finish

Coutet   tasted 1986
Mid/deep gold
Complex honeyed nose
Good fruit and concentration
Balanced acidity on finish

d'Yquem   tasted 1977
Mid gold
Superb delicate balance and finesse
Beautiful balance and finesse on nose
Perfect balance, very slight acidity, almost almond finish

d'Yquem   tasted 1980
Mid gold
Lovely rich, marmalade nose
Very full, hot, rich, superb fruit and balance

d'Yquem   tasted 1986
No change

d'Yquem   tasted 1988
No change

Gilette crème de tête (bottled 1979)   tasted 1987
Very deep gold
Very rich concentrated hot nose
Lovely, rich melon/marmalade taste
A superb wine

Guiraud   tasted 1976
Pale gold, good solid honeyed nose, lacks depth and centre, expected more on the palate than the nose suggested

Guiraud   tasted 1978
Mid gold
Light, complex and botrytised, honeyed
Hottish, drying out on finish, losing its fruit

Guiraud   tasted 1985
Mid/deep gold
Honeyed nose, slightly medicinal
Good rich fruit in centre, fades on finish

Lafaurie-Peyraguey   tasted 1976
  Deep gold
  Lovely rich nose
  Full, well balanced

Lafaurie-Peyraguey (half bottles, L.B.
Percy Fox)   tasted 1978
  Deep gold
  Good depth and sweetness and
  nutty on nose
  Good balance and weight, depth
  and nutty flavour, long finish

Lafaurie-Peyraguey   tasted 1987
  Mid gold
  Lovely rich marmalade nose
  Superb fruit and richness. Long
  finish

Rieussec   tasted 1978
  Mid gold, nice botrytis nose,
  slightly lemony depth and hot
  extract, good weight and body
  No sign of fading, fresh finish

Rieussec   tasted 1984
  Mid gold
  Superbly rich botrytised nose
  Lovely, full of fruit; long finish

Suduiraut   tasted 1978
  Deep gold
  Rich honeyed, marmalade nose
  Good depth and weight
  Hot finish

Suduiraut   tasted 1988
  Deep gold and pale Cognac brown
  Hot, rich, lovely depth of fruit
  with botrytis
  Complex, delicate finish. Great
  finesse and balance

1960
A big crop producing largely
undistinguished wine. Picking
started 9th September.
Climens   tasted 1985
  Mid gold
  Quite appley with botrytis
  Good fruit and richness; dry finish
d'Yquem   tasted 1974
  Nice fruit and acidity, not
  combined yet
d'Yquem   tasted 1978
  Mid gold
  Good rich nose, very good balance
  and finish
d'Yquem   tasted 1981
  Bright Cognac colour
  Sweet lemon, spirity nose
  Light and mature, slightly losing
  fruit. Appears to be older (maybe
  an odd bottle)
d'Yquem   tasted 1986
  Mid/deep gold
  Rich marmalade nose

Good rich fruit, nicely balanced
finish
Guiraud   tasted 1986
  Mid gold
  Light lemony nose
  Lacks depth and concentration
Rieussec   tasted 1986
  Deep gold
  Good rich fruit
  Lovely complex wine; drying on
  finish

1961
A small harvest. Picking started 19th
September. Not a classic vintage but
it produced good wines, if somewhat
lightweight in style and lacking in
extract.
Climens   tasted 1976
  Mid gold, solid nose, hint of
  mustiness
  Quite light with a woody taste
  underneath — short finish

Climens   tasted 1985
  Mid gold
  Slightly leafy nose
  Light on centre and finish

Coutet   tasted 1971
  Light and slightly green tinge
  Good appley nose
  Soft but full, slight tannin

Coutet (magnum)   tasted 1972
  Pale gold
  Good appley nose
  Big appley taste, long finish

Coutet   tasted 1978
  Pale gold, light eggy yeasty nose,
  fairly full centre, light finish

Coutet   tasted 1982
  Mid gold
  Light eggy nose
  Lightweight

Doisy-Védrines   tasted 1981
  Pale/mid gold
  Light, sweet nose
  Lacks body and finish

d'Yquem   tasted 1974 (must weight
17.6°)
  Beautiful
  Delicate but slightly unbalanced

d'Yquem   tasted 1978
  Dark gold
  Tight, acidity and botrytis,
  slightly earthy
  Tight, slightly burnt, light, not
  quite ready but lightweight

d'Yquem   tasted 1987
  Deep gold
  Slightly earthy, sweet nose
  Nicely balanced fruit
  Lightweight, drying on finish

Gilette crème de tête (bottled
1979)   tasted 1987
  Deep gold
  Lovely rich concentrated
  marmalade nose
  Great depth and extract;
  concentrated finish

Gravas   tasted 1987
  Very deep gold and brown
  Lovely rich botrytis
  Thick, rich mouthful

Guiraud   tasted 1978
  Deep gold, well balanced with
  good extract
  Good fruit and balance. Slight
  acidity on finish
  One of the better 1961s

Guiraud   tasted 1985
  Deep gold
  Good rich nose with botrytis
  Good depth of extract; long finish

Lafaurie-Peyraguey   tasted 1976
  Mid gold
  Good nose
  Full and fruity, pleasant finish

Lafaurie-Peyraguey   tasted 1980
  Mid gold
  Light, sweet nose
  Quite good fruit and finish

Rieussec   tasted 1972
  Mid gold
  Nice balanced nose
  Good fruit, nice balance, light
  finish

Rieussec   tasted 1984
  Mid gold
  Light honeyed nose
  Quite sweet, light finish

Roumieu-Lacoste   tasted 1975
  Mid gold
  Light, slight honeyed nose
  Lacks finesse and balance

Sigalas-Rabaud   tasted 1973
  Mid gold
  Lovely fruity nose
  Good fruit nice balance, light
  finish

1962
A big crop and very fine quality.
Picking started 1st October. Most
probably near their best in the late
1970s but the finest will hold for
many years.
Caillou   tasted 1982
  Deep gold
  Good botrytised, appley nose
  Well balanced; lovely rich finish

Caillou   tasted 1985
No change

Climens   tasted 1969
Characteristic Barsac nose, darkish barley-sugar flavour, good extract

Climens   tasted 1975
Mid gold
Superb fruit, apple nose
Full, well balanced, long perfect finish

Climens   tasted 1978
Still perfection

Climens   tasted 1981
Pale/mid gold
Good appley complex botrytis nose
Great finesse, very rich centre, beginning to dry on finish

Climens   tasted 1988
No change

Coutet   tasted 1976
Mid gold
Very big appley nose
Long, fully open and developed, at its peak
Superb finish

Coutet   tasted 1978
Mid/deep gold
Strong smell of almonds
Very full, luscious, but just turning

Coutet   tasted 1988
Mid/deep gold
Lemon marmalade nose
Quite rich centre, slightly drying on finish

de Malle   tasted 1966
Very perfumed and a very distinct savour
Light and fruity
Most attractive wine

de Malle   tasted 1984
Pale gold
Eggy, lightweight nose
Lacks depth, centre and finish

Doisy-Daëne   tasted 1963
Interesting because this is the first vintage to be made wholly under a new method of vinification, *méthode carbonique*
Wine very promising, very sweet and fruity but not heavy

Doisy-Daëne   tasted 1969
More powerful than '61 and extremely unctuous on the nose
A very fine wine
Beautiful flavour, fuller and broader than '61

Doisy-Daëne   tasted 1969
Fine nose — hint of limes, good flavour, not a heavyweight but great charm

Doisy-Daëne   tasted 1976
Mid gold
Good, luscious, slight acidity and appley
Good balance, heavyweight, fairly short finish
Acidity on finish

Doisy-Daëne   tasted 1977
Markedly finer and richer than in 1969

Doisy-Védrines   tasted 1972
Deep gold, nice nose with hint of marmalade, taste as nose, good texture and finish

Doisy-Védrines   tasted 1985
Deep gold
Good fruity, rich, well balanced nose
Good rich fruit; long finish

d'Yquem   tasted 1966 (must weight 18.5°)
Light in colour
Full unctuous bouquet
Wine very rich but without heaviness
Soft and delicate finish

d'Yquem   tasted 1969
Marvellously deep and full nose and flavour, markedly oily texture

d'Yquem   tasted 1974
Sweet and direct nose
Soft, well balanced, more sugar than fruit at present

d'Yquem   tasted 1976
Mid gold
Treacle, light closed
Good balance closed, questionable balance on finish

d'Yquem   tasted 1977
Lots of character and backbone, hasn't really opened out yet
Will be great

d'Yquem   tasted 1977
Mid gold
Tight closed, good depth
Good balance and weight, tannin and acidity but an unpleasant overtaste almost earthy, tangy

d'Yquem   tasted 1988
Mid/deep gold
Honeyed, leafy nose
Fairly light, medicinal grassy flavour
Lightweight finish

Guiraud   tasted 1971
Pale gold
Perfect balance

Guiraud   tasted 1972
Mid gold
Soft full nose
Big fruit, luscious long beautiful finish

Guiraud   tasted 1975
Deep colour, classic bouquet, good flavour and texture

Guiraud   tasted 1980
Deep gold
Superb richness; complex nose
Rich with great finesse

Guiraud   tasted 1984
Pale gold
Light, complex nose with botrytis
Good fruit in centre; long finish

Pajot   tasted 1978
Mid gold
Light, delicate and has finesse
Slight tannin, delicate, light centre, good finish

Petit-Mayne   tasted 1987
Deep gold
Very deep and rich, lots of botrytis
Pure barley-sugar
Superbly rich. Elegant finish

Rayne-Vigneau   tasted 1984
Mid gold
Light, sweet nose
Quite rich but lightweight finish

Rieussec   tasted 1972
Attractive honeyed nose, good flavour
Good acidity balance
Well shaped and fine finish

Rieussec   tasted 1976
Pale gold
Closed nose almost sharp
Very big future but not ready yet

Rieussec   tasted 1983
Deep gold
Good rich honeyed nose
Quite full and rich in centre and finish

Suduiraut   tasted 1963
A remarkable wine of amazing richness
Magnificent savour
Should have great future

Suduiraut   tasted 1967
A very big wine
Still a little raw, needs more time

Suduiraut   tasted 1983
Mid gold
Marmalade, rich and acidity
Full, lovely honeyed finish

Suduiraut   tasted 1987
   No change

1963

A poor vintage producing thin,
acidic wines. Picking started 3rd
October.
d'Yquem   tasted 1972
   Very deep gold/brown
   Acidic, unattractive nose
   Light, thin, acidic, poor fruit, thin
   short finish

d'Yquem   tasted 1986
   Deep brown
   Spicy, acidic nose
   Very light on fruit, thin and high
   acidity
   Some sweetness on the finish
   Untypical d'Yquem style

Rayne-Vigneau   tasted 1985
   Deep gold
   Grassy medicinal nose
   Dry and acidic

1964

A mediocre vintage which produced
a few attractive wines. Picking
started 2nd September. No d'Yquem
made. No Filhot made.
Caillou   tasted 1977
   Mid gold
   Fresh, lemony, slightly stony
   Good weight and balance, fresh
   acidity on finish
Climens   tasted 1974
   Very deep gold, good deep classic
   honeyed nose
   Taste characteristics similar, fair
   finish

Climens   tasted 1977
   Pale gold, good weight
   Good apple nose
   Nice balance, slightly watery
   finish
   Lightweight generally

Climens   tasted 1981
   Pale/mid gold
   Attractive botrytis, appley nose
   Light balance and finish

Climens   tasted 1983
   Pale gold
   Light delicate appley nose
   Fairly lightweight and short finish

de Malle   tasted 1982
   Mid gold
   Sweet nose
   Lightweight centre and finish

Guiraud   tasted 1976
   Mid gold
   Nice honeyed nose, botrytis
   Good fruit and weight, good finish

Guiraud   tasted 1985
   Mid/deeper gold
   Nice honeyed nose
   Light and sweet, good finish

La Tour-Blanche   tasted 1971
   Fairly full honey nose
   Lightweight but good finish, nice
   balance

La Tour-Blanche   tasted 1976
   Mid gold, hint of diesel fuel,
   lightweight, not a lot of depth

La Tour-Blanche   tasted 1976
   Good gold, good marmalade-
   honey nose
   Fine, delicate in mouth, not heavy,
   quite soft and 'peachy'

Lafaurie-Peyraguey   tasted 1986
   Mid gold
   Light honeyed nose
   Not great but sweet finish

Rayne-Vigneau   tasted 1978
   Pale gold
   Eggy, yeasty and so₂
   Light, lacks depth in centre, weak
   finish

Rieussec   tasted 1972
   Rich barley-sugar nose, with
   similar characteristics in mouth

Rieussec   tasted 1977
   Mid gold
   Good honeyed nose
   Lightweight but good fruit and
   light finish

Rieussec   tasted 1988
   Deep gold
   Honeyed nose with botrytis
   evident
   Medium weight; nice finish

1965

A poor vintage but a few properties
produced attractive wines. Picking
started 2nd October.
d'Yquem   tasted 1976 (must weight
17.7°)
   Mid gold
   Fairly light nose and acidity
   Quite a thick mouthful, fruity,
   quite high acidity, firm finish

d'Yquem   tasted 1980
   Mid gold
   Finesse and lovely rich fruit
   Light centre with lovely balanced
   finish

d'Yquem   tasted 1984
   Mid gold
   Fairly rich marmalade nose
   Quite thick and honeyed. Good
   rich finish

d'Yquem   tasted 1987
   Mid gold
   Lightish honeyed nose
   Quite rich but showing age

Lafaurie-Peyraguey   tasted 1983
   Mid gold
   Complex botrytised nose
   Good fruit and finish

Rayne-Vigneau   tasted 1984
   Deep golden
   Crème brulée nose
   Lightweight but sweet finish

Rieussec   tasted 1977
   Mid gold
   Light but full botrytis nose
   Full, good weight and balance,
   long finish, very slight acidity

Suduiraut   tasted 1966
   Good colour
   Very pleasant and delicate, true
   Sauternes flavour
   Light, short at the finish at the
   moment but should round off well
   in bottle

Suduiraut   tasted 1978
   Mid gold
   Lacks botrytis
   Slight smell of so₂
   Quite weighty but lacks fruit and
   depth

Suduiraut   tasted 1978
   Bronze colour
   Mature nose but lacks fruit and
   sweetness

Suduiraut   tasted 1986
   Mid gold
   Light, musty nose
   Sweet but lacks balance on finish

1966

Quite a good vintage but rather
variable. Picking started 26th
September. The good wines have
matured early and will probably not
have a very long life.
Climens   tasted 1982
   Pale/mid gold
   Good fruity, slightly eggy nose
   Slightly leafy finish

Coutet   tasted 1967
   Intense nose, fine and elegant nose
   but fairly light

Coutet   tasted 1972
   Attractive but lightish in style and
   character

Coutet   tasted 1977
   Pale gold
   Nice full apple nose
   Light on fruit, but well made and
   balanced

de Malle   tasted 1987
   Pale/mid gold
   Slightly woody nose
   Drying in centre and finish

d'Yquem   tasted 1986
   Mid gold
   Good rich nose, medium extract
   Good fruit but lacking depth of
   concentration

Guiraud   tasted 1967
   Really fine wine
   Very fruity
   Light attractive wine
   Only medium sweet

Lafaurie-Peyraguey   tasted 1976
   Pale gold
   Disappointing, musty nose
   Lacks charm and depth

Lafaurie-Peyraguey   tasted 1985
   Pale/mid gold
   Strange leafy nose
   Lacks balance. Lightweight finish

Rayne-Vigneau   tasted 1974
   Beautiful classic Sauternes nose
   and taste, distinctly oily texture,
   quite good balance and finish

Roumieu (Swiss bottled)   tasted 1987
   Rich, unctuous with botrytis
   Marmalade flavour
   Good-quality wine

Sigalas-Rabaud   tasted 1977
   Pale gold
   Light but fruity nose
   Light, nice balance, not a big finish

Sigalas-Rabaud   tasted 1984
   Pale/mid gold
   Light, sweet nose
   Quite sweet; light finish

Suduiraut   tasted 1967
   Very powerful distinctive nose
   Very sweet and rich
   Fine, very typical

Suduiraut   tasted 1978
   Mid gold
   Slightly flabby nose
   Rich but not much depth. Woody
   flavour (could be an odd bottle)

Suduiraut   tasted 1986
   Mid gold
   Good, rich well balanced nose
   Rich, sweet; good finish

Trillon (half bottles, bottled by
Block, Grey and Block)   tasted 1977
   Good medium gold, nice rich
   honeyed botrytis nose — perhaps a
   hint of orange; good balance in
   mouth
   Rich, honeyed, good fruit,
   surprisingly long finish

1967
A very variable harvest. Picking
started 2nd September. Château
d'Yquem quite exceptional, some
attractive wines near their peak in the
mid-1970s, many others light and
undistinguished.
Bouyot   tasted 1983
   Mid gold
   Deep woody concentration
   Good fruit and finish

Climens   tasted 1980
   Mid gold
   Great depth, full botrytis
   Superb rich wine with excellent
   balance

Climens   tasted 1981
   Pale/mid gold
   Good appley botrytis
   Well balanced, rich. Thick finish

Coutet   tasted 1975
   Pale gold
   Apple nose, good but light
   Light, fairly fruity, slight acidity

Coutet   tasted 1978
   Pale gold
   Light apple nose and yeast
   Lightweight, lacks depth, watery
   finish

Coutet   tasted 1982
   Mid gold
   Quite good botrytis and fruit
   Quite eggy, light centre and finish

Coutet   tasted 1986
   No change

de Fargues   tasted 1975
   Very beautiful, delicate balance
   Soft, fruity and acidity

de Fargues   tasted 1986
   Deep gold
   Lovely rich marmalade nose
   Good, tight botrytised centre and
   finish

Doisy-Védrines   tasted 1976
   Quite light gold, odd nose
   Fragrant, flowery with a hint of
   sulphur
   Fruit and sugar all right but an odd
   harshness at the end

d'Yquem   tasted 1973 (must weight
20.5°)
   Beautiful balance
   Rich fruit and tannin — closed
   finish

d'Yquem   tasted 1977
   Mid gold
   Delicate, fragrant, a lot of depth
   Superb balance, still tannin and
   acidity, long finish, long way to go

d'Yquem   tasted 1980
   Mid gold
   Tight, rich, superb botrytis and
   marmalade
   Great depth, closed, tight on palate
   Years to go

d'Yquem   tasted 1984
   No change

d'Yquem   tasted 1987
   No change

d'Yquem   tasted 1988
   No change

d'Yquem   tasted 1989
   Deep gold
   Tight, closed and concentrated
   honey nose with full botrytis
   Thick in the mouth, still very tight
   with a harsh youthful acidity on
   the finish from new oak

Fayau (Cadillac)   tasted 1988
   Mid gold
   Rich, tight, honeyed; good extract
   Full, luscious with balanced
   acidity. Long finish

Filhot   tasted 1988
   Deep gold
   High sulphur on herby nose
   Quite rich but with a medicinal
   finish

Guiraud   tasted 1974
   Deep colour, little suggestion of
   botrytis on nose
   Some depth of flavour, texture
   quite oily
   Rather lacking in sugar

Guiraud   tasted 1978
   Very deep gold
   No fruit on nose
   Completely dried out

Guiraud   tasted 1988
   Very deep gold
   Good, rich honeyed nose
   Full, rich centre. Lightweight
   finish

La Chartreuse   tasted 1978
   Good colour
   Superb botrytis nose
   Lovely balance and finish

Lafaurie-Peyraguey   tasted 1976
   Mid gold
   Good nose
   Nice balance

Lafaurie-Peyraguey   tasted 1987
   Mid gold
   Good rich botrytised nose
   Well balanced; full finish

Rabaud-Promis   tasted 1983
   Mid/deep gold

Good rich fruity nose
Full centre but falling short on
finish

Rieussec   tasted 1977
Mid gold
Excellent balance on nose
Good fruit, good finish, one of the
better '67s

Rieussec   tasted 1988
Deep gold
Rich honeyed nose with good
botrytis
Rich centre; slightly drying on
finish

*Ste-Croix-du-Mont Syndicat
Vinicole*   tasted 1987
Mid gold
Rich botrytised barley-sugar nose
Full, well balanced

Sigalas-Rabaud   tasted 1985
Mid gold
Light, sweet nose
Lacks finesse; sweet finish

Suduiraut   tasted 1976
Good deep gold, nice but rather
slight nose, good classic qualities
in the mouth but not a
heavyweight

Suduiraut   tasted 1985
Deep gold
Full, fat, rich, honeyed nose with
good botrytis
Good depth and concentration of
fruit; long finish

Suduiraut   tasted 1987
No change

Suduiraut   tasted 1988
No change

1968
A very poor harvest indeed. Picking
started 1st October. Almost entirely
declassified wines. Château
d'Yquem still showing some
character.
d'Yquem   tasted 1976
Deep brown/gold
Full 'peachy' nose, noticeably
glutinous texture, deep firmness at
end
Not as much sugar as some but lots
of character

d'Yquem   tasted 1977
Odd chemical flavour at the end,
not nearly so impressive

d'Yquem   tasted 1977
Mid gold
Nice balance, attractive light nose
Good balance
Slightly bitter after-taste

d'Yquem   tasted 1978
Deep gold
Nice complex, honeyed nose
Tight, firm, with acidity, closed
with life to come

d'Yquem   tasted 1988
Mid/deep gold
Honeyed nose with botrytis
Delicate fruit, sweet complex
finish

Rayne-Vigneau   tasted 1984
Mid gold
Leafy, medicinal nose
Quite sweet; dry finish

1969
Rather an undistinguished vintage
producing mainly lightweight wines
which will not have a very long life.
Picking started 1st October.
Barbier   tasted 1974
Some richness on nose, quite good
all-round qualities in mouth
Has not really opened out yet

Climens   tasted 1981
Pale/mid gold
Quite rich, slight botrytis
Fairly full, well made, drying on
finish

Coutet   tasted 1982
Mid gold
Slightly stalky
Light centre; slightly medicinal
finish

Doisy-Védrines   tasted 1987
Pale/mid gold
Sweet, rich nose
Quite rich centre, but slightly
lightweight on finish

d'Yquem   tasted 1977
Pale gold
Light, honeyed, closed, slight
acidity and almond nose

d'Yquem   tasted 1988
Mid gold
Honeyed, balanced nose
Rich and sweet. Good honey finish

Filhot   tasted 1988
Deep gold
Delicate, botrytised nose
Quite light, hollow centre with
some sweetness
Drying on finish

Guiraud   tasted 1978
Mid gold
Slight botrytis, acidity, high
muscadelle
Closed, good balance, will
develop

Lafaurie-Peyraguey   tasted 1976
Pale gold

Light, lacks acidity and depth
Tannin, closed, but good balance,
generally lightweight

Lafaurie-Peyraguey   tasted 1988
Pale/mid gold
Lightweight but sweet nose
Lacks centre and finish

Rieussec   tasted 1987
Mid gold
Good rich balanced nose
Nicely balanced, sweet honey
finish

Rieussec   tasted 1988
No change

Sigalas-Rabaud   tasted 1986
Pale gold
Light, eggy nose
Lacks balance; light finish

Suduiraut   tasted 1978
Mid gold
Slight botrytis
Lightweight but nice balance

Suduiraut   tasted 1983
Pale/mid gold
Good rich nose with botrytis in
evidence
A well made 1969 with a good,
rich, fruity finish

Suduiraut   tasted 1988
Deep gold
Good depth of concentration and
marmalade with botrytis
Lovely rich long botrytis finish

1970
A big vintage of very good quality on
the whole. Picking started 1st
October. Most of the best wines have
very good extract and will last well;
some properties produced wines
rather light in style with a much
shorter life.
Climens (L.B.)   tasted 1977
Pale gold
Slightly rubbery smell
Light on fruit, disappointing finish

Climens   tasted 1981
Pale gold and green
Light, leafy with botrytis
Slightly bitter, medicinal, dry
finish (could be an off bottle)

Climens   tasted 1986
Mid gold
Tight, appley nose
Quite sweet, not of great depth
Tight finish

Clos Haut-Peyraguey   tasted 1978
Very pale and green
Light eggy yeasty nose
Lacks depth of fruit (on nose)
Lightweight, lacks depth, fruit and
extract

Coutet tasted 1982
Pale/mid gold
Sulphur on nose with acidity
Light centre and finish

Coutet tasted 1984
No change

de Malle tasted 1984
Mid gold
Lightweight, but nicely balanced nose
Quite rich centre; light finish

Doisy-Daëne (half bottles) tasted 1976
Pale young lemon
Classic Barsac appley nose
Lots of depth and fruit slightly closed, firm

Doisy-Daëne tasted 1987
Deep gold
Lovely, rich botrytised nose
Well balanced, tight honeyed finish

Doisy-Védrines tasted 1974
Nose quite attractive
Quite nice creamy taste but odd suggestion of mustiness

Doisy-Védrines tasted 1980
Mid gold
Good, fruity, racy nose
Rich fruit; long finish

Doisy-Védrines tasted 1984
Mid gold
Good, rich nose
Nicely balanced; full finish

d'Yquem tasted 1978
Pale gold
Tight closed with acidity, a lot of depth and finesse
Enormous depth and good balance
Closed tight finish

d'Yquem tasted 1981
Mid gold
Great depth and finesse
Very rich extract, closed, tight tannic finish

d'Yquem tasted 1987
Mid gold
Honeyed nose
Open, beginning to show signs of age

Filhot tasted 1988
Deep gold
Rich botrytised marmalade nose
Slightly roasted taste; short finish

Guiraud tasted 1977
Pale green tinge
Good botrytis, fairly light
Good depth and balance
Slightly tight, good fruit, good finish

Guiraud tasted 1986
Pale/mid gold
Light on fruit
Lacking depth and finish

La Chartreuse tasted 1974
Nose rather closed, taste too
Plenty of depth but seems to lack sugar
Perhaps obscured by acidity at present
Could develop well

Lafaurie-Peyraguey tasted 1976
Tight
Unbalanced
Lacks acidity

Lafaurie-Peyraguey tasted 1977
Attractive if rather light Sauternes nose
Good in mouth, again lightish in extract but elegant and charming

Lafaurie-Peyraguey tasted 1984
Mid gold
Very light eggy nose
Lacks depth and character

Lafaurie-Peyraguey tasted 1985
No change

La Tour-Blanche tasted 1986
Pale gold
Light, sweet nose
No great depth; eggy finish

Les Ramparts tasted 1980
Mid gold
Rich nose, slightly eggy
Good concentration; well made

Piada tasted 1976
Slightly *maderisé*
Over-sweet without balance

Rabaud-Promis tasted 1978
Good mid gold
Attractive, fragrant, but lightish lemon nose
Quite light in the mouth, delicate with firm finish

Rieussec tasted 1974
Good nose
Creamy flavour, good texture
Rather 'dark' and hard as yet

Rieussec tasted 1977
Pale gold
Tight closed good nose
Fruity, closed, long way to go

Rieussec tasted 1987
Pale/mid gold
Lovely deep rich nose
Nicely balanced fruit, good balanced finish

Ste-Croix-du-Mont Syndicat Vinicole tasted 1987
Pale gold
Barley-sugar nose
Rich fruit and botrytis
Good finish

Suduiraut tasted 1976
Pale gold
Luscious, slight acidity, very forward
Heavyweight, full and tannin, well made

Suduiraut tasted 1981
Mid gold
Quite rich and deep, slightly leafy nose
Quite rich, open and developing quickly

Suduiraut tasted 1988
Mid/deep gold
Fairly rich, earthy nose
Short on fruit in centre and finish

1971
A good vintage. Picking started 1st October. Some excellent wines produced which will last well, most somewhat lightweight in style and extract, drinking well in the 1980s.

Broustet tasted 1983
Mid gold
Lovely, rich, full botrytised nose
Good fruit and extract

Caillou tasted 1984
Mid gold
Light balanced nose
Good fruit and acidity; light finish

Climens tasted 1985
Mid gold
Good rich deep nose
Lovely fruit, slightly light finish

Climens tasted 1988
Mid gold
Rich, open, honeyed nose
Good centre; drying on finish

Coutet tasted 1977
Pale yellow
Good nose and botrytis
Light but nice balance, creamy, appley
Light acidity on finish

Coutet tasted 1981
Pale gold
Eggy and yeasty
Some weight but clumsy

Coutet tasted 1982
Pale gold
Lightweight, slightly eggy
Lacks depth and body; eggy finish

Coutet tasted 1986
No change

d'Arche crème de tête   tasted 1977
  Mid gold
  Finesse and depth, fairly
  lightweight
  Good depth and balance
  Long finish with finesse, fairly
  lightweight

d'Arche   tasted 1985
  Pale/mid gold
  Good, rich, honeyed nose
  Well balanced, fruity finish

Doisy-Daëne   tasted 1980
  Pale gold
  Fairly lightweight with sweet nose
  Lacks weight and body; slightly
  bitter finish

Doisy-Védrines   tasted 1976
  Pale gold
  Good fruit, slightly eggy nose
  Forward, nice extract, good
  balance
  Ready to drink

Doisy-Védrines   tasted 1980
  Pale and green
  Slightly leafy nose
  Lightweight, lacks centre but good
  finish

Doisy-Védrines   tasted 1984
  Mid gold
  Light, leafy nose
  Quite lightweight, but good,
  fruity finish

d'Yquem   tasted 1977
  Pale gold
  Superb botrytis rich nose, slightly
  cloudy
  Excellent balance, fruit, tight firm
  finish
  Long way to go

d'Yquem   tasted 1981
  Mid gold
  Deep closed honeyed with great
  concentration
  Thick, closed, great extract
  Very good balance; years to go

d'Yquem   tasted 1986
  No change

Filhot   tasted 1979
  Well balanced but overall light and
  eggy

Filhot   tasted 1988
  Mid/deep gold
  Nice delicate botrytised
  marmalade nose
  Well made and balanced, with soft
  sweet marmalade finish

Guiraud   tasted 1981
  Deep gold
  Lightweight nose
  Light centre and finish (odd
  bottle?)

Guiraud   tasted 1981
  Mid gold
  Soft and leafy
  Quite good depth

Haut-Bommes   tasted 1977
  Pale; yeast and so$_2$; slight botrytis
  Light, eggy on finish, not full

La Chartreuse   tasted 1978
  Good colour
  Superb rich nose
  Good balance and finish

Lafaurie-Peyraguey   tasted 1981
  Pale gold
  Lemony, eggy
  Quite rich with acidity

La Tour-Blanche   tasted 1981
  Pale gold
  Lightweight, lacks depth
  Soft but thin and lacks fruit
  No botrytis evident

Loubens   tasted 1980
  Pale gold
  Good, rich fruit
  Well balanced, honeyed finish

Raymond-Lafon   tasted 1986
  Deep gold
  Mature, honeyed, lemon
  botrytised nose
  Fairly lightweight in mouth,
  lacking in centre
  Light, dry finish

Rayne-Vigneau   tasted 1981
  Pale gold
  Very light and eggy
  Thin, lacks depth
  No botrytis evident

Rieussec   tasted 1977
  Mid gold
  Good botrytis nose
  Full, good balance, nice acidity
  Good now but will improve

Rieussec   tasted 1981
  Pale/mid gold
  Good honeyed botrytis nose
  Quite rich, good balance and finish

Romer-du-Hayot   tasted 1987
  Pale gold
  Perfumed richness on nose
  Quite rich and full, lime flavour

Sigalas-Rabaud   tasted 1983
  Pale/mid gold
  Light, honeyed nose
  No great depth, light finish

Suduiraut   tasted 1978
  Pale gold
  Marmalade/lemon nose
  No botrytis evident
  Lightweight, thin finish

1972
A poor year. Much of the wine was
declassified; some properties
produced an acceptable wine for
early consumption.
Broustet   tasted 1978
  Pale gold/green
  High yeasty, quite high so$_2$, slight
  botrytis
  Fairly light, lacks depth, short
  finish

Broustet   tasted 1982
  Pale gold
  Thin and lightweight
  Lacks body; lightweight finish

Climens   tasted 1981
  Very pale and green
  Light, eggy, leafy
  Eggy, quite sweet. No botrytis

Climens   tasted 1985
  Pale gold
  Light and thin
  Quite sweet but lacking in body
  and finish

Climens   tasted 1988
  Pale gold
  Light, slightly leafy; some botrytis
  Falls away fast; light finish

Nairac   tasted 1980
  Pale gold
  Good fruity honeyed nose
  Well balanced, good fruity finish

Rabaud-Promis   tasted 1977
  Pale gold
  Slightly honeyed nose
  Light, very little fruit

Rieussec   tasted 1978
  Pale gold
  Very light, botrytis, quite high
  acidity but nice fruit
  Fruit, slightly yeasty and earthy
  finish

Suduiraut   tasted 1978
  Pale gold
  Strong lemon nose, no botrytis
  evident
  Thin, lightweight

Suduiraut   tasted 1986
  Pale/mid gold
  Sweet, light nose; slightly leafy
  No great depth of fruit; light finish

1973
Rather lightweight wines produced
on the whole, most of which will
have a comparatively short life.
Caillou   tasted 1987
  Mid/gold
  Slight botrytis evident
  Light, earthy dryish finish

Climens   tasted 1983
  Mid gold
  Creamy nose with botrytis
  Good balance; full, rich finish

Climens   tasted 1988
  No change

Coutet   tasted 1977
  Light gold, well balanced good
  nose
  Good balance; fruit; firm, tight
  finish

Coutet   tasted 1982
  Mid gold
  Lightweight, slightly leafy nose
  Becoming unbalanced; clumsy
  finish

d'Arche-Lafaurie (second wine of
Château d'Arche)   tasted 1977
  Light gold, full honeyed nose
  Good balance, nice fruit and depth
  Lacks subtlety

de Malle   tasted 1986
  Mid gold
  Forward, sweet nose
  Quite rich, with good finish

Doisy-Daëne   tasted 1978
  Pale gold and green
  Strong sémillon and youthful
  acidity
  Slightly eggy and yeasty
  Young, tight, with acidity, firm,
  nice balance
  Slightly lacking depth of fruit

d'Yquem   tasted 1982
  Mid/pale gold
  Marmalade nose, good depth of
  extract
  Rich, thick with balanced acidity
  Still a long way to go

Grand Enclos du Cérons   tasted 1975
  Light-medium gold
  Pleasant nose, hint of botrytis
  richness and in mouth, but rather
  light

Guiteronde   tasted 1980
  Pale gold
  Good fruit and balance
  Open, well balanced finish

Lafaurie-Peyraguey   tasted 1981
  Pale yellow
  Very lightweight nose
  Lacks fruit and finish

Liot   tasted 1983
  Pale gold
  Good, rich fruit
  Nice weight and depth

Loupiac-Gaudiet   tasted 1982
  Pale gold

Light nose, not a lot of depth
Short on fruit and finish

Mazarin (Loupiac)   tasted 1984
  Mid gold
  Light on fruit
  Lacks depth

Nairac   tasted 1977
  Pale gold, appley nose, hint of oak
  Clean light, well balanced, fresh
  finish

Nairac   tasted 1985
  Mid gold
  Good, tight nose
  Fairly lightweight finish

Rabaud-Promis   tasted 1977
  Pale gold
  Thin nose and SO_2
  High acidity, after-taste not quite
  clean

St-Amand   tasted 1980
  Pale gold
  Lovely rich nose
  Good balance; lovely, rich finish

Voigny   tasted 1980
  Pale gold
  Sweet, open nose
  Quite well balanced; sweet finish

1974
A poor vintage, on the whole,
producing light rather
undistinguished wines, many of
which were declassified.
Climens   tasted 1983
  Pale/mid gold
  Sulphur, woody nose
  Fairly light and thin. Lacks body

Climens   tasted 1988
  Pale gold
  Oaky, sulphur nose. Some
  botrytis underneath
  Drying on finish

de Malle   tasted 1977
  Pale and green
  Light creamy nose
  Marked sauvignon
  Lacks depth, light finish

Filhot   tasted 1977
  Mid gold, flowery nose
  Muscadelle prominent
  Forward, lacks acidity, short
  finish, lacks depth

La Tour-Blanche   tasted 1977
  Delicate
  Well balanced, good finesse on
  nose, good fruit
  Good finish

Nairac   tasted 1978
  Pale yellow

Fresh nose
Lightweight but good extract

Rayne-Vigneau   tasted 1977
  Pale gold, light, lacks depth on
  nose
  Dryish light finish
  Not quite clean, little body

Rieussec   tasted 1982
  Pale gold
  Light with some botrytis
  Light in centre; short finish

1975
Small harvest due to spring frost
especially in Barsac. Early dry, warm
summer. Very hot July/August.
Some rain in September but warm
and sunny. Clear, dry October
therefore very good botrytis and
balanced acidity. Picking started 29th
September. Wines very rich with
great depth and superb balance and
future.
Bouyot   tasted 1983
  Pale gold
  Reminiscent of burnt apples
  Quite rich but falls short on finish

Brousset   tasted 1977
  Pale gold
  Quite light, fruity appley nose
  Light and fruity
  Well balanced, no great depth

Brousset   tasted 1978
  Pale, nice balance
  Quite weighty but mutage
  Fairly forward

Brousset   tasted 1982
  Mid gold
  Light, sweet nose
  Not a lot of depth; sweet finish

Cantegril   tasted 1978
  Very pale
  Nice depth and yeast
  Slightly burnt, nice balance
  Tight, heaps of flavour, quite
  forward

Climens   tasted 1983
  Mid/pale gold
  Good, tight, rich nose with some
  sulphur
  Well balanced fruit and acidity;
  good tight finish
  Will develop well

Climens   tasted 1987
  Mid gold
  Lovely botrytis on nose with
  barley-sugar
  Full, intense; rich finish, with good
  balance

Climens   tasted 1988
  No change

Clos Haut-Peyraguey   tasted in cask
1977
Pale gold
Lightweight nose
Lemony, lacks weight and depth
Rather unbalanced, high acidity,
little fruit

Clos Haut-Peyraguey   tasted in bottle
1977
Pale gold
Creamy nose, lacks depth and
weight
Light eggy finish

Coutet   tasted 1977
Mid gold/good balance
Alcohol high in mouth, lovely
balance and fruit and finish

Coutet   tasted 1982
Pale/mid gold
Rich, soft
Very full and intense; tight finish

Coutet   tasted 1984
Mid gold
Lovely, rich, deep nose
Very good balance and finish

Coutet   tasted 1987
Mid gold
Lovely rich nose
Good fruit and concentration

d'Arche   tasted 1978
Mid gold, tight closed
Lightweight, quite forward, light
centre
Lacks weight

d'Arche   tasted 1983
Mid gold
Light, sweet nose
Quite forward, lacks balance

d'Arche   tasted 1987
Mid gold
Forward, sweet nose. Lacks
botrytis
Commercial finish

de Cérons   tasted 1983
Mid gold
Light, sweet nose
Not great but quite good finish

de Malle   tasted 1986
Mid gold
Full, rich honeyed nose
Good depth of fruit; long, rich
finish

Doisy-Daëne   tasted 1977
Very pale gold/green
Light, soft fruity nose
Forward, lacks depth, but
attractive to drink now

Doisy-Daëne   tasted 1978
Pale and green

Very forward, big sémillon
Big, forward, commercial

Doisy-Daëne   tasted 1984
Mid/deep gold
Nice botrytised nose
Open, sweet; slightly unbalanced
finish

Doisy-Védrines   tasted 1980
Mid gold
Sweet nose and balanced acidity
Good depth of fruit; long finish

d'Yquem   tasted 1983
Pale gold
Great extract of honey and botrytis
Full; very rich underneath. Still
closed

d'Yquem   tasted 1986
Mid/pale gold
Very full, concentrated, honeyed
botrytised nose
Superb richness. Tight, closed
finish

d'Yquem   tasted 1987
No change

Filhot   tasted 1977
Mid gold
Good fruit and balance
Long fruity finish, soft, forward

Filhot   tasted 1978
Pale and green
Forward, mutage
Lightweight, forward, eggy, thin
finish

Filhot   tasted 1981
Mid gold
Quite rich nose
Open, commercial blend

Filhot   tasted 1988
Mid gold
Sweet, eggy nose
Apricots; bland, lacks character
and finesse

Guiraud   tasted 1977
Pale gold
Complex, good nose, slight SO_2
Perfect balance, superb long finish

Guiraud   tasted 1978
Tight with acidity
Delicate and fine
Quite forward, good depth and
extract
Great finish and tannin

Guiraud   tasted 1980
Pale gold
Superb rich depth of fruit and
botrytis
Tight, intense; a long way to go

Haut-Bergeron   tasted 1978
Pale and green, tight, closed

Depth, closed, light centre, well
made
Quite forward

Haut-Bommes   tasted 1978
Pale and green
Light, yeasty
Light, lacks weight and depth, thin
finish

Lafaurie-Peyraguey   tasted 1977
Pale gold, slightly yeasty nose
Good balance, good fruit and
acidity
Firm finish

Lafaurie-Peyraguey   tasted 1978
Very pale and green
Medicinal, and unclean, mutage
Light, forward, lacks depth and
extract

Lamothe   tasted 1977
Pale gold/green
Light, attractive
Good balance
Lacks depth, light finish

La Tour-Blanche   tasted 1977
Green/gold, well-balanced nose
Good fruit
Slightly light centre, closed, not
ready

La Tour-Blanche   tasted 1978
Very pale and green
Artificial, a little medicinal
Yeasty taste
Creamy and open
Very open, unsubtle, forward

La Tour-Blanche   tasted 1984
Mid gold
Slightly musty nose
Lacks body and finish

La Tour-Blanche   tasted 1986
Mid gold
Barley-sugar nose
Lacks complexity — disappointing

Les Justices   tasted 1987
Deep gold
Lovely rich botrytised fruit
Fairly full; tight, delicate finish

Loubens (Ste-Croix-du-Mont)
tasted 1983
Pale gold
Lovely, honeyed nose
Quite rich; well balanced finish

Mazarin (Loupiac)   tasted 1985
Pale/mid gold
Light barley-sugar nose
Lacks depth; light finish

Nairac   tasted 1977
Pale gold
Good depth
Closed, excellent balance

Nairac   tasted 1987
Pale gold
Good, rich, tight nose
Well balanced; tight finish

Rabaud-Promis   tasted 1977
Mid gold, green tinge
Good full nose
Nice fruit, good fruit

Rabaud-Promis   tasted 1985
Deep gold
Good rich botrytised nose
Initially good but fades in the
mouth leaving a short finish

Rabaud-Promis   tasted 1987
Deepish gold
Sweet nose, lacking depth
Lightweight, short finish

Raymond-Lafon   tasted 1978
Pale, good tight extract
Tight closed and acidity
A lot of depth, good future

Rayne-Vigneau   tasted 1977
Pale gold
Light, high sauvignon
Lacks depth
High acidity

Rayne-Vigneau   tasted 1978
Pale and green
Very light
Slightly herbal, unctuous,
lightweight, no depth

Rieussec   tasted 1977
Mid gold
Closed on nose
Full fruit in mouth, long finish,
closed

Rieussec   tasted 1978
High sémillon
Great depth and extract
Very closed, good balance and
weight
Slightly light centre
Long finish

Rieussec crème de tête   tasted 1982
Very deep brown gold
Deep rich, superb botrytised
marmalade nose
Immensely rich and intense
Amazing thickness in the mouth
A superb wine

Rieussec   tasted 1982
Mid/deep gold
Wonderful rich botrytis
Tight, closed; rich finish

Rieussec   tasted 1984
Deep gold
Intense marmalade nose
Superb richness; tight finish

Rieussec   tasted 1987
Full rich botrytised nose

Opened up over the years to
develop well

Roumieu   tasted 1978
Pale, closed and earthy
Slightly unclean, petrol smell
Light and nice balance
Lacks depth, light finish

St-Amand   tasted 1978
Pale, tight, closed and acidity
Good depth and extract, a great
future

*Ste-Croix-du-Mont Syndicat
Vinicole*   tasted 1987
Deep gold
Good botrytised, barley-sugar
nose
Lovely, rich deep concentrated
fruit

Sigalas-Rabaud   tasted 1977
Pale gold/green
Good depth on nose, nice balance
Light in mouth and finish

Sigalas-Rabaud   tasted 1978
Pale and green and acidity
Closed, a lot of depth, good
extract and balance, finishes short

Sigalas-Rabaud   tasted 1986
Pale/mid gold
Sweet, commercial nose
Lacks balance and finesse
Clumsy finish

Suduiraut   tasted 1977
Mid gold
Forward nose
Good balance, fairly light
Lacks weight and depth, thin finish

Suduiraut   tasted 1983
Mid gold
Light, sweet nose, slightly closed

Suduiraut   tasted 1988
Mid/deep gold
Rich, botrytised nose with nicely
balanced acidity

Voigny   tasted 1984
Pale gold
Sweet nose lacking in finesse
Quite short; light finish

1976

Early flowering, long hot summer,
with rain just before and during the
vintage. Picking started 21st
September. Large crop with lower
acidity than 1975. Very high
percentage of botrytis. Very rich
wines with an abundance of botrytis.
However, some wines lack balance.
Broustet   tasted 1977
Mid gold
Light nose, honeyed, closed

Good balance of fruit and acidity
Luscious, alcohol in mouth

Broustet   tasted 1986
Mid/deep gold
Nice delicate honeyed nose
Well balanced; good finish

Caillou   tasted 1980
Pale gold
Good, rich, deep botrytis
Thick, rich mouthful. Good finish
although lighter than some

Climens   tasted 1977
Pale green/gold
Tight closed
Good depth and acidity, closed
Light in style for Climens

Climens   tasted 1981
Pale gold
Rich, barley-sugar nose
A lot of concentration
Will develop well

Climens   tasted 1983
Pale/mid gold
Deep, rich, closed nose
Tight with good extract

Climens   tasted 1987
Pale/mid gold
Nice, rich, botrytised nose with
good balance
Full, rich with a good, tight finish

Climens   tasted 1988
No change
Will develop into a great wine with
finesse rather than a blockbuster

Clos Haut-Peyraguey   tasted 1977
Pale gold
Lightweight and so$_2$ on nose
Nice weight and balance, quite
high acidity, closed

Clos Haut-Peyraguey   tasted 1986
Mid/pale gold
Light, sweet nose
Slightly unbalanced centre and
finish

Coutet   tasted 1977
Pale gold, full nose, well balanced
Firm finish, very good future

Coutet   tasted 1982
Pale gold
Light, appley nose
Quite tight; light finish

Coutet   tasted 1983
Pale gold
Light, delicate nose
No great depth, finishes a little
short

Coutet   tasted 1987
Pale gold
Lightweight nose
Lacks balance and finish

Doisy-Daëne   tasted 1977
Pale gold/green
Complex nose, lacks depth
Tight, closed, light — for early
drinking

Doisy-Daëne   tasted 1983
Pale gold
Light, sweet nose. Pleasant
No great depth; light finish

Doisy-Védrines   tasted 1977
Mid gold, closed, rich, complex
Excellent balance and depth

Doisy-Védrines   tasted 1980 (14°
alcohol + 4° unfermented sugar
retained)
Mid gold
Tight and closed. Good botrytis
Well balanced, rich finish

Doisy-Védrines   tasted 1984
Mid gold
Quite rich; a lighter style '76
Good balance but falls slightly
short

Doisy-Védrines   tasted 1986
Deepish gold
Appley acidity
Light. Not as rich as would be
expected

d'Yquem   tasted 1983
Pale gold
Great depth of fruit and botrytis
Superb balance; still very young
Many years to go

d'Yquem   tasted 1987
Pale gold
Very concentrated, botrytised
nose
Great depth. Fantastic balance
Not ready yet

Filhot   tasted 1977
Mid gold, very good complex
nose
Botrytis evident, full, perfect
balance
Fairly forward

Filhot   tasted 1980
Mid gold
Nice, rich nose
Thick, full and very forward
No great centre but rich, sweet
finish

Filhot   tasted 1981
Mid gold
Rich, open nose
Good weight, quite forward

Filhot   tasted 1982
Mid gold
Quite rich and full
Forward with sweet finish

Filhot   tasted 1983
Mid gold
Full blown, rich nose
Concentrated sweetness. Very
open and blousy

Filhot   tasted 1987
Open, sweet nose
Quite rich with apricots but
slightly drying on finish

Filhot   tasted 1988
No change

Guiraud   tasted 1977
Gold, complex, full, good botrytis
Full palate, superb balance, firm
finish

Guiraud   tasted 1980
Mid gold
Deep, rich botrytis. Closed
Tight, oaky, good depth of fruit

Guiraud   tasted 1983
Mid/deep gold
Fairly rich and deep with botrytis
Full, good rich centre; slightly
burnt finish

Guiraud   tasted 1987
Deepish gold
Quite rich, botrytised nose
Slightly drying on finish

Lafaurie-Peyraguey   tasted 1977
Pale gold
Well balanced nose
Good fruit, firm finish
Nice balance in mouth

Lafaurie-Peyraguey   tasted 1986
Mid gold
Fairly light nose
Quite sweet; tight finish

Lamothe   tasted 1977
Pale gold/green
Light, good balance and botrytis,
hint of SO_2
Good balance in mouth, nice fruit,
quite forward

Lamothe   tasted 1980
Pale gold
Well balanced, botrytised nose
Good fruit and finish

La Tour-Blanche   tasted 1977
Pale green
Closed nose, good fruit and depth
Long flavour, firm, good balance

La Tour-Blanche   tasted 1985
Mid gold
Good, rich marmalade nose
Well balanced; good, rich finish

Les Justices   tasted 1982
Pale gold
Lovely balanced sweet nose
Good depth and finish

Liot   tasted 1983
Pale gold with green
Quite a light, lemony nose
Quite thin; lacking in depth and
finish

Loupiac-Gaudiet (Loupiac)
tasted 1980
Pale and green
Light, eggy, slight botrytis
Lightweight; eggy finish

Nairac   tasted 1984
Deep gold
Good, tight nose. Rich and deep
with tannin
Very oaky finish

Nairac   tasted 1987
Mid gold
Good, tight botrytised nose
Very good balance. Still youthful
but developing very well

Padouen   tasted 1981
Pale gold/yellow
Soft, eggy, sweet nose
Lightweight. Lacks depth and
finish

Peyrat (Cérons)   tasted 1980
Pale gold
Slightly grassy nose
Quite sweet but lacks body

Rabaud-Promis   tasted 1977
Mid gold
Well-balanced nose, good fruit
Good weight and depth

Rabaud-Promis   tasted 1987
Mid gold
Good, sweet concentrated nose
Well balanced; rich finish

Rayne-Vigneau   tasted 1984
Mid gold
Quite rich and sweet
Sweet and full, but lacks finesse

Rieussec   tasted 1977
Deep gold
Deep botrytis nose
Very rich, full, honeyed, superb
balance
Long rich finish

Rieussec   tasted 1981
Deep gold
Closed and tight
Great depth underneath

Rieussec   tasted 1982
Deep gold
Rich marmalade nose
Very full with very long finish

Rieussec   tasted 1983
Deep gold
Lovely, deep, very rich in botrytis
Thick, amazing extract and
concentration

Rieussec   tasted 1987
  Deep gold
  Full, rich marmalade nose
  Lots of richness

Rieussec (half bottles)   tasted 1987
  Deep, rich gold
  Marmalade, botrytised nose
  Full blown. Great depth of extract;
  slightly drying on finish

*Ste-Croix-du-Mont Syndicat
Vinicole*   tasted 1987
  Mid gold
  Lightweight but good botrytis
  Quite rich, firm finish

Sigalas-Rabaud   tasted 1977
  Pale gold — good nose
  Light but nice depth, good
  balance, well made

Sigalas-Rabaud   tasted 1980
  Pale gold
  Quite sweet nose
  Nice balanced centre; slightly light
  finish

Suduiraut   tasted 1982
  Mid gold
  Rich, deep nose with good botrytis
  Full, tight. Lovely finish

Suduiraut   tasted 1983
  Mid gold
  Good botrytis and balance
  Full, quite rich. Good balance and
  finish

Suduiraut   tasted 1987
  Mid gold
  Lovely, rich, full nose
  Good balance of fruit with finesse

1977
Heavy spring frosts at the end of
March/beginning of April caused
great damage. Poor summer with
little sun. Picking started 20th
October resulting in a small crop
approximately 50% less than usual.
Poor vintage. Many châteaux did not
produce wine under their château
label. Wines generally thin and
lacking in balance.
Caillou (30 barrels only
produced)   tasted 1987
  Quite deep gold
  Slightly dry, earthy nose
  Sweet, lacks botrytis but a pleasant
  wine
  Dryish finish

Climens   tasted 1983
  Pale yellow/gold
  Sulphur and slight volatile acidity
  Sweet and short; lacks finesse

Climens   tasted 1988
  Pale gold

Some botrytis, slightly medicinal
Hollow centre; short finish

Coutet   tasted 1987
  Pale yellow/gold
  Green, grassy with sulphur and
  medicinal undertones on nose
  Lacks balance and finesse

Doisy-Védrines   tasted 1980 (13.5°
alcohol + 3.5° unfermented sugar
retained)
  Pale gold
  Lightweight
  Lacks depth and finish

d'Yquem   tasted 1987
  Mid/deep gold
  Good rich botrytised marmalade
  nose
  Quite full and concentrated
  Medium weight on finish

Filhot   tasted 1984
  Pale gold
  Lightweight nose
  Sweet, but lacks character

Guiraud   tasted 1980 (14.0° + 4°)
  Mid gold
  Lightweight with slight botrytis
  Light on fruit and finish

Lafaurie-Peyraguey   tasted 1987
  Light/mid gold
  Fruity marmalade nose
  Roasted, good rich, fruity wine

Rayne-Vigneau   tasted 1985
  Mid gold
  Sweet, open nose
  Well balanced, but short finish

1978
Hot dry summer. Weather not
humid enough during September/
October to spread botrytis. The
resultant wines were fairly rich and
sweet and high in alcohol but with
little botrytis and therefore untypical
although of reasonable quality.
Caillou   tasted 1982
  Pale gold
  Sweet without botrytis
  Light, slightly eggy finish

Climens   tasted 1983
  Pale gold
  Light, sweet without botrytis
  Lacks depth and finish
  Lightweight

Climens   tasted 1988
  Very pale gold
  Light, sweet, eggy, leafy nose
  Short finish

Doisy-Védrines   tasted 1980 (13.5°
alcohol + 3.5° unfermented sugar
retained)

Pale gold
Light, eggy nose
Sweet but no great depth in centre
or finish

d'Yquem   tasted 1987
  Pale yellow/gold
  Light, delicate honeyed nose
  Not of great depth. Fairly full
  finish

Filhot   tasted 1980
  Pale and green
  Lightweight. Lemon nose
  Very light, almost demi-sec. Short
  finish

Guiraud   tasted 1980 (in cask) (14.5°
+ 4.6°)
  Pale gold
  Pleasant, slightly botrytised leafy
  nose
  Medium weight; short finish

Lafaurie-Peyraguey   tasted 1986
  Pale/mid gold
  Light, commercial nose
  Lacks fruit and extract

Lamothe   tasted 1987
  Pale and green
  Fairly fruity, eggy nose
  Slightly yeasty in the mouth
  Quite full and good balanced fruit

Rabaud-Promis   tasted 1983
  Mid gold
  Sweet, with slight botrytis
  Thin, lacks finesse and finish

Raymond-Lafon   tasted 1983
  Pale/mid gold
  Creamy, oaky nose without
  botrytis
  Good concentration with oak and
  tannin. Long finish
  A well made '78

Rayne-Vigneau   tasted 1985
  Mid gold
  Medicinal undertones
  Lacks depth of fruit; light finish

Rieussec crème de tête   tasted 1980 (in
cask)
  Mid gold
  Rich, superb, botrytised nose
  Heavyweight, deep, rich extract
  Very long, superb finish

Rieussec crème de tête   tasted 1983 (in
bottle)
  No change

Rieussec   tasted 1982
  Pale gold
  Sweet and rich without botrytis
  Lacks centre and body
  Lightweight

Suau   tasted 1985
Mid/pale gold
Eggy nose; no botrytis
Sweet, quite good fruit but lacks
finesse

Suduiraut   tasted 1983
Pale gold
Creamy, lemony nose without
botrytis
Quite sweet, but lacks character

Suduiraut   tasted 1988
Pale gold
Light, leafy, medicinal nose
Sweet but light and eggy. Delicate
finish

1979
A late harvest with rain starting 15th
November. Good quality for those
growers who picked before this date.
Good spread of botrytis. Lightly
balanced acidity. A good vintage but
not a lot of lasting power, developing
rather quickly. Attractive to drink
now.
Climens   tasted 1987
Mid gold
Oaky and appley nose
Rich extract, good balance and
depth of honeyed fruit and botrytis
Long, full finish

Coutet   tasted 1987
Pale gold
Tight, stalky nose
Slightly medicinal, musty taste
Short finish

de Cérons   tasted 1987
Mid gold
Light, quite thin
Lacks centre and finish

de Malle   tasted 1984
Mid/pale gold
Quite woody and slight volatile
acidity
Lightweight, lacking in depth

Doisy-Védrines   tasted 1980 (13.5°
alcohol + 4° unfermented sugar
retained)
Mid gold
Nicely balanced, botrytised nose
Well balanced centre and finish

du Haire   tasted 1981
Mid gold
Slightly eggy but with good depth
Light in centre but good finish

d'Yquem   tasted 1987
Mid gold
Fully developed, rich nose with
some peachiness
Full, good extract, developing
well

Filhot   tasted 1988
Pale gold
Lightweight, lacking botrytis
Thin, hollow, lightweight with
dry finish

Filhot Cask 1 (80% sémillon 20%
sauvignon)   tasted 1980
Pale and green
Dry and light lacking in botrytis
Medium/sweet; dry finish

Filhot Cask 2 (60% sémillon 40%
sauvignon)   tasted 1980
Pale
Light, slight botrytis
Leafy and medicinal

Filhot Cask 3 (100%
sémillon)   tasted 1980
Pale gold
Deep, rich nose
Thick in mouth but lightweight
finish

Filhot Cask 4 (70% sémillon 30%
sauvignon)   tasted 1980
Pale gold
Light lemon nose
Fairly sweet, short finish

Guiraud   tasted 1980 (in cask) (14.5°
+ 5°)
Very pale gold
Lightweight nose
Fairly rich. Tight sauvignon nose

Guiraud   tasted 1983
Mid gold
Good balance with delicate
botrytis
Rich, fairly full. Light finish

Guiraud   tasted 1986
Mid gold
Attractive hint of botrytis
Not of great depth

La Tour-Blanche   tasted 1987
Mid gold
Good tight, rich nose
Well balanced, good extract and
firm finish

Les Justices   tasted 1987
Mid gold
Light, flowery nose
Lightweight on centre on finish

Liot   tasted 1987
Mid gold
Honeyed nose
Quite rich. Unsubtle; drying on
finish

Nairac   tasted 1984
Mid gold
Good, rich deep nose
Long, full, tannic finish

Nairac   tasted 1983
Pale gold

Closed and tight with good depth
Rich, full and well balanced; tight
finish

Raymond-Lafon   tasted 1986
(picking mid-October)
Mid gold, slightly browning
Rich, slightly burnt nose. Good
depth
Long, rich, full of fruit and
botrytis

Rayne-Vigneau   tasted 1985
Mid gold
Medicinal nose
Lacks fruit and depth. Slightly
bitter after-taste

Rieussec tête de cuvée   tasted 1983
Mid gold and green
Tight, rich, closed with huge
botrytis
Immense extract, tight, closed,
enormous depth
A very great future

Rieussec   tasted 1982
Pale/mid gold
Lovely botrytised, marmalade
nose
Full and rich; tight finish
Well balanced

Romer-du-Hayot   tasted 1987
Mid gold
Slightly eggy nose
Lacks finesse. Short centre and
finish
Slightly medicinal and cloying

St-Amand   tasted 1987
Mid/deep gold
Well balanced botrytis and barley-
sugar
Well made, full and rich. Tight
finish

Suduiraut   tasted 1983
Pale gold
Good balance of fruit and botrytis
Full, rich, tight finish

Suduiraut   tasted 1988
Mid gold
Good botrytis, tight and oaky
Oily and thick, good
concentration
Long, tight, rich botrytised finish

1980
Small crop. Cold, wet spring, very
cold early summer. Poor flowering.
Fine August, very hot September,
rained during most of October, fine
November. A very late vintage
benefiting from the late sun after the
rains; quite a lot of botrytis. Nicely
balanced wines but fairly forward,
light and quite charming.

Climens   tasted 1983
  Pale gold
  Light, creamy nose with botrytis
  Quite rich with firm finish

Climens   tasted 1987
  Pale/mid gold
  Sweet nose with botrytis. Slightly
  grassy
  Quite good depth of fruit on
  finish, but fairly light centre
  Forward

Coutet   tasted 1987
  Pale gold
  Light, sweet nose
  Very forward and sweet. Lacks
  depth of fruit

d'Yquem   tasted 1987
  Pale and green
  Rich, deep, fruity marmalade
  nose. Light on botrytis
  A full, rich mouthful; still quite
  tight

Guiraud   tasted 1983
  Pale gold
  Closed, tight with good balance
  Quite rich — a good 1980

Guiraud   tasted 1984
  Pale/mid gold
  Good rich balance with botrytis
  Good balance — rich finish

Guiraud   tasted 1987
  Mid/pale gold
  Nicely balanced fruit and botrytis
  Good weight with sweet finish

Lafaurie-Peyraguey   tasted 1987
  Pale and green
  Lightweight. Lacks finesse on nose
  Fairly sweet, but characterless

La Tour-Blanche   tasted 1987
  Pale yellow
  Grassy/medicinal with sulphur
  Very light, almost *demi-sec*. Short
  finish

Nairac   tasted 1987
  Pale/mid gold
  Very oaky with richness
  underneath
  Quite full but a little out of balance

Raymond-Lafon (picking end
October)   tasted 1986
  Mid gold
  Quite good botrytis with slightly
  grassy nose
  Light on fruit, lacks depth of
  concentration
  Quite full with fairly light, earthy
  finish (could be an off bottle)

Raymond-Lafon   tasted 1987
  Mid/deep gold

Delicate botrytis with finesse
Nicely balanced with botrytis
Forward, fairly lightweight

Rieussec tête de cuvée   tasted 1982
  Pale gold
  Very tight and closed botrytis
  Very good depth of fruit and
  richness
  Closed finish
  A long future

Rieussec   tasted 1982
  Pale gold with green
  Good, rich, deep, closed nose with
  lanolin
  Tight, fairly rich. Closed finish

Rieussec   tasted 1983
  No change

Rieussec   tasted 1984
  Pale and green
  Good depth, opening nicely
  Well balanced finish

Rieussec   tasted 1987
  Mid gold
  Rich, honeyed nose
  Good fruit and balanced finish

Suduiraut   tasted 1987
  Mid gold
  Lightweight nose. Not much
  depth
  Fairly sweet, but lacks balance

Domaine de Thibaut   tasted 1988
  Pale and green
  Eggy with sulphur
  Fairly rich, hollow finish

1981
Early, warm spring becoming cooler
later. Some frost at the end of April.
Good weather in June followed by a
cold, wet July. Very hot August with
rain September/October. Fine and
warm in the latter half of October.
Harvesting went on well into
November with a lot of botrytis
evident; fairly low acidity. Very
attractive wines with a good future.
Caillou   tasted 1983 (14.5° alcohol +
4.5° unfermented sugar retained)
  Pale gold
  Tight, lemony nose with good
  fruit
  Closed, tannic. Long way to go

Caillou   tasted 1987
  Mid gold
  Lovely bouquet of apples and oak
  Quite rich and still quite tight on
  finish

Climens   tasted 1983
  Pale gold and green
  Soft, tight nose with sulphur

Rich fruit, still closed. Well
balanced
A good future

Climens   tasted 1987 ·
  Pale gold and green
  Very good depth with lots of
  botrytis. Lovely bouquet of honey
  and apples
  Good deep concentration. Closed
  on finish

Coutet   tasted 1987
  Mid gold
  Nice, tight fruit and botrytis
  Good balance, tight, closed. Long
  finish

de Ségur (second wine of Château
Broustet)   tasted 1988
  Pale lemon
  Eggy, sulphurous nose
  Light, tight, hollow centre. High
  acidity on finish

Doisy-Dubroca   tasted 1987
  Mid gold
  Good fruity nose
  Good depth of extract. Long finish

d'Yquem   tasted 1987
  Mid gold
  Beautiful balance of richness and
  botrytis
  Still very closed
  Good depth of fruit and acidity
  Will develop into a good wine

Filhot   tasted 1988
  Pale gold
  Lemon/honey nose
  Quite rich, well balanced centre
  Fairly short finish but attractive

Guiraud   tasted 1983
  Pale and gold
  Good depth with botrytis
  Closed; good future

Guiraud   tasted 1987
  Pale and green
  Lovely rich honeyed nose with
  good botrytis
  Quite good weight and fruit in
  centre. Good finish

La Tour-Blanche   tasted 1987
  Pale and green
  Fairly rich nose with botrytis
  Quite full centre with slightly
  short finish

Nairac   tasted 1987
  Mid gold
  Full, rich, oaky nose. Still quite
  closed
  Tight and closed in the mouth but
  will develop well

Raymond-Lafon (picking second week
October–second week November;
bottled 1985)   tasted 1986

Mid gold
Closed, delicate and honeyed
Tight, good depth. Long future

Raymond-Lafon   tasted 1987
Mid gold
Good marmalade, botrytised nose
Good weight in the centre and
finish
A well made 1981

Rayne-Vigneau   tasted 1987
Pale and green
Quite rich nose — fairly forward
Lacks centre but pleasant finish

Rieussec   tasted 1982 (in cask)
Pale gold and green
Good rich depth on nose. Good
botrytis
Closed — will develop well

Rieussec   tasted 1983
Mid/deep gold
Lovely botrytis showing, but still
tight
Still closed but rich depth

St-Amand   tasted 1987
Mid gold
Lovely balanced, botrytised
honeyed nose
Still quite tight; well made with
good fruit. Long, tannic finish

Suduiraut   tasted 1987
Mid gold
Lightweight nose and lacking in
charm
Quite rich but little botrytis
Finishes rather short

1982

A hot, dry summer with a lot of rain
in October starting 3rd October.
Vintage started in September for
some growers. Some of the crop had
been picked before the rains. These
wines are good although some are
slightly lacking in botrytis. This is a
vintage to judge by tasting as some
châteaux tended to blend some of the
crop picked during the rain.

Bouyot   tasted 1983 (15° alcohol + 5°
unfermented sugar retained)
Pale with lemon
Light, racy, appley nose
Good concentration with quite
good botrytis
Rich finish. Well made

Broustet   tasted 1982
Pale/mid gold
Lemony, eggy nose
Tight and fairly sweet but slightly
unbalanced finish

Caillou   tasted 1983 (15.2° alcohol +
4.3° unfermented sugar retained)

Pale and green
Light and closed
Well balanced with good tannin
Good finish

Caillou   tasted 1987
Mid gold
Appley and slightly earthy nose
Quite rich; slightly earthy finish

Climens   tasted 1987
Pale and green
Quite deep concentration of fruit
and botrytis
Lightweight centre but a good
finish

Clos Haut-Peyraguey   tasted 1987
Pale/mid gold
Light, lemony nose
Lacks finesse and body with short
finish

Coutet   tasted 1987
Mid gold
Lightweight, sweet nose
Light on fruit but nice, sweet finish

d'Arche   tasted 1987
Pale gold
Lightweight sweetness
Lacks body. Light finish

de Malle   tasted 1987
Mid gold
Quite tight, forward; nice balance
Quite rich with forward finish

de Ricaud (Loupiac)   tasted 1987
Pale yellow
Light, sweet, forward but lacks
finesse
Very light, almost *demi-sec*

de Rolland   tasted 1987
Mid gold/yellow
Lightweight, lacking in botrytis
Tight, lacks weight. Grassy, bitter
after-taste

Doisy-Daëne   tasted 1987
Mid gold
Tight, sweet nose
Lightweight. Slightly cloying on
finish

Doisy-Védrines   tasted 1987
Pale gold
Good balanced nose
Quite rich with well balanced
finish
A good 1982

du Mont (Ste-Croix-du-Mont)   tasted
1987
Mid gold
Lovely marmalade nose
Good fruit, rich finish
A good 1982

d'Yquem   tasted 1987
Pale gold
Concentrated nose with lots of
botrytis
Thick, rich and firm although very
young
Still tannic with quite a long,
honeyed finish

Filhot   tasted 1985 (13.5° + 4°)
Pale gold
Almost dry nose
Forward, lightweight. Eggy finish

Filhot   tasted 1987
Mid gold
Light — lacks botrytis
Quite sweet with concentration
but without much botrytis

Guiraud   tasted 1983
Pale gold
Tight, closed, good fruit with
sulphur
Thick, concentrated. Short on
botrytis but finishes well

Guiraud   tasted 1984
Pale gold
Good tight oaky nose
Good balance, light on botrytis

Guiraud   tasted 1987
Mid gold
Sweet, open, oaky nose
Quite forward

Haura cuvée Madame (Cérons)   tasted
1987
Mid gold
Good, rich nose
Good botrytised fruit, full finish
A good 1982

Lafaurie-Peyraguey   tasted 1987
Mid gold
Forward — fairly rich nose
Quite good balance and richness
A good 1982

La Tour-Blanche   tasted 1987
Mid gold
Slightly grassy/medicinal nose
Lightweight, lacks finesse
Short finish

Les Justices   tasted 1987
Mid gold
Seductive, honeyed nose
Good rich texture with plenty of
character

Le Tarey (Loupiac)   tasted 1987
Pale yellow
Thin, very light. Lacks body and
finish

Nairac   tasted 1983
(a) sauvignon and muscadelle
only

Pale gold
Sulphur and new oak
Fruity without richness
(b) 100% sémillon
Mid gold
Good, thick botrytis
Very full bodied

Nairac   tasted 1987
Mid gold
Good botrytised, oaky nose
Good fruit with predominant oak

Nairac   tasted 1988
No change: a well made 1982

Rabaud-Promis   tasted 1985
Pale gold
Quite forward, sweet with slight
sulphur
Lacks depth; sweet, forward finish

Rabaud-Promis   tasted 1988
Deep gold
Open, sweet nose
Fairly rich centre but lightweight
finish

Raymond-Lafon (picking started 15th
September)   tasted 1985
Mid gold
Lemony nose with sulphur
Good depth, well balanced; long
finish

Raymond-Lafon   tasted 1986
Mid gold
Tight, honeyed nose but short on
botrytis
A well made 1982 — quite forward

Raymond-Lafon   tasted 1987
No change

Rayne-Vigneau   tasted 1985
Mid/pale gold
Light, lacks finesse, eggy
Short on fruit, lacks depth; very
light finish

Rayne-Vigneau   tasted 1988
No change

Rieussec   tasted 1983
Mid gold
Good botrytis and fruit
Rich, full, well balanced. Quite
forward

Rieussec   tasted 1987
Mid gold
Marmalade nose with botrytis
Full, rich with a good fat finish

St-Amand   tasted 1987
Mid gold
Nice barley-sugar and botrytis
Quite rich — good concentration
A good 1982

Suau   tasted 1987
Mid gold and green

Slightly medicinal
Light, thin. Lacks finesse and body

Suduiraut   tasted 1983 (14° + 5°)
Pale gold
Lovely, rich, lemony nose
Full, rich, honeyed
A well made 1982

Suduiraut   tasted 1987
Mid gold
Nice, rich nose with botrytis and
barley-sugar
Good balance. Open and forward
A good 1982

Suduiraut   tasted 1988
No change

Suduiraut cuvée Madame   tasted 1987
Mid gold
Very full and rich with botrytis
Very good balance. Excellent
concentration with long finish

Suduiraut cuvée Madame   tasted 1988
No change

1983

Wet spring, very hot July and a little
rain. Some rain in August and quite
hot which produced a lot of acidity.
Dry, warm September. Hot humid
October — perfect conditions.
Botrytis arrived late towards end of
October/beginning of November:
therefore the châteaux who picked
early lack botrytis whereas the
properties who picked later had an
abundance of botrytis and produced
superb wines. A great vintage with
wines of great depth and quality.
Long lasting.

Bastor-Lamontagne   tasted 1987
Pale gold and green
Quite good weight and fruit
Fairly forward
Nicely balanced finish; not a
heavyweight wine

Bougat (Ste-Croix-du-Mont)   tasted
1987
Mid gold
Lovely botrytised nose
Well made, tight, closed
A good future

Broustet   tasted 1987
Mid gold
Lightweight, lemony nose
Light on depth of fruit and finish

Caillou   tasted 1987
Pale gold and green
Tight, deep and good, oaked
botrytis. Classic appley Barsac
Lovely, rich, full, long but closed
A wine with a great future

Climens   tasted 1987
Mid gold
Very deep, rich fruit with oak
Tight, slightly closed but with lots
of complex depth underneath
Very well made with good balance
A great wine

Clos Haut-Peyraguey   tasted 1987
Pale gold and green
Sulphur, grassy — lacks character
Very light, lacking body and
finesse

Coutet   tasted 1987
Pale gold and green
Lightweight, appley nose
Quite thin, lacks centre
Lightweight finish

Domaine du Coy   tasted 1987
Pale gold and green
Slightly medicinal and eggy
Light, thin with a bitter after-taste
similar to Château Suau 1983

d'Arche   tasted 1987
Mid gold
Quite tight and rich nose
Good concentration and extract
Rich finish
Slightly light on botrytis

de Fargues   tasted 1987
Pale gold
Very well balanced nose with
excellent fruit and botrytis
Tight, tannic with years to go
Great depth underneath

de Malle   tasted 1987
Pale gold
Tight and closed with good fruit
underneath
Quite light and delicate with a
good finish
Well made

de Rolland   tasted 1987
Pale gold and green
Clean, lemony with some botrytis
Quite well balanced; light finish

de Veyres   tasted 1987
Yellow
Forward and lightweight
Open. Drinking well now

Doisy-Daëne   tasted 1987
Pale gold
Good depth of botrytis
Full, deep with a good fruity finish

Doisy-Védrines   tasted 1987
Pale gold/yellow
Lovely, classic nose. A delicate,
appley Barsac
Very well balanced. Lovely rich
finish
Classic

d'Yquem   tasted 1987
Pale/mid gold
Exceptional vanilla richness and
depth. Tremendous concentration
with lots of botrytis
Still very tight and youthful but
with an immense underlying depth
of fruit and extract
Superb — a great classic

Filhot (picking 6th October–6th
November)   tasted 1987 (13.8°
alcohol + 4° unfermented sugar
retained)
Mid gold
Tight, lemony and botrytis
Quite light in centre. Tight finish,
lacking in depth

*Grand-Peyrot (Ste-Croix-du-
Mont)*   tasted 1987
Mid gold
Lovely, botrytised nose
Full, rich. Very well made. Long
future

Gravas tête de cuvée   tasted 1987
Mid gold
Oaky, earthy; quite rich
Full, rich with an oaky finish

Guiraud   tasted 1984
Pale gold
Very good depth, tight but lovely
and thick, very full and rich
Very long future

Guiraud   tasted 1987
Mid gold
Oaky, closed but with much depth
Thick, rich, closed
A great wine with a long future

Labatut-Bouchard (Cadillac)   tasted
1987
Pale gold
Light, thin nose
Short, thin finish; lacks depth

Lafaurie-Peyraguey   tasted 1987
Mid gold
Tight — good depth of fruit and
botrytis
Very good depth and weight
Lovely, rich finish

Lamothe-Guignard   tasted 1987
Mid gold
Light, lemony nose
Quite good depth; forward

La Tour-Blanche   tasted 1987
Mid gold
Fairly tight, fruity nose
Quite light centre with tight,
sweet finish

Les Justices   tasted 1987
Pale gold and green
Quite tight and closed but with
finesse

Well balanced with firm acidity
Light/forward finish

Nairac   tasted 1987
Mid gold
Good depth of fruit, botrytis and
oak
Lovely, rich, full wine with a great
future

Rabaud-Promis   tasted 1987
Mid/deep gold
Quite good depth of fruit and
botrytis
Good, rich balance; tight finish

Raymond-Lafon (picking started
September, bottled October
1986)   tasted 1986
Pale gold
Very tight and closed, but deep
underneath
Hidden fruit as the wine is very
closed with good tannin
A great future

Raymond-Lafon   tasted 1987
Mid gold
Very rich; closed with great depth
Thick, tight, good botrytis. Long
finish and tannin

Rayne-Vigneau   tasted 1987
Mid gold
Lightweight on nose; lacks depth
Quite sweet, but does not have
depth of concentration

Rieussec   tasted 1987
Mid gold
Rich, marmalade nose with good
botrytis
Full, tight with a lot of depth
Very well made

Romer-du-Hayot   tasted 1987
Mid gold and green
Sweet, tight, grassy with sulphur
Forward on the nose
Lightweight; lacks depth and
centre

St-Amand   tasted 1987
Pale/mid gold
Closed but very well balanced fruit
underneath
Thick, well balanced. Good, tight,
tannic finish

St-Marc   tasted 1987
Mid gold
Medicinal, grassy nose with
sulphur
Lightweight, lacks body,
unbalanced fruit

Suau   tasted 1987
Pale gold and green
Slightly bitter/medicinal nose
Light, thin, eggy. Lacks botrytis
— short finish

Suduiraut   tasted 1987
Mid gold and green
Fairly rich with slightly botrytised
nose
Quite full and rich but with a light
finish
Fairly unbalanced; lacks the finesse
of an 1983

Suduiraut   tasted 1988
No change

1984

A lot of rain resulting in light, watery
wines with the exception of a few
châteaux whose selection is more
rigorous and who produced quite
deep, rich wines with botrytis and
good balance. Only a small quantity
of wine was produced —
approximately 50% of 1983.

Les Cypres de Climens   tasted 1987
(18 months in cask)
Pale gold and green
Nice clean nose with good depth of
fruit
Quite sweet, forward; good finish

Coutet   tasted 1988
Pale and green
Light, lemony nose. No botrytis
evident
Light on fruit, eggy, short finish

d'Arche   tasted 1987
Mid yellow/gold
Quite sweet and concentrated for a
1984
Delicate, quite light but nicely
balanced

de Rolland   tasted 1987
Pale gold and green
Slightly medicinal, sulphur, with
some botrytis underneath
Lightweight with grassy finish

du Tich (Ste-Croix-du-Mont)   tasted
1987
Pale gold
Eggy nose
Lightweight with thin finish

Filhot   tasted 1987 (13.5° alcohol +
2.5° unfermented sugar retained)
Pale gold/yellow
Lemony with slight barley sugar
Light, lacks botrytis. Short, sweet

Grand Peyruchet (Loupiac)   tasted
1987
Pale yellow
Thin, watery nose and high
sulphur
Quite fruitless

Guiraud   tasted 1988
Pale and green
Honeyed, lemon nose
Light centre, tight, dry finish

Lafaurie-Peyraguey   tasted 1988
Pale/mid gold
Light delicate nose
Lightweight but a nice, balanced finish

Lamothe-Guignard   tasted 1987
Mid gold
Quite sweet, clean nose
Forward, commercial with a sweet finish

La Tour-Blanche   tasted 1987
Mid gold
Quite nice tight fruity nose
Well balanced with depth
A good 1984

Nairac
No wine produced under the Château Nairac label

Rabaud-Promis   tasted 1988
Mid gold and green
Slightly lemony nose with some botrytis
Lightweight with fairly short finish

Raymond-Lafon   tasted 1986
Pale gold
Lemony and botrytised nose with some astringency
Good balance, quite light with a nice botrytised finish

Raymond-Lafon (bottled 2nd October 1987)   tasted 1987
Pale yellow/gold
Good botrytised nose. Fairly forward and oaky
A well made 1984. Long finish

Rayne-Vigneau   tasted 1988
Mid/pale gold
Light, no depth
Very light, lacks depth and finesse
Very short finish

Rieussec   tasted 1987
Mid gold
Marmalade, nicely balanced nose, slight sulphur
Good weight for a 1984. Tight, slightly bitter after-taste with short finish

St-Amand   tasted 1987
Pale gold
Light mango bouquet with slight botrytis
Quite delicate with finesse. Light, but a well made 1984

St-Amand   tasted 1988
No change

Suduiraut   tasted 1987
Pale gold
Light, sweet, lemony nose

Quite sweet but lacks elegance
Light centre and finish

Suduiraut   tasted 1988
No change

1985
A difficult year with hail and frost in the spring. Due to a very dry August and September botrytis was slow to develop and particularly in Preignac and Barsac some growers picked too early and missed the botrytis which arrived later around 15th–20th October. Some growers were picking well into December. Small vintage of indifferent quality; careful selection is required.

Bastor-Lamontagne   tasted 1987
Pale gold and green
Quite light, sweet nose
Lacks centre. Slightly cloying finish

Broustet   tasted 1987
Pale gold/lemon
Very light, tight delicate nose
Quite good weight in the centre
Slightly short finish

Caillou   tasted 1987
Pale yellow/gold
Tight, sweet nose with sulphur
Quite rich and sweet. Nice balance

Climens   tasted 1987
Mid gold
Well balanced, good botrytis on nose
Good fruit, rich with botrytis
A very well made 1985

Coutet   tasted 1988
Pale gold
Light, sweet nose, lacks finesse
Short of weight and fruit. Thin finish

Clos Haut-Peyraguey   tasted 1987
Mid yellow/gold
Light lemon nose
Very light, lacks depth and finish

d'Arche   tasted 1987
Pale gold
Quite nicely balanced, honeyed, oaky nose
Lightweight but good, delicate balance

de Malle   tasted 1987
Pale gold
Quite sweet and light
Not of great depth and character

de Malle   tasted 1988
No change

de Rolland   tasted 1987
Pale lemon

Eggy, slightly false sweetness on nose
Cloying, lacking in finesse
Slightly bitter finish. Short

Doisy-Daëne   tasted 1987
Pale gold
Lightweight nose — lacks botrytis
Clean, light on fruit and finish

Doisy-Dubroca   tasted 1988
Very pale and green
Very light, eggy with sulphur
Lightweight throughout

Doisy-Védrines   tasted 1987
Pale gold
Light, delicate, appley nose and sulphur
Good depth, nice balance and finish

Filhot (picking November until December. 6 *tries*)   tasted 1987
(14.5° alcohol + 3° unfermented sugar retained)
Pale yellow and green
Lemony and slightly honeyed
Light, short on fruit and botrytis
Quite thick and oily in mouth
Short finish

Gravas   tasted 1987
Mid gold
Light, tight nose
Forward, easy to drink

Guiraud   tasted 1987
Mid gold
Lovely, rich, oaky, balanced nose
Tight and concentrated
Big, rich, good extract. Delicate finish — quite forward

Lafaurie-Peyraguey   tasted 1987
Mid gold
Nice botrytis with good depth
Full, rich. Well made with long finish

Lamarque (Ste-Croix-du-Mont)   tasted 1987
Pale yellow/gold
Thin, light nose
Short on fruit. Very light finish

Lamothe-Despujols   tasted 1987
Pale gold
Light sweetness
Lacks concentration. Short finish

Lamothe-Guignard   tasted 1987
Mid gold
Quite tight and light peach sweetness. Very little botrytis
Lacks character and finesse
Lightweight finish

La Tour-Blanche   tasted 1987
Pale yellow/gold

Light, forward, sweet nose
Lacks depth, lightweight and short
finish

Les Justices   tasted 1987
  Mid gold
  Light, delicate nose
  Well balanced. Good extract and
  finish

Mademoiselle de Ste-Marc (second
wine of Château La Tour-
Blanche)   tasted 1987
  Mid gold
  Light, forward
  Very lightweight; lacks depth of
  concentration

Nairac   tasted 1987
  Pale gold and green
  Closed nose with oak
  Good concentration of extract and
  botrytis. Closed finish
  A good 1985

Rabaud-Promis   tasted 1987
  Pale gold and green
  Forward, lemony, oversweet
  Very light, lacks any depth of fruit

Rayne-Vigneau   tasted 1987
  Pale gold
  Good balance of fruit and some
  botrytis on nose
  Good extract and finish

Rayne-Vigneau   tasted 1988
  No change

Rieussec   tasted 1987
  Pale gold and green
  Slightly bitter, medicinal nose
  Thin, light, eggy. Lacking in
  botrytis. Short finish

Romer-du-Hayot   tasted 1987
  Pale gold
  Tight, grassy nose
  Lacks balance and finesse with a
  false, sweet finish

St-Amand (bottled September
1987)   tasted 1987 (14.2° + 5°)
  Pale gold/yellow
  Tightly knit fruit and sulphur
  Fairly rich, tight. Well balanced

Suau   tasted 1987
  Pale gold and green
  Slight eggy, unbalanced nose
  Lightweight. Short on fruit

Suduiraut   tasted 1987
  Pale gold
  Light, lacks depth with green,
  medicinal nose
  Unbalanced, light, lacks
  concentration. Short finish

1986

Botrytis arrived late September in
ideal weather conditions and spread
like wildfire during October
resulting in a superb vintage with
good quantities. The wines are rich
and concentrated slightly lacking
acidity but a great vintage
nonetheless.

Bastor-Lamontagne   tasted 1987
  Pale gold and green
  Good depth, open, sweet nose
  Quite forward, good balance, firm
  finish

Broustet   tasted 1987
  Pale gold and green
  Lightweight, appley nose
  Not as much depth and weight as
  would be expected

Caillou   tasted 1987
  Pale yellow to green
  Classic appley/Barsac nose —
  good concentration
  Very well balanced with long
  finish

Clos Haut-Peyraguey   tasted 1987
  Mid gold
  Grassy/medicinal nose
  Light, lacks depth and finesse

Clos Haut-Peyraguey   tasted 1988
  Mid gold
  Light, eggy nose
  Light with short, acidic finish

Coutet cuvée Madame   tasted 1987
  Pale gold to green
  Good depth on nose which is still
  closed
  Well balanced, good rich finish

Coutet   tasted 1987
  Pale and green
  Lightweight. Lacks centre and
  concentration — eggy finish

de Malle   tasted 1987
  Pale gold
  Good depth of fruit
  Lightweight but well made

de Malle   tasted 1988
  Pale and green
  Lemony nose with tight, delicate
  balance of botrytis
  Good fruit, light finish

d'Arche   tasted 1987
  Pale gold
  Good extract with botrytis on nose
  Quite rich and full with a well
  balanced finish

de Ricaud (Loupiac)   tasted 1987
  Mid gold to green
  Soft, sweet nose with acidity

Quite fruity but short in the centre
Sweet finish and forward

de Rolland   tasted 1987
  Mid/pale gold
  Nice botrytised nose
  Slightly lacking in balance on the
  palate

Doisy-Daëne   tasted 1987
  Pale/mid gold and green
  Light, delicate nose
  Quite forward, good balance and
  finish

Doisy-Védrines   tasted 1987
  Pale gold and green
  Good depth of fruit and
  concentration with a classic
  appley/Barsac nose
  Well balanced, good extract. A
  well made wine

Filhot (picking 6th October–6th
November)   tasted 1987
  Pale gold and green
  Lemon nose with botrytis
  Fairly rich marmalade; quite
  forward

Gravas   tasted 1987
  Pale gold and green
  Light, lemon nose
  Forward, sweet; well balanced

Guiraud   tasted 1987
  Mid gold
  Tight, honeyed, well balanced
  nose with some oak
  Good weight and extract. Great
  finesse. Tight finish

Lafaurie-Peyraguey   tasted 1987
  Pale gold and green
  Tight, with good depth
  Well balanced, good finish
  A good 1986

Lamothe-Despujols   tasted 1987
  Pale and green
  Light, lemony nose
  Lacks both depth and weight with
  a short finish

Lamothe-Guignaud   tasted 1987
  Very pale gold and green
  Light, lemon nose with botrytis
  Quite sweet, forward with light
  finish

La Tour-Blanche   tasted 1987
  Pale/mid gold
  Good balance on the nose with
  extract
  Well made, good concentration
  Long finish

Les Justices   tasted 1987
  Pale gold and green
  Sweet, lemon nose

Lightweight sweetness. Fairly
forward

Liot   tasted 1988
   Pale and green
   Lightweight, honeyed nose
   Fairly full, forward. Pleasant finish

Nairac   tasted 1987
   Pale/mid gold
   Nice, delicate, closed nose
   Well balanced, good extract. A
   good future

Rabaud-Promis   tasted 1987
   Pale gold and green
   Quite forward with an open
   sweetness
   Fair balance, but lacks finesse and
   charm

Rayne-Vigneau   tasted 1987
   Pale and green
   Well balanced nose with good,
   tight extract
   Good concentration and full finish
   Well made

Rayne-Vigneau   tasted 1988
   No change

Rieussec   tasted 1987
   Pale gold
   Thick lemon, oaky nose. Good
   extract
   Closed, but great depth of fruit
   underneath
   Tight, tannic finish which is very
   thick in the mouth
   A good 1986 with very good
   balance

Rieussec   tasted 1988
   No change

Romer-du-Hayot   tasted 1987
   Pale/mid gold
   False sweetness lacking in botrytis
   Oversweet, cloying, very forward

Sigalas-Rabaud   tasted 1988
   Mid gold and green
   Lemony, sulphur, eggy, lacking in
   botrytis
   Quite tight, hollow centre. Very
   short finish

Sigalas-Rabaud   tasted 1989
   Pale gold with green tinge
   Some depth of oak and botrytis,
   slightly eggy
   Lightweight, with a hollow
   centre. Short finish

St-Amand   tasted 1987
   Mid/pale gold
   Well balanced with tight, closed
   nose
   Very good weight, tight. Good
   future

Suau   tasted 1987
   Very pale yellow and green
   Open, forward, lacks botrytis
   False sweetness, lacks finesse

Suau   tasted 1988
   No change

Suduiraut   tasted 1987
   Pale gold to green
   Quite light, lemony on nose
   Not of great depth. Lacks centre
   and finishes short

Suduiraut   tasted 1988
   No change

1987
Cold January, some frost damage
in parts of Barsac and Preignac.
Fine spring, then wet June with
long irregular flowering. Near
optimum ripening weather in

August and September. Botrytis
was quite well established in some
properties when the rains came and
lasted, on and off, through most of
October. Some quite good wines
made notwithstanding.

1988
After an abnormally mild winter
the spring and early summer were
warmer and wetter than usual. The
next three months however were
exceptionally sunny and dry. There
was some botrytis in early
October, but because of the long
dry spell it did not really spread
until the last ten days of the month,
after some rain, by which time
some properties had already
picked. The quality of these
properties who picked late should
be very fine.

1989
Very early flowering, in the last
week of a very hot May. Hot
summer with gales in July and
August and a very severe hail storm
on the 6th July which badly
damaged some of the leading
properties of Bommes and
sauternes. At the end of September,
beginning of October there were
several light showers and this combined with cold nights created a
very good spread of botrytis at just
the right time. Early picking started
at the end of September and
finished at the beginning of
October with some very high con-
centrations (26 degrees beaume
recorded at Caillou and 27 degrees
at Rieussec). It shows every sign of
being an exceptional vintage.

Glossary

Assemblage The mixing of the grape varieties.

Balance The perfect proportion of fruit and acidity.

Barrique Barrel holding 225 litres.

Baumé Degrees of unfermented sugar.

Bentonite A fining agent used to clarify wine.

Cépage Grape variety.

Chai Wine cellar.

Cuvée The contents of a particular vat, either of one wine or a blend. It can also refer to the entire contents of a cellar or production of a vineyard.

Débourbage Resting the must before fermentation.

Égrappoir A machine to detach grape stalks.

Émietteur A machine to break up the cake of pressed grape skins.

Epoxy Plastic lining of vats.

Extract Depth of fruit and flavour.

Fermentation The action of yeasts on the natural sugar in the grape juice which produces alcohol and carbon dioxide.

Fining Clearing the wine of impurities.

Fouloir A machine to crush (not press) grapes.

Hectare 2.4 acres.

Hectolitre 22 gallons.

Inox Stainless steel lining for vats.

Lees The deposit left in cask after wine has been drawn off or racked.

Maderisation A condition of white wines caused by oxidation; the wine often develops a brownish colour and tastes rather like a very nasty madeira.

Mélange *see assemblage*.

Muscadelle The third and least-used grape variety of Sauternes.

Must Unfermented grape juice.

Mutage Stopping fermentation with SO_2.

Négociant Wine broker.

Oidium Powdery mildew.

Oxidation A fault in wine caused by over-exposure to air.

Peronospora Downy mildew.

Phylloxera Insect whose larval form attacks the roots of vines.

Racking Transferring the wine to a fresh tank or cask.

Sauvignon Second grape variety of Sauternes.

Sémillon Predominant grape variety of Sauternes.

Sulphur dioxide (SO_2) A chemical stabiliser for Sauternes also used to stop fermentation.

Tonneau 900 litres.

Trie Selective picking of grapes affected by botrytis.

BIBLIOGRAPHY

ALLEN, H. WARNER, *The Wines of France*, 1954

ALLEN, H. WARNER, *White Wines and Cognac*, Constable & Co., 1952

AMERINE, M. A., *The Technology of Wine Making*, AVI Publishing Co., 1972

BROADBENT, MICHAEL, *The Great Vintage Wine Book*, Mitchell Beazley, 1980

BROOK, STEPHEN, *Liquid Gold*, Constable & Co., 1987

DE CASSAGNAC, PAUL, *French Wines*, Chatto and Windus, 1930

COCKS ET FERET, *Bordeaux and its Wines*, various editions from 1883

DENMAN, J. L., *The Vine and its Fruits*, Longman, Green & Co., 1875

DUIJKER, HUBERT, *The Good Wines of Bordeaux and the Great Wines of Sauternes*, Mitchell Beazley, 1983

DUSSAUT, *Les Grands Vins de Bordeaux*, INAOC, 1977

FRUMKIN, LIONEL, *The Science and Technology of Wine*, H. C. Lea & Co., 1965

GINESTET, BERNARD, *Barsac/Sauternes*, Jacques Legrand, 1987

GOLD, ALEC (Editor), *Wines and Spirits of the World*, Virtue Publishing Co., 1968

GOUABET, JEAN, *Les Grands Vins de Bordeaux*, La Société de l'Annuaire de la Gironde, 1856

GOUNOUILHOU, *Bordeaux et la Gironde*, 1895

HEALY, MAURICE, *Claret and the White Wines of Bordeaux*, Michael Joseph

JOHNSON, HUGH, *The World Atlas of Wine*, Mitchell Beazley, 1971

JOHNSON, HUGH, *Wine*, Nelson, 1966, and Sphere Books

LARMAT, LOUIS, *Atlas de la France Vinicole*, Larmat, 1949

LICHINE, ALEXIS, *Encyclopedia of Wines and Spirits*, Cassell, 1967

MASSEL, ANTON, *Basic Oenology*, Heidelberg Press, 1971

MASSEL, ANTON, *Basic Viticulture*, Heidelberg Press, 1971

MORTON SHAND, P., *A Book of Wine*, Guy Chapman, 1926

OLNEY, RICHARD, *Yquem*, Dorling Kindersley, 1986

DES OMBIAUX, MAURICE, *Le Gotha des Vins de France*, Payot, 1925

PARKER, ROBERT, *Bordeaux — The Definitive Guide*, Dorling Kindersley, 1985

PASTEUR, *Studies on Fermentation*, McMillan & Co., 1879

PATTON, REV. W., *Laws of Fermentation*, National Temperance Society, 1871

PENNING-ROWSELL, EDMUND, *The Wines of Bordeaux*, Penguin Books Ltd., 1969

PEPPERCORN, DAVID, *Bordeaux*, Faber and Faber, 1982

PEPPERCORN, DAVID, *Pocket Guide to the Wines of Bordeaux*, Mitchell Beazley, 1986

PONSOT, M., *Complete Yearbook of French Quality Wines*, 1945

ROBINSON, JANCIS, *Vines, Grapes & Wines*, Mitchell Beazley, 1986

ROGER, J. R., *Les Vins de Bordeaux*, André Deutsch, 1955

ROUDIE, PHILLIPE, *Les Vignobles Bordelais*, Privately published, 1973

SEELY, JAMES, *Great Bordeaux Wines*, Secker & Warburg, 1986

SICHEL, ALLAN, *A Book of French Wines*, 1965

SIMON, ANDRE, *In Vino Veritas*, Grant Richards, 1912

TENNENT, EMERSON, *Wine*, James Madden, 1852

VIZETELLY, *Wines of the World*, Ward, Lock & Tyler, 1875

WARDER, *Vineyard Culture*, R. Clarke & Co., 1867

WINE AND SPIRIT TRADE RECORD, *Clarets and Sauternes*, 1920

WINKLER, A. J., *General Viticulture*, California Press, 1974